DESIGNING OUTDOOR ENVIRONMENTS *for* CHILDREN

DESIGNING OUTDOOR ENVIRONMENTS *for* CHILDREN

Landscaping Schoolyards, Gardens, and Playgrounds

LOLLY TAI
MARY TAYLOR HAQUE
GINA K. McLELLAN
ERIN JORDAN KNIGHT

McGRAW-HILL

NEW YORK | CHICAGO | SAN FRANCISCO | LISBON
LONDON | MADRID | MEXICO CITY | MILAN | NEW DELHI
SAN JUAN | SEOUL | SINGAPORE | SYDNEY | TORONTO

The McGraw·Hill Companies

Cataloging-in-Publication Data is on file with the Library of Congress.

1 2 3 4 5 6 7 8 9 0   DOC/DOC   0 1 0 9 8 7 6

ISBN 0-07-145935-9

The sponsoring editor for this book was Cary Sullivan and the production supervisor was Richard C. Ruzycka. It was set in Plantin by Matrix Publishing Services. The art director for the cover was Handel Low.

Printed and bound by RR Donnelley.

 This book is printed on recycled, acid-free paper containing a minimum of 50% recycled, de-inked fiber.

McGraw-Hill books are available at special quantity discounts to use as premiums and sales promotions, or for use in corporate training programs. For more information, please write to the Director of Special Sales, McGraw-Hill Professional, Two Penn Plaza, New York, NY 10121-2298. Or contact your local bookstore.

This book is dedicated to generations of parents and teachers who have instilled a love of nature in children and to future generations who will engage in conserving natural landscapes and creating outdoor play and learning places for children. With special tribute to our parents:

Kuang Ming Tai and Kuo Hua Li Tai

Edmund Rhett Taylor, Sr., and Mary Herbert Taylor

Raymond J. Kooiman and Margaret Darring Kooiman

William F. Jordan and E. Rosaline Jordan

who facilitated discovery and nurtured our appreciation of the natural environment when we were children.

CONTENTS

ACKNOWLEDGMENTS

This book has become a reality through a concerted team effort, and we wish to thank everyone on that team. We acknowledge three groups of people, all important contributors to the final product but in different ways.

First, we would like to thank Cary Sullivan, our senior editor at McGraw-Hill, who made our vision of publishing this book possible. We also thank our team of colleagues and collaborators who provided direct assistance with case studies, images, artwork, formats, and information. There are too many to name each of you, but special thanks go to:

Mary Allinson, Section Gardener at Longwood Gardens, for meeting with us and for editing the text of the Bee-aMazed Children's Garden.

Natalie Andersen, Vice President for Education at NYBG, for meeting with us, for permission to use images, and for editing the text of Everett Children's Adventure Garden at the New York Botanical Garden.

Heather Bergerud, Volunteer Coordinator of the CGLSP for editing the text of the Children's Garden at Linky Stone Park.

Sandra Bolain, former Associate of Marshall Tyler Rausch Landscape Architects, for sending us images of the Children's Healthcare of Atlanta Children's Garden.

Angie Bruhjell, Science Specialist at Whitehall Elementary School, for her assistance with information and photographs.

Elliot Buff, former landscape architecture student at Clemson University, for the sketch of a tree detail.

Sofiya Cabalquinto, Public Affairs Coordinator at BBG, for assistance with tours, photographs, edits, interviews, and information about the Brooklyn Botanic Garden Children's Garden.

Jenny Carey, Board Member of Awbury Arboretum, for meeting with us to tour and discuss Awbury Arboretum.

Doris Cole, former Principal of Whitehall Elementary School, for her leadership in design and providing information about their children's outdoor learning environments.

Linda Cotilla, Head Librarian of Suburban Campus Libraries at Temple University–Ambler, for compiling the references, list of public children's gardens, list of selected school gardens and youth gardening educational programs, and list of organizations/selected internet resources.

Gage Couch, former landscape architecture student at Clemson University, for his illustrations.

Jennifer Dykes, Coordinator of Public Relations and Events at CCG, for meeting with us and for permission to use images of Camden Children's Garden.

Linda Eirhart, Curator of Plants at Winterthur, for meeting with us and for editing the text of the Enchanted Woods.

Karin Emmons, Department of Parks, Recreation and Tourism Management at Clemson University, for answering endless questions, handling hundreds of photographs, and formatting figures.

Patricia Evans, Publicity Coordinator at Longwood Gardens, for permission to use images and for editing the text of the Bee-aMazed Children's Garden.

Fletcher Group, Inc. for permission to use images of the Children's Garden at Linky Stone Park.

Vivian Flores, Administrative Assistant for Education Division at NYBG, for sending us images of Everett Children's Adventure Garden at the New York Botanical Garden.

Rick Forest, for use of his preliminary sketches of *The Secret Garden* mural in The Children's Garden at Linky Stone Park.

Val Frick, Director of Education of CCG, for editing the text of the Camden Children's Garden.

Tres Fromme, Lead Designer at Longwood Gardens, for permission to use images and for editing the text of Longwood Garden's New Indoor Children's Garden.

Brice Hipp, Chair of the CGLSP, for editing the text of Children's Garden at Linky Stone Park.

Crystal Huff, Director of Visitor Services of the CGHG, for permission to use images and for editing the text of the Children's Garden at Hershey Gardens.

William Jordan, Coordinator of Sprouting Wings at the South Carolina Botanical Gardens, Clemson University, for providing photographs for multiple chapters.

Gerald Kaufman, Education Director of AA, for meeting with us and for editing the text of Awbury Arboretum.

R. Scott Kelly for providing the image of child on a "tree house."

Renee Keydoszius, Plant and Environmental Sciences graduate student at Clemson University, for her design drawings and renderings.

David Knight for providing photographs for multiple chapters.

Leeann Lavin, Director of Public Affairs at BBG, for assistance with tours, interviews, images, edits, and information about the Brooklyn Botanic Garden Children's Garden.

Albert Lynn, former landscape architecture student at Clemson University, for the sketch of a tree detail.

Ted Maclin, former manager of BBG's Children's Garden, for assistance with interviews and information about the Brooklyn Botanic Garden Children's Garden.

Denise Magnani, Curator/Director of the Landscape Division at Winterthur, for meeting with us to discuss the Enchanted Woods.

Jill Manley, Director of Marketing and Public Relations, for permission to use images of the Children's Garden at Hershey Gardens.

Kevin Mercer, Youth Programs Manager at CHACG, for editing the text of the Children's Healthcare of Atlanta Children's Garden.

Emily Crow Neely, Program Manager at Upstate Forever's Active Living Office in Spartanburg, SC, for editing the text of multiple chapters.

Barbara Siegel-Ryan, student at Temple University, for numerous drawings and renderings.

Colleen M. Seace, photographer at Hershey Gardens for the images of the Children's Garden at Hershey Gardens.

Jason Smit, former landscape architecture student at Clemson University, for his *Alice in Wonderland* Storybook Garden illustrations.

W. Gary Smith Design, Inc., Landscape Architect, for meeting with us, for permission to use images and for editing the text of the Enchanted Woods.

Marilyn Smith, Director of Children's Education at BBG, for assistance with interviews and for information about the Brooklyn Botanic Garden Children's Garden.

Kevin Snow, Principal of Whitehall Elementary School, for his leadership in service learning landscape designs and information about school landscapes.

The Sustainable Universities Initiative, for support with K–12 Schoolyard Habitat research and outreach design projects.

Landscapes for Learning, Clemson University, for financial and technical support of children's gardens throughout South Carolina.

Jane Taylor, Founding Curator of the Michigan 4-H Children's Garden, for permission to use the image of the site plan and for editing the text of the Michigan 4-H Children's Garden.

Cindy Tyler, principal at the firm of Marshall, Tyler, Rausch, Landscape Architects, for permission to use images and for editing the text of the Children's Healthcare of Atlanta Children's Garden.

Upstate Forever, for use of several images in Chapter 1.

Upstate Mulch, for use of the image of children playing on Tumblesafe® Playground Mulch.

USDA: Parts of this book are based upon work supported by the Cooperative State Research, Education and Extension Service, U.S. Department of Agriculture, under Agreement No. 2002-38411-12122. Any opinions, findings, conclusions, or recommendations expressed in this publication are those of the authors(s) and do not necessarily reflect the view of the U.S. Department of Agriculture.

Venturi, Scott Brown and Associates, Inc., for permission to use images of Camden Children's Garden and Andrea Abramoff for sending us the images.

Elsie Viehman, Education Director of AA, for meeting with us, for permission to use images, and for editing text of Awbury Arboretum.

Brent Whiting, Senior Technology Support Specialist at Temple University, for his work on the preliminary book layout.

Second, thank you to everyone who contributed time and expertise to the development of the children's environments we featured in the book. Some were mentioned above, and others include:

The hundreds of people involved in planning and implementing the *Clemson Elementary Outdoors* project including Dr. Paul Prichard, Clemson Elementary School Principal during the planning and early implementation of *Clemson Elementary Outdoors*, for his ongoing support and belief that this elementary school should and would have great outdoor environments for play and learning; the teachers and staff at Clemson Elementary for their ongoing cooperation and involvement in too many ways to list; David Allison, whose architectural expertise and parental enthusiasm assured the physical linkage of the school with its outdoor areas; Donza Mattison, project architect with McMillian, Smith and Partners, Architects, PLLC; Bond Anderson, owner of SoundPlay and extraordinary designer of outdoor musical instruments, who worked diligently with volunteers to build the music garden; Jimmy Burke, with GameTime Playground Equipment Company, who really listened to ideas for a different approach to playgrounds and accommodated those ideas in equipment designs; Kathy McInnis, Gail Collins, and Mary Ann Hill, Clemson Elementary School teachers, who have set benchmarks for environment-based education, and have expanded the reach of *Clemson Elementary Outdoors* with the addition of creative and versatile gardens; Chris Nigro, the "Brawn" of the *Clemson Elementary Outdoors* project, whose ability to enlist volunteers and get things done exceeded the greatest expectations; Dr. Serji Amirkanian and Dr. Scott Schiff, civil engineering professors at Clemson University, who led their students in service learning projects to build concrete thematic garden elements and bridges for gardens and the nature trail; Renee Roux, Carolyn Taylor, Vic Shelburne, Barbara Weaver, Clemson Elementary PTA, and the hundreds of parent volunteers who contributed their time and organizational skills to the development of *Clemson Elementary Outdoors;* to the many generous financial donors; to James F. Barker, President of Clemson University, for his personal interest and effort in making *Clemson Elementary Outdoors* a reality; to the Departments of Parks, Recreation and Tourism Management, Horticulture, and Landscape Architecture for their generosity in contributing faculty, student, and staff time to *Clemson Elementary Outdoors*; to the more than 1,000 Clemson University students, who, through service learning projects helped to design and build the *Clemson Elementary Outdoors* project; and finally, to the hundreds of Clemson Elementary School students who dreamed up the ideas for *Clemson Elementary Outdoors* and worked so hard to help make their dreams come true.

Many partners made the Children's Garden at Linky Stone Park possible. Leadership Greenville Class XXX, the visionary group who initiated and led the project; Brice Hipp, Chair of LG XXX, whose leadership made the project possible; Heather Bergerud, Volunteer Coordinator, who organized our workdays and tasks; Paul Ellis, Director of Parks and Recreation and Don Shuman, Assistant Administrator of Parks and Grounds for the City of Greenville and their staff, without whose support our garden would not exist nor could it be sustained; Jordan Franklin and the Falls Park Staff, whose dedicated maintenance of the garden allowed us to create the detailed, plant-based discovery garden children most desire; our talented and generous volunteers: Eric Bergerud; The Clarice Wilson Garden Club; Fletcher Group, Inc.; David Gillespie; Dr. Jim Faust of Clemson University and his 2005 Annuals and Perennials horticulture students; Greenville Master Gardeners; Bill Jordan; Megan Logsdon; Stephen Nix; Cal Pilgrim; all the other volunteers who assisted with workdays, wrote or illustrated educational signage, assisted with carpentry, art, or implementation; the children who played major roles in the garden's planning and implementation: Joshua Cooke; Mireille Fehler; Children of the Greenville County School System; Karen and Carlie Kerechanin; Lauren and Jake Lampley; Brooks and Lee Leavitt; Erica Mullinax; Oakview Elementary School Garden Club; Abbie Slade; the contracted construction/installation team members.

And third, thank you to those closest to us who provided encouragement and support throughout the entire process. We appreciate the support of our employers, Temple University, Clemson University, and Upstate Forever, in our goal of writing this book. We thank the children in our lives, Lara McLellan, Mariana Haque, Omar Haque, and Noman Haque, who contributed more to our passion for children's environments than they will ever realize, and the biggest thanks of all to our husbands J. Michael Kelly, Imtiaz Haque, Bob McLellan, and David Knight, because we know that without their encouragement and help, this book would simply not have happened.

The Faerie Cottage at The Enchanted Woods™, Winterthur Museum & Country Estate, Winterthur, Delaware, Gary Smith, Landscape Architect. (COURTESY OF WINTERTHUR AND W. GARY SMITH)

Introduction

A Natural Childhood: Giving Children the World

Childhood is a time for discovery, and for many children the most wonderful, powerful, life-changing discoveries they will ever make lie hidden in nature (Figure I-1). Studies indicate that during our formative years we are genetically predisposed to explore our world and seek to understand it. In fact, the drive for exploration is a trait we share with all of our primate relatives. Yet these motivations cannot be explained simply by need for food, water, or survival. Biologist and developmentalist Jean Piaget has researched human development and determined that this urge is particularly intense during childhood (Verbeek and de Waal, 2002). Louise Chawla, International Coordinator of the Growing Up in Cities Program of UNESCO, supports this conclusion, stating that ages 6–12, commonly referred to as "Middle Childhood," is the natural period during which children are genetically programmed to form a bond with nature. She hypothesizes that this is due to the fact that our species originally would have developed survival skills during this age (Nixon, 1997). Far too

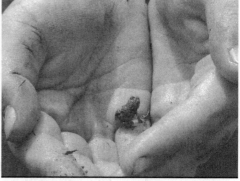

FIG I-1. Children make important, formative discoveries in nature. (COURTESY OF ERIN JORDAN KNIGHT.)

many of us lose the willingness to seek understanding of nature and to become a part of it as we grow older.

A child's relationship with nature is a perfect one; both partners have something critically important to offer and something essential to gain. As much of the research represented within this book suggests, children benefit from interaction with nature in all aspects of their development: physical, mental, moral, and emotional. The critical bond between nature and a child benefits the natural world as well, for research indicates that it is during childhood that people form their values concerning nature. In fact, the vast majority of people who grow up to devote themselves to conservation—or to live environmentally responsible lives—attribute their attitudes to the love born in their childhood and to the adults who taught them through example the importance of nature.

There was once a time when a nature-based childhood was the *natural* condition, but that is not the case today. More children today lack daily contact with natural environments than ever before (Nabhan and Trimble, 1994). A major factor contributing to this trend is that more children are growing up in urban and suburban environments (Figure I-2). According to the United Nations *Report of the Secretary General on World Demographic Trends*, published in April 2005, half the world's population will live in cities by 2007. In the United States, 87% of the population lives in cities (World Demographic Trends, 2005). When nature no longer occurs naturally in childhood, it is imperative that parents, educators, designers, planners, policy makers, and others work to provide ample opportunities for children to explore nature and develop that innate bond.

FIG I-2. Children are isolated by the impacts of sprawl: development that outpaces population growth. (COURTESY OF UPSTATE FOREVER.)

Current trends toward providing nature-based experiences—such as gardens, parks, restoration habitats, and a variety of environmental education opportunities for children—are enthusiastic, innovative, and widespread. The scale of successful projects can vary from the low-budget restoration of an undeveloped green space for neighborhood children to the creation of a dynamic fully staffed public children's garden.

A lifeless landscape of concrete is no substitute for natural spaces and gardens. It is through a partnership between eager children and supportive adults that nurturing landscapes can be created and provided so that no child will suffer the void of a desolate landscape.

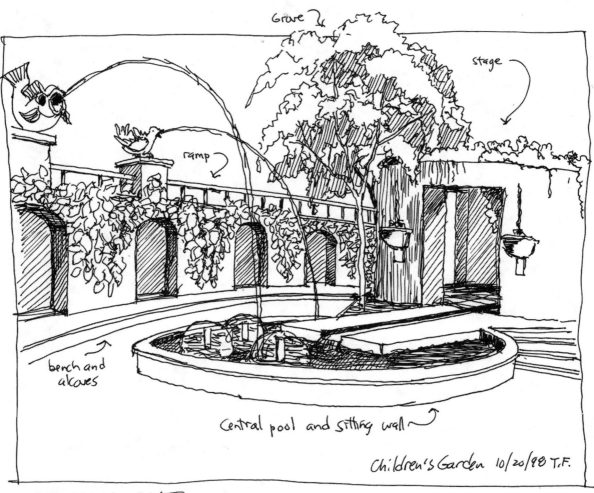

Grove

stage

ramp

bench and alcoves

Central pool and sitting wall

Children's Garden 10/20/98 T.F.

CENTRAL COVE

The Central Cove at The New Indoor Children's Garden, Longwood Gardens, Kennett Square, PA.
(COURTESY OF LONGWOOD GARDENS, TRES FROMME, LEAD DESIGNER.)

CHAPTER 1

History and Development

The History of Children's Gardens

THE CHILDREN'S LANDSCAPE UNDERGOES A REVOLUTION

In the cyclical nature of history, the themes that have shaped children's play spaces over centuries still impact their world today. Likewise, the progressive breakthroughs in children's environments, education, and literature that resulted from the deficiencies of the landscapes of childhood throughout history can inspire and instruct today's innovators.

The need for the creation of special natural spaces for children was first recognized during the Industrial Revolution in Europe (Dannenmaier, 1998). There is great discrepancy regarding the beginning and ending dates of this economic revolution that brought about the widespread use of power-driven machinery for manufacturing; some experts argue that it continues today (Rempel, 2005). This was a time of great changes in lifestyles and landscapes, as cities grew and consumed the surrounding natural land and resources. This altering of the landscape, as well as a mass migration of people from the country to the city, brought about an absence of natural surroundings in the lives of many children. Experts of the age believed that children deprived of nature suffered physically, mentally, and morally (Dannenmaier, 1998).

As Molly Dannenmaier, author of "A Child's Garden" discusses, literature of this time period reflected these attitudes. *Heidi*, a children's

FIG 1-1. Literature of the Industrial Revolution reflects attitudes toward childhood. Spyri, the author of Heidi, writes of the detrimental effects of city life and the restorative powers of nature. (COURTESY OF BARBARA SIEGEL RYAN.)

novel written by Johanna Spyri, is one such example (Figure 1-1). In the country, Heidi is happy and healthy. Although she is surrounded by wealth when she moves to the city, she suffers physically, mentally, and emotionally. She recovers upon her return to the Alps and to nature. When Clara, her city-friend who is confined to a wheelchair, comes to visit, she grows strong enough to overcome her handicap and walk (Spyri and Leslie, 1956).

Frances Hodgson Burnett uses a similar theme in *The Secret Garden*, a book inspired by her move from industrialized Europe to rural Tennessee in 1865 (Penguin Group USA, 2005) (Figure 1-2). Mary, who is emotionally troubled, ill-tempered, and sickly, and her cousin Colin, who has both severe emotional and physical problems, are both healed by the "magic" of a garden (Burnett, 1987).

It was not only through literature of this era that nature was being empowered with the ability to teach, heal, and shape children. Friedrich Froebel, an educator of the Industrial Period, invented the kindergarten, a phrase meaning "Garden of Children," in 1837. These schools were based on the premise that play areas should mimic the country life of which most children were deprived. This program for young children integrated plants and animals as well as building materials and props, all utilized under the guidance of expert educators (Dannenmaier, 1998). So, while the Industrial Period was one with many overwhelmingly negative impacts on the life of a child, these detriments did not go unnoticed, and some innovation in child development resulted (Figure 1-3).

FIG 1-2. In *The Secret Garden*, children find physical, mental, and emotional growth in a garden; they call this healing power "magic." (COURTESY OF RICK FOREST.)

The Industrial Revolution's impacts on the natural environment and human attitudes toward it are dramatic to this day. Massive deforestation of Scotland robbed that nation of a forest, described in "The Forest of Forgetting" by Guy Hand as "grand as any on earth. Elms, ash, alder and oak shaded the low-lying coastal plains and inland valleys; aspen, hazel, birch, rowan and willow covered the hills; and beautiful, red bark Scots pine clung to the glacial moraines and steep granite slopes. The Romans called it the Forests of Caledonia, 'the woods on heights' and it clung to the Scottish soil for millennia."

Today, the Scottish highlands are one of the most deforested regions on the planet, and the rich forests that once stood are so thoroughly forgotten by most Scots today, that according to Hand, most have virtually no concept of a forest. Peter H. Kahn, Jr., psychologist and professor, calls this phenomenon *environmental generational amnesia*, which refers to each generation's acceptance of the degraded state of the natural environment during their childhood as the "natural" state (Kahn, 2002). If applied to the state of rapid development the United States is undergoing today, environmental generational amnesia and the lessons we can learn from history have frightening implications of a constant degradation of the acceptable condition of the natural world.

Kahn suggests that although there are no easy answers to the problem of environmental generational amnesia, it is important to note that its genesis lies in childhood. We can combat its impacts by attempting to shape the attitudes of today's children. Kahn offers the "structural development approach" as a first step toward a solution; children need environmental interaction to form their own values concerning it. The dilemma is that the environment will be continually degraded in quality, which will limit the richness and diversity of their experience (Kahn, 2002). We are experiencing massive declines in biodiversity with

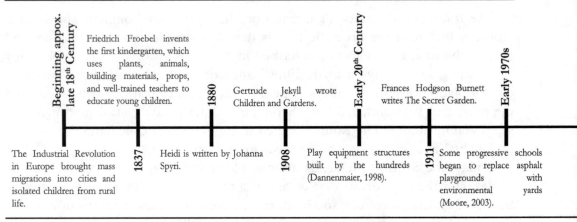

FIG 1-3. Children's landscapes in the last century. (COURTESY OF ERIN JORDAN KNIGHT.)

15,000–30,000 species extinctions a year and severe declines in many other species (Kellert, 1997, 2002; Wilson, 1992).

The process can be further refined by discussions with children about what "used to be," hoping that this dialogue can help shape the future. Reclaiming and restoring land through the use of indigenous plants of the region is another solution, and one that can give children great fulfillment while teaching valuable scientific lessons. This concept goes a step beyond the average park, for its intent is not only to provide green space but to restore native plant communities, such as meadows, wetlands, forests, and creeks, into the ecosystems where they would naturally occur. Finally, it is important to help children experience pristine nature, so they can build associations and begin to understand what was lost before they were there to experience it (Kahn, 2002).

CHILDREN'S LANDSCAPES IN THE LAST CENTURY

In the early 1900s, constructed play structures designed for physical recreation became the primary focus of outdoor spaces for children. From 1905 to 1909, hundreds were constructed, and early ideals of mimicking nature were abandoned for steel structures, which dominated children's play areas (Dannenmaier, 1998). These structures not only neglect children's need for nature, but pose far more safety concerns than the plant-based play yard. They are still prominent features of children's play spaces today.

During the 1900s, Gertrude Jekyll rejected the popular new children's garden design concepts and concentrated on the experience of the child (Jekyll, 1991).

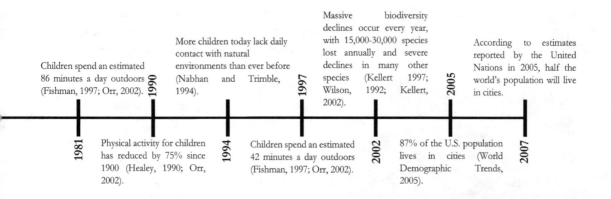

Children spend an estimated 86 minutes a day outdoors (Fishman, 1997; Orr, 2002).

1990
More children today lack daily contact with natural environments than ever before (Nabhan and Trimble, 1994).

1997
Massive biodiversity declines occur every year, with 15,000-30,000 species lost annually and severe declines in many other species (Kellert 1997; Wilson, 1992; Kellert, 2002).

2005
According to estimates reported by the United Nations in 2005, half the world's population will live in cities.

1981

1994

2002

2007
Physical activity for children has reduced by 75% since 1900 (Healey, 1990; Orr, 2002).

Children spend an estimated 42 minutes a day outdoors (Fishman, 1997; Orr, 2002).

87% of the U.S. population lives in cities (World Demographic Trends, 2005).

Jekyll wrote *Children and Gardens,* which recommended a playhouse with a working kitchen, pantry, parlor, and screen porch. The purpose of this elaborate play space was the cultivation of domestic skills (Dannenmaier, 1998). Naturally, this was not a concept every child could afford, and yet Jekyll's concept is based on the enduring art of building rustic forts, playhouses, and hideouts during childhood. This urge to build occurs particularly between the ages of 8 and 11, according to philosopher David Sobel (Sobel, 1993). Sobel suggests that this desire may represent or stem from an emotional metamorphosis that helps a child develop a sense of self (Nixon, 1997) (Figure 1-4).

In the early 1970s, some progressive schools began to replace asphalt play yards with environmentally rich play and learning opportunities for the school and community. Washington Elementary in downtown Berkeley, CA, partnered with local organizations including the UC Berkeley campus to create an Environmental Yard. The acre and a half of asphalt became a variety of ecosystems representative of the region (Moore, 2003).

Convinced of the Environmental Yard's many benefits over the traditional play space, progressive schools and communities worldwide now use this model and other similar hands-on learning environments (Figure 1-5). Robin Moore, professor of landscape architecture and expert in design of play and learning environments, and educator Dr. Herb Wong found

FIG 1-4. Children are drawn to the building of forts and treehouses, in which they can escape adult supervision and survey their surroundings. Sobel suggests this urge may help children develop a sense of self. (COURTESY OF BARBARA SIEGEL RYAN.)

FIG 1-5. Nature can inspire creativity, and may even increase intelligence, as its ever-changing state stimulates children's cognitive development. Learning landscapes like this school courtyard use nature as a teaching tool. (COURTESY OF ERIN JORDAN KNIGHT.)

that aggression incidents decreased and imagination and creative social interaction increased following the conversion of a schoolyard from asphalt to an Environmental Yard with plants and a pond (Chawla, 2002). *Closing the Achievement Gap*, a 1998 survey of 40 K–12 schools in 13 states that used open spaces to create hands-on learning opportunities for students, demonstrated that such environments are associated with great improvements in a child's ability to learn. In particular, the study reports that standardized achievement scores of at-risk children improved (Moore, 2003). Another study (Kirkby, 1989) observed that in a schoolyard with both built equipment and plant material, the most dramatic play occurred near bushes and other vegetation (Chawla, 2002). Countless studies support the theory that children thrive in play areas with diverse natural elements as their tools, and their cognitive and social development is enriched by such imaginative and unrestricted play.

Today, popular trends to provide imaginative hands-on learning environments rich with natural learning recall the ideals of the "garden of children" conceived during the Industrial Revolution—another time period when massive migrations into urban environments changed the landscape of childhood. This chapter will further explore the beneficial aspects of nature on childhood development and the detriments children can suffer when deprived of it.

Nature and Development

Researchers have drawn impressive correlations between direct contact with nature during childhood and all aspects of development: mental, physical, and emotional. The richness of nature in childhood even seems to impact and shape values that form life-long behavioral patterns. It may also determine the course of one's adult life goals and ambitions.

COGNITIVE DEVELOPMENT

There is strong evidence that nature, in its constantly changing and growing state, increases intelligence. Studies show that neural connections in the brain increase and become more complex when people or animals are surrounded by dynamic environments, such as those provided in nature. However, those deprived of rich environments tend to lack energy, and are often more prone to violent behavior (Dannenmaier, 1998).

Through interaction with the physical and social environment, children build on knowledge and understanding (Kahn, 2002). Social ecologist Stephen R. Kellert proposes that there are three kinds of contact with nature:

FIG 1-6. Kellert suggests that direct contact with nature is important to childhood development, and yet it is less common than symbolic nature experiences. Here, children watch sensitive plant withdraw from their touch. (COURTESY OF ERIN JORDAN KNIGHT.)

- ❧ direct, physical contact, free of human controls (Figure 1-6);

- ❧ indirect contact, which is the product of human manipulation, such as a zoo, museum, or arboretum;

- ❧ vicarious or symbolic experience, with the absence of actual contact with nature. This could consist of watching a nature program on television or reading a book, magazine, or Web site (Kellert, 2002).

Due to the dramatic increase in symbolic experience as opposed to direct, physical experience in many childhoods today, fewer children can experience the complex, enriching cognitive development Kahn has documented crossculturally in many nations. Yet, Kahn's studies found that there was a similarity to the structure of children's affiliations with nature across cultures and regardless of that child's exposure to unblemished natural environments. Kahn attributed this phenomenon to the universal appeal and availability in all environments to "bugs, pets, plants, trees, wind, rain, soil, sunshine." In one example he shared, an urban child can bond with nature by moving a worm off the sidewalk. Although not as nature-based or as rich as a rural child's experience, that child can still seek and find the affinity with nature he or she was predisposed to have (Kahn, 2002) (Figure 1-7).

FIG 1-7. Sometimes, the urban nature experiences available to a child within an undeveloped lot or park space can be rich and inspiring. Here, a child sketches Sliding Rock Creek in Greenville, SC, on a makeshift sewer line seat. This incongruous juxtaposition of distinctly urban and natural features does not always detract from the child's exploration experience. (COURTESY OF ERIN JORDAN KNIGHT.)

In some ways, educators have used nature as a major teaching tool. Nature is a dominant theme in many of the stories, fables, myths, and legends of childhood, which adds excitement to the discovery of nature and stimulates the imagination. Nature is a major teaching tool in the first stage of cognitive development, as evidenced by the majority of young children's books that rely heavily on anthropomorphized animals as opposed to objects, to teach counting, naming, and categorizing. Elizabeth Lawrence used the term "cognitive biophilia" to describe the use of such symbols of nature for the development of human intellect (Kellert, 2002).

According to Charles Lewis, a horticulturalist who studies human response to nature, by age 12 children have experienced most of the learning for which they are biologically predisposed. He suggests that "innate responses to environmental stimuli provoke unforgettable cognitive imprints." A deficiency of such environments may also negatively impact a child's development of intuition (Dannenmaier, 1998).

The extent of the partnership between nature and the development of cognition is still an issue for greater scientific study, but the interrelationship between the two already revealed through research is astonishing. A partnership as old as mankind rests between man and nature, and perhaps it was at the dawn of our species that nature first began to play a role in our development when we relied on our intelligence for survival and nature could be a teacher—sometimes nurturer or provider, sometimes adversary.

PHYSICAL DEVELOPMENT

Nature's impact is also significant on the physical development of a child, but is perhaps best observed in terms of the negative effects suffered when that child is isolated from nature. Today's altered state of childhood immobility and improper eating habits is creating a health crisis in which 15% of children ages 6 to 19 are obese or overweight, according to the Center for Disease Control and Prevention, as are 1 in 10 2- to 5-year-olds (Moore, 2003). Ten thousand ads a year, according to one study, appeal to children to eat fatty and sugary foods (Orr, 2002). Despite these alarming statistics, school districts across the nation have reduced recess time or eliminated it completely (Moore, 2003) (Figure 1-8).

One major contributor to the obesity factor of children and adults today is the sprawling state of many U.S. cities. Sprawl is defined by the nonprofit organization Smart Growth America as the process by which the spread of development across the landscape far outpaces population growth. Public health lecturer Ross Lopez used a 100-point scale to rate urban sprawl in the United States and compare it to physical activity statistics. As sprawl increased point by point, physical activity decreased and obesity increased (Dahlgren, 2003). As cities become more sprawling, residents live further and further from city centers where they work, so they spend more time in their cars, and walking, biking, or using other alternative means of transportation becomes more problematic (Figure 1-9). Children have to be bussed or driven to schools as communities become unwalkable, due to crowded streets, narrow or nonexistent sidewalks, and the consolidation of the neighborhood schools into larger learning centers further from homes. In short, sprawl is an isolating force that encourages residents to get in the car for every trip and errand they need

FIG 1-8. Studies indicate that children are more interested in eating vegetables and fruits when they participate in growing them, and they exercise in the process. (COURTESY OF ERIN JORDAN KNIGHT.)

FIG 1-9. Sprawl leads to more time spent in the car and less opportunity for exercise and time in nature. The solution is to combat these negative impacts with smart growth, which incorporates principles of quality of life into the development equation. (COURTESY OF UPSTATE FOREVER.)

FIG 1-10. Principles of traditional neighborhood development (TND) encourage active living and foster a sense of community. Schools, shopping, and other destinations are located within walking distance of residential areas. Sidewalks with tree-lined buffers between them and the road make walking safe and pleasant. (COURTESY OF UPSTATE FOREVER.)

to make. It hinders the development of a sense of community and greatly impacts childhood, as children do not have the freedom to safely explore their environment. They become dependent on parents or other adults to drive them around, and wild, natural environments are beyond most children's reach for exploration on a regular basis (Figure 1-10).

Many find the allure of technological entertainment indoors more appealing than active play outdoors in these manicured, homogenized environments, which further decreases their activity levels. This decline in exercise compounds child health problems. By some estimates, physical activity among children has been reduced by 75% since 1900 (Healey, 1990; Orr, 2002). Another study showed that children ages 3 through 12 spent 86 minutes a day outdoors in 1981 but only 42 minutes a day in 1997 (Fishman, 1999: Orr, 2002).

The necessity of increasing exercise and activity for children is particularly poignant for children suffering additional problems, such as behavioral disorders like attention deficit hyperactivity disorder (ADHD). It is estimated that 8% of children ages 3 to 17 suffer from ADHD, and the statistic is rising, probably due to improvements in diagnosis. In school environments, there is not only a greater need for hands-on learning and more physical activity in the classroom to better meet the needs of an ADHD child, but it is also likely that other children who have varied learning types will respond to this healthy approach (Moore, 2003).

EMOTIONAL DEVELOPMENT (AFFECTIVE MATURATION)

Nature also stimulates complex emotional development, referred to by Kellert as "affective maturation." Not only does nature inspire joy, excitement, and wonder in a child, but also fear and challenge. These conflicting feelings are motivators for learning and development, and for personal growth (Kellert, 2002).

Middle childhood is a critical bonding period for children with nature. During this time, they use nature to develop autonomy, according to Harold Searles (1959). They also begin to see nature as separate from themselves, while they simultaneously seek affinity with it (Kellert, 2002). This stage in a child's life has also been referred to as the child's "earth" period.

Sobel experimented with children at different ages and levels of development to study their varying relationships to space. He asked the participants in the study to draw maps, which helped him understand the places that made up their world and were important to them. To summarize his findings:

- *Age 4*—They begin exploring. Until age 7, their home is the center of their world.

- *Ages 8—11*—Their homes become unimportant and their representation moves to the map's periphery. Children explore lots, woods, ditches, and other interesting places around their home.

- *Age 12*—Social world of malls appeals to them, their "earth period" wanes.

- *Age 17*—Their "gasoline period" begins, with the car at the center of their world. Often, it never ends (Nixon, 1997).

Finally, something beyond the mental or physical occurs for many children who spend time in nature (Figure 1-11). It is most closely akin to an emotional experience, but it surpasses emotional development as well and falls more acutely in the realm of profound, formative experience.

For some children, bonding with nature can be a spiritual experience, and it will make an impact on their lives that is lasting and moving. In a survey of a heterogeneous group conducted by Sebba, 96.5% of participants indicated that the outdoors was the most significant environment of their childhood. Another study polling 700 of the past (those who had attended over the last 25 years) and present participants of well-known outdoor programs such as Outward Bound, the National Outdoor Leadership School, and the Student Conservation Association had similarly positive results. A large majority reported the experience as being one of the most important in their lives and claimed it impacted their per-

FIG 1-11. From ages 8 to 11, children explore woods, ditches, and vacant lots near their homes, according to the studies of Sobel. These wanderings help children develop autonomy and form important bonds with nature that can impact their values throughout their lives. (COURTESY OF ERIN JORDAN KNIGHT.)

sonality and development (Kellert, 2002). Most further claimed that the experience helped their self-esteem and ability to problem solve, their coping capacity and ability to meet challenges, and their ability to function in a city. Their nature appreciation and support of conservation, as well as their future level of activity in the outdoors were all favorably influenced by that singular adolescent experience in nature (Kellert and Derr, 1998; Kellert, 2002).

According to Chawla, most children like spending time in the outdoors, even if they do not become a naturalist as an adult (Nixon, 1997). According to Chawla's research, of those who do grow up to devote themselves to the protection of the environment, the study of nature, or some other related field, 77% identified one of two factors that led them to their field; either they had positive childhood experiences that inspired their life's work, or a family role model demonstrated a love of nature and passed the sentiment to them (Chawla, 2002). With outstanding testimonies such as these, it seems evident that the best way to inspire stewardship for a more responsible future is to instill a love of nature during childhood.

CHILDHOOD TODAY: THE CURRENT MASS MIGRATION TO THE CITIES

The importance of nature experiences in childhood is irrefutable, and yet it is a condition in crisis. In America, we lose a million acres annually to urban sprawl and infrastructure development (Orr, 2002) (Figure 1-12). Since the middle of the 20th Century, world fossil fuel consumption has increased by five times, and freshwater use has doubled. At that rate of increase, these resources could be exhausted by the end of this century (Crenson, 2001). This continued depletion of natural resources, paired with the predominance of technology in the average child's life, is depleting nature experiences.

FIG 1-12. In the United States, a million acres are lost annually to sprawl and infrastructure development. (COURTESY OF UPSTATE FOREVER.)

The average young person watches 4 hours of television a day (Orr, 2002). According to the American Academy of Pediatrics, by age 18, a child has seen an estimated 360,000 television ads and 200,000 violent acts on television (*Environment and Health Weekly*, 2000). Over 1,000 studies show that TV violence increases aggressive behavior in some children and youth, desensitizes them to violence, and convinces them that the world is a dangerous place (Orr, 2002). Television's other effect is to replace children's discovery of nature with knowledge of another and far less valuable sort. A 2002 study from Britain reports that 8-year-olds surveyed identified Pokemon characters with far greater ease than they could recognize "otter, beetle, and oak tree" (Louv, 2005). Another study found that children could name over 1,000 corporate logos but only a few plants and animals.

Internet addiction is another threatening problem for today's generation of children. One study showed that even a few hours a week online led to a "deterioration of social and psychological life" and increased depression and a sense of isolation in subjects that were otherwise normal (Orr, 2002). Richard Louv, author of a variety of child development books including *Last Child in the Woods,* uses the phrase "nature deficit disorder" to describe the possible impacts these factors have on a child, potentially hindering both mental and physical development (Louv, 2005). In *The Thunder Tree*, Robert Michael Pyle dubs the phenomenon of the transformation of the natural special places of childhood into shopping malls and game rooms "the extinction of experience" (Pyle, 1993). These poignant terms begin to emphasize the extremity of the potential loss today's children—and tomorrow's—are facing.

Even though they are often deprived of nature, studies show children still crave and seek it; although children spend less than 15% of their time in natural environments, they consider them their favorite places (Nixon, 1997) (Figure 1-13). We live in an age of competing interests for children's attention. There are a number of negative trends, such as the isolation from direct daily contact with nature, which must be combatted by passionate adults, many of whom probably look back to their own nature-rich childhoods for inspiration as they seek a better future for their children. Although critically important, parks and gardens cannot wholly replace pristine nature, or the lessons the natural experience alone can provide (Kahn, 2002). However, conservation of the most special untouched wildernesses and the development of a green network of parks and open spaces throughout urban and suburban regions can work together. They can provide children with a nature-rich childhood by integrating both the convenience of discovery, play, and educational experiences within the urban fabric on a daily basis (Figure 1-14).

FIG 1-13. Although children spend less time in nature today than in the past, they still consider it among their favorite places. It is the responsibility of adults to provide nature opportunities to youth who so clearly seek them and benefit from them in many ways. (COURTESY OF BILL JORDAN.)

FIG 1-14. Green space such as parks within cities is easily accessible for large numbers of people and provides children with opportunities to interact with nature on a daily basis. (COURTESY OF LOLLY TAI.)

A Place of Their Own: Giving Nature Back to Children

Children should not only be folded into the adult-scale greenscape, but should have special spaces of their own. These children's parks and gardens should be designed with their own significant and particular needs in mind and with their input and involvement (Moore, 2003). In some ways, children and adults have the same needs. A love of trees and a feeling of safety within their shelter is a common comfort felt by all ages. A study by Kuo, Sullivan, Coley, and Brunson (1998) found that public housing residents living adjacent to public areas with trees and grass used common areas more, had more neighborhood social connectivity, and felt safer and better adjusted than those whose spaces lacked natural elements (Figure 1-15). Coley, Kuo, and Sullivan (1997) similarly found that twice as many children played in spaces with many trees as those with few in the 64 public Chicago spaces of their study. The play observed in treed areas was also more creative, and adults were found to be more attentive and engaged in children's play (Chawla, 2002).

FIG 1-15. Landscapes with trees make people feel more at ease and inclined toward social behavior. (COURTESY OF WILLIAM JORDAN.)

However, simply "green" is not good enough, when it comes to design for children. This text will elaborate in some detail on the development of design, but in general, these spaces must be child-centered and memorable, inviting repeat visits, and thus increasing the likelihood of making a lasting impact on a child's memory and development (Moore, 2003) (Figure 1-16).

This text examines many of the issues involved in providing landscapes designed for children, from safety to designing with children in mind to sustainability. This complex web of considerations may seem daunting, but the beautiful truth about the creation of a children's garden is that one person cannot and should not do it alone. A reader who finds parts of the process beyond his or her expertise can find reassurance in the community of a project team. Anything beyond the simplest project is going to need collaboration. Even a landscape architect experienced in the creation of children's spaces should involve the children whom the garden will serve to create a successful project. Parents, teachers, the community, maintenance staff, and anyone else with interest in the concept should also be included in the collaboration. Children's gardens are projects with life. It may not be easy to realize your goals and create a child's vision, but passion, collaboration, and the proper guidance, starting with the fundamentals of this text, will help your garden grow.

FIG 1-16. Landscapes for children should be memorable and inspiring so children will want to visit them many times and constantly discover new intriguing details. Such spaces are more likely to make a profound impact on the development of children who visit them. (COURTESY OF LOLLY TAI.)

There is no shortage of studies and reports indicating the value of nature to children, and there is no lack of evidence that adults who are passionate about the natural world developed that bond during their own childhoods. Yet most of the adults reading this text, seeking better understanding of ways in which they can bring a generation of children closer to a natural world they see slipping away, don't need statistics to feel the urgency of the need. They still feel a thrill of wonder at the indefinable power of a vast wilderness that always holds discovery, hope, joy, and beauty (Figure 1-17). Once we find our way back to those vacant lots, flower-filled meadows, and laughing streams of our own youth, we will know how to take today's children back there with us.

FIG 1-17. Those who provide gardens for youth must seek to inspire wonder, joy, and passion for nature while providing pleasure for children. (COURTESY OF ERIN JORDAN KNIGHT.)

Concept sketch of The Dinosaur Garden at The Children's Healthcare of Atlanta Children's Garden, Atlanta, Georgia. (COURTESY OF CINDY TYLER, TERRA DESIGN STUDIOS.)

CHAPTER 2

The Design Process

Schoolyards, gardens, and playgrounds are outdoor places where children can interact, play, and learn. The spaces within these settings comprise the framework of a designed outdoor learning environment. To create these spaces, a three-step design process is used. The steps include: (1) research, site inventory, site analysis, program development and user needs; (2) design; and (3) construction documentation, cost estimating, and implementation. This problem-solving process involves the organization of information, thoughts, and ideas that lead to a design solution. A sensitive design can often fit the design to the site and help save trees and wildlife habitat areas, reduce grading and erosion, and save money.

The design of outdoor environments for children begins with the evaluation of the specific design problems and objectives. It is based on a variety of considerations that are analyzed in a systematic manner that leads to informed decisions. Creating a design is not a simple process. It doesn't just happen. Many elements of the project need to be considered, including the existing site features, the requirement and purpose of the project, and the required construction and landscape materials, such as the pavement and furnishings as well as trees, shrubs, groundcovers, and flowers. Arranging these elements with functional and aesthetic purposes in mind ultimately produces a built project that provides a fun, interesting, safe, and rich learning environment for children. The exploration of design alternatives helps to identify the best solutions to the problem. Before starting the design process, it is essential to formulate a design team.

The Design Team

Development of the design team is the first step toward creating a successful design. The project team for schoolyards, gardens, or play yards should consist of administrators (i.e., school principal, garden director, community or civic leaders, etc.); users (i.e., children, parents, and the community); designers (i.e., landscape architects and architects); and others necessary to support the project (i.e., arborist, ecologist, educators, engineers, horticulturist, child psychologist, color psychologist, maintenance staff, and wildlife biologist).

It is important to actively involve the design team throughout the design process. Ultimately, it is their strong interest and commitment that will help to realize and maintain the project for the long run.

In a school setting, for example, it is imperative to develop a strong team to ensure a successful program. One determined educator or an excited parent cannot carry the project without an organized group of supporters equally committed to the continued health and success of the project. On this team, children are the most important members. Their ideas should define the components, structure, and goals of the project (White and Vicki, 1998) (Figure 2-1). Educators should be involved as mentors to the children, offering resources, facilitating student ideas and goals, and acting as co-workers with the children. The next partner is the school administrator and staff. Budget concerns, future building plans, liability issues, community relations, and funding opportunities are issues in which their assistance is fundamental. Most administrators see garden development as a valuable asset. They improve the image of the school, offer cost savings, provide teaching opportunities in all aspects of the curriculum (Figure 2-2), and foster student involvement and development within the project. The maintenance staff is an important asset to the team. They must have a clear understanding of the project's scope so they can offer assistance in assessment of the tools and equipment needed for the work, as well as advice

FIG 2-1. Children can be involved in every phase of the design and implementation process. They are the most important elements when developing component, structure, and goals of the project. (COURTESY OF GINA K. MCLELLAN.)

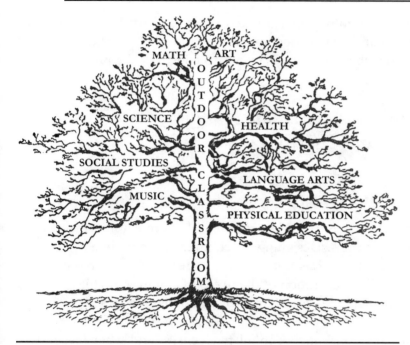

FIG 2-2. The outdoor classroom can become a vehicle for teaching subjects across the curriculum. (COURTESY OF BARBARA SIEGEL RYAN AND ERIN JORDAN KNIGHT.)

on issues of construction and long-term maintenance. Parents, too, must be included and involved, not only so the project is successful, but also so its goals and ideals can be reinforced in the home environment. Local businesses and civic organizations are great resources and team members as well, for they often offer technical support, material contributions, grants, volunteers, and other donations. Finally, resource professionals are important to the team. Landscape architects have invaluable knowledge and design expertise.

After the team is defined and formed, a clear and workable goal should be set and a time line determined. Planning, budget, and material needs should be estimated, and areas where assistance is needed should be identified. These lists and estimates may change after the site analysis, and updates may be needed as information becomes available.

Steps of the Design Process

There are three basic steps to the design process (Figure 2-3). The first step, research, site inventory and analysis, and program development, is critical to understanding the issues and conditions of the site. The

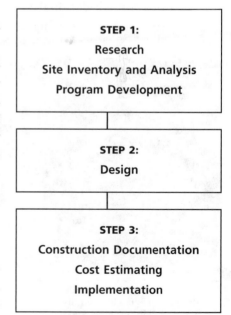

STEP 1:
Research
Site Inventory and Analysis
Program Development

STEP 2:
Design

STEP 3:
Construction Documentation
Cost Estimating
Implementation

FIG 2-3. Steps of the design process.

second step, design, organizes the information in step one into a workable design solution. The third step, construction documentation and implementation, builds on step two and provides the necessary drawings to construct the project.

Step 1: Research, Site Inventory, Site Analysis, Program Development and User Needs

RESEARCH

Why Should One Explore This Topic?

The first step in any project is research. It is ideal to assemble as much information as possible about the project goals. Designing for children, whether in a residential, public, or school setting, requires not only an understanding of basic landscape design but also special consideration of the needs of children. A child's safety, stimulation, and development are crucial principles in designing these special garden spaces.

Five senses: a child's garden should appeal to all five senses, and whenever possible, bring wildlife into a child's world (Moore, 1997). Such gardens are not only educational and fun, but instill in children a love of nature that will grow into stewardship and environmental sensitivity. Gardens that appeal to all the senses also provide many opportunities for discovery (Figure 2-4), an essential element of childhood. Through a child's opportunity to define the parameters of his or her play, creative and constructive activity occurs. As described by Molly Dannenmaier in *A Child's Garden*, plant life (Figure 2-5), wildlife, heights, enclosure, construction with loose parts, and games of make-believe (Figures 2-6 and 2-7) all provide opportunities for discovery.

Scale: It is important to identify both the common needs of children and adults, and special needs particular to the young. Although adults see the world on

FIG 2-4. At the Children's Healthcare of Atlanta Children's Garden, children discover the phenomenon of the honey-making process and are eager to test the taste of honey. (COURTESY OF LOLLY TAI.)

a large scale, children are attentive to details. Gary Nabhan, co-author of *The Geography of Childhood*, recalls a time he gave his young son a camera for photographs of a trip to several western National Parks (Nabhan and Trimble, 1994). Upon viewing his son's photos, Nabhan was struck by the difference between the subjects of his son's pictures and those of his own. Although amazing vistas dominated his own photographs, the child seemed more interested in rocks, twigs, lizards, and other more tactile, small-scale objects he could explore on an intense level. Children are intrigued by the miniscule details that give an object beauty or interest; adults often take the simple and small elements for granted, preferring to see the "big picture" from a more distant standpoint. When designing for children, this is an important fact to remember, and when designing for adults, it may be challenging and beneficial to encourage them to see the same level of detail, as through a child's eyes (Figure 2-8).

FIG 2-5. Opportunity for discovery is provided at Awbury Arboretum when children learn about plant and animal life and the process of decomposition of a tree. (COURTESY OF ELSIE VIEHMAN.)

FIG 2-6 (left) and FIG 2-7 (right). Children find discovery when they make believe in the Acorn Tearoom and in the Bird's Nest at the Enchanted Woods™ at Winterthur Museum & Country Estate. (COURTESY OF W. GARY SMITH.)

FIG 2-8. When designing for children, it is important to pay attention to the scale of children and to view details at their level. Average heights were determined by averaging the boys' stature for age and girls' stature for age in the 50th percentile of the pediatric growth charts developed by the National Center for Health Statistics in collaboration with the National Center for Chronic Disease Prevention and Health Promotion (2000, http.//www.cdc.gov.growthcharts "Pediatrics. Growth Charts for Boys and Girls." About.com. 26 August 2005. http.//pediatrics.about.com/cs/growthcharts2/l/bl_growthcharts.html, accessed 2005). (COURTESY OF BARBARA SIEGEL RYAN.)

> *"We can be there with them as they climb on rocks, play in streams and waves, dig in the rich soil of woods and gardens, putter and learn. Here, on the land, we learn from each other. Here, our children's journey begins."*—Stephen Trimble, co-author of The Geography of Childhood.

Safety: It is important to consider design principles alongside safety precautions to create successful children's spaces. A design cannot be masterful without meeting the safety needs of children, yet issues of safety and liability cannot overshadow the various desires and needs of the child. The two are not exclusive, and when used successfully in cooperation with one another, provide the best spaces children can have to further their development, happiness, and health. (For further discussion and guidelines about safety, refer to Chapter 4: Schoolyards, Playgrounds, and Backyards.)

Two of the most desirable elements in a children's landscape, water and heights, are often omitted due to liability and safety concerns (as well as costliness). However, there are many ways to provide both safely in ways appealing to children. Perhaps the greatest joy for children discovering a landscape is found in water (Figure 2-9).

Heights give children a sense of escape, providing a unique and exciting perspective. Well-designed treehouses and play towers with appropriate fall zone surfaces below allow children to experience safe height exploration (Figure 2-10).

Thoughtful design of spaces, paired with safety education for children, minimizes risk.

Retreat: It is essential to realize the similarities between children and adults as well as the differences. Many adults treat children with less respect or attention than they would a peer. However, adults must remember that children are individuals, with varied and dynamic personalities that add immeasurable insight to the design process. Children express the same range of emotions that adults do, but the source of their feelings may be alien to an adult perspective. Some adults see childhood as a time for play, free of the stress and care common to later life. Just as adults need private spaces in which to relax and escape, children must have a retreat. Gardens are wonderful, safe spaces to fulfill this need.

One way children retreat is to seek enclosure. Children need places where they feel safe and can think and play privately, away from the constant supervision of adults. This is essential to the development of a sense of autonomy, and gives children a place for creative play. Spaces for enclosure should be situated within a safe environment so adults can remain nearby and assure safety of the child, without invading the private space the child seeks (Dannenmaier, 1998). Safe spaces of enclosure may be built structures, such as tree houses or the tubes of a plastic fabricated play structure. They

FIG 2-9 (top). Two of the most desirable elements in a children's landscape are water and heights. Children cannot keep their hands off the Flower Fountain in the Bee-aMazed Children's Garden at Longwood Gardens. (COURTESY OF MARY TAYLOR HAQUE.) FIG 2-10 (bottom). Atop a "treehouse" in a residential backyard, a child can look and search for creatures through a telescope. (COURTESY OF SCOTT R. KELLY.)

FIG 2-11. Children need places where they feel safe, can ponder, and play privately. At the Camden Children's Garden, they can hide and play in the Red Oak Run Maze. (COURTESY OF CAMDEN CHILDREN'S GARDEN.)

may also be part of a natural garden environment (Figure 2-11). Woven willow branches can create sculptural spaces for children to hide in or move through, and vines trained over a low, simple arbor can create a private space through a screen of greenery. Creative spaces for enclosure can be very beautiful and fitting to a garden setting that adults use as well. Ideas for such structures can be found in books and magazines; a good source is Sharon Lovejoy's *Roots, Shoots, Buckets, and Boots* (Lovejoy, 1999). Many gardens described in her book give children a sense of privacy within walls constructed purely of plant material, such as the Sunflower House. With walls made of sunflowers of varying heights, and a roof of flowering vines clinging to a grid of twine strung between the tallest sunflowers, a beautiful and magical space is created.

Play: Play has important roles beyond recreation; it is the exploration of a world still fresh from the perspective of a child (JOPERD, 1994). Some play, such as games of make-believe and role-play, or investigative play such as exploration of nature, develops the mind of a child and expands the thought processes. Other play is more active, and directly effects a child's development of motor skills and physical fitness. Yet another kind of play is the controlled and deliberate release of feeling, an expression of self, such as drawing a picture or making any unique and artistic object. Each type of explorative play contributes to a child's education.

Active play: Physical development is currently the primary focus of outdoor spaces for children. Although children's mental and emotional needs must be met to ensure healthy childhood development, it is also crucial to maintain safe places where children can be physically active (Moore, 1997) (Figure 2-12).

Development of motor skills and physical health is essential, but it is important to realize that different children need different types of spaces for movement and physical play. Some children enjoy group activities, but others prefer active games they can play alone.

The skill level of the child may reflect greatly on their preferred physical play (Sawyers, 1994). It is important to allow physical development to occur in a non-threatening atmosphere in which the child has control of his or her type of involvement. Children who fear the ridicule of their peers in team sport situations or group games can gain confidence before interacting in situations in which they must prove their skill. Movement and physical play should be enjoyable and comfortable for every child, and spaces should be versatile to meet children's varied needs and skill levels.

Creative play: Imaginative play is one of the most important exercises of childhood. Often, creativity is strongest in childhood, but when it is not cultivated, it can be lost. When encouraged and stimulated by a healthy play environment, a child's imagination will thrive, improving his or her mind, thought process, and potential (Figure 2-13).

Spaces for make-believe are easy to provide, by definition. Children can fill in the details of their games with their minds, and have entertainment with very rudimentary tools or no tools at all. However, a natural environment is best for encouraging creativity, for within nature are many elements that children can adapt into their play (White and Vicki, 1998). Sticks, leaves, acorn caps, and rocks can represent the dishes and food of a tea party, or be fashioned into tiny houses and miniature figures to inhabit them. When a child's mind is given tools to create a new world, the possibilities are endless.

Through play with loose elements such as dirt, twigs, cones, and leaves, children develop skills in construction and creation. For a

FIG 2-12. Physical development is currently the primary focus of outdoor spaces for children. At the Bee-aMazed Children's Garden at Longwood Gardens, children get plenty of physical exercise running around the Buzz Trail. (COURTESY OF LONGWOOD GARDENS.)

FIG 2-13. Children develop skills with construction and creation at the Dinosaur Garden at the Children's Healthcare of Atlanta Children's Garden through play with loose elements of sand and water. (COURTESY OF LOLLY TAI.)

FIG 2-14 (left). Selection of plant materials requires careful consideration when designing for children. Pumpkins are one of the most popular plants for kids. (COURTESY OF BILL JORDAN.) FIG 2-15 (right). Children are attracted to the color and smell of plants at the Children's Garden at Hershey Gardens. (COURTESY OF COLLEEN M. SEACE PHOTOGRAPHY AND HERSHEY GARDENS.)

child, comprehension of these principles may be as basic as knowing that wet soil can be sculpted better than dry, or that flowing water will eventually break a dam of twigs and sand (Dannenmaier, 1998).

Plants: Selection of plant material requires careful consideration when designing for children (Figure 2-14). Plants should be hardy, interesting to children, and safe for their environment (Dannenmaier, 1998). Two primary dangers must be considered: plants that are poisonous or have poisonous parts, and plants with hazardous parts, such as thorns, barbs, or sharp blades.

Many common plants, or their parts, can be hazardous or fatal to children if consumed (Moore, 1993). Anemone, caladium, foxglove, hydrangea, lantana, mistletoe, and philodendron are poisonous if eaten. The bulbs of amaryllis and daffodil, the leaves of apple and privet trees, the seeds of apple and wisteria, and berries of holly and privet are all poisonous (Dannenmaier, 1998). Should these be totally eliminated, or should children be taught to respect their dangers? This is a question any parent, supervisor, or designer for children should answer for his or her particular situation and landscape.

Some plants provide particular attraction and interest to children, often based on bright color, unusual behaviors, fruits, flowers, or plant parts that can be used creatively for play, projects, and crafts (Figure 2-15).

Wildlife: Plants are essential, beautiful elements for children's outdoor spaces. Often, these plants serve a double function, by attracting wildlife into children's spaces. Observation of wildlife is a favorite pastime of childhood, and is beneficial both in developing a sense of the wonders of nature and in teaching children about animals (Dannenmaier, 1998). It is simple to invite animals into a landscape. Birds and butterflies are particularly easy to accommodate, and can come into children's lives even in a city setting. The National Wildlife Federation (NWF) has many helpful guidelines for the attraction of wildlife into the landscape, and will certify spaces in schoolyards or backyards that meet the criteria demanded by animals (NWF, 2001). To attract wildlife such as birds and butterflies or deer, rabbits, and other larger animals, four essentials are necessary: food, water, shelter, and a place to raise young (Figure 2-16).

Food: When creating a wildlife habitat and providing food, it is best to utilize natural sources, which means implementing native vegetation. Trees, shrubs, and other plants that produce acorns, nuts, berries, and other seeds are great attractions, while leaves, buds, catkins, nectar, and pollen are also important. By providing food for the animals through the natural food chain, children learn about ecology while animals get the best possible source of nutrition. According to the NWF, native plants can support 10 to 15 times as many species of wildlife as nonnative species (NWF, 2001). Most states have a native plant society, and contacting a local chapter is a good way to learn about native species.

FIG 2-16. Observation of wildlife is a favorite pastime among children. Brooklyn Botanical Garden's Discovery Garden provides the essentials of a wildlife habitat including food, water, shelter, and a place to raise young. (COURTESY OF LOLLY TAI.)

Natural food can be supplemented by feeders, and particularly in winter, this is a great benefit to animals. The best foods for feeders include sunflower, niger, safflower, millet seed, cracked corn, meal worms, and suet, according to the NWF. Each type attracts particular kinds of birds, and a variety of feeders and food types ensures a diverse bird population. In warm months, humming bird feeders containing four parts water to one part sugar can supplement the hummingbird's diet.

When providing feed, there are several important rules to follow. Make sure feeders have proper drainage holes and are covered to keep seed dry, so mildew won't develop. Do not place feed directly on the ground, for mold, mildew, animal droppings, lawn fertilizers, pesticides, and bacteria can contaminate the seed and harm birds. Also, keep in mind that bird droppings may accumulate under the feeder, so avoid areas where the mess will cause problems. Follow these steps, and children will enjoy hours of watching and listening to birds of all kinds.

Water: All animals need water throughout the year for drinking and bathing. Adding a water feature to the garden is the best way to ensure that birds will be attracted to the site. Water is helpful to the health and happiness of birds because clean feathers insulate the bird, and bathing helps prevent parasites. Birdbaths provide for this necessity, but a few basic rules apply to ensure that they are safe and beneficial to birds. Basins should be no more than 1.5 to 3 inches (38 mm to 76 mm) deep, with small pebbles in the basin to provide areas for perching and preening. They must be placed in an open area safe from predators, but with cover available nearby, and should be 15 feet (4.6 meters) from feeding areas. Fresh water should be added every 2–3 days.

Shelter: To provide shelter for wildlife, it is again advisable to look to the natural state of the area. The same plants that feed wildlife often provide natural sanctuary. Brush piles, fallen logs, rock piles, and other natural elements can give animals safety and shelter. A variety of sizes, heights, and densities of material is preferable. Evergreen and deciduous plant material should be combined to provide for animals' needs throughout the year. Often, the same spaces can also be used for courting, nesting, and raising young.

Man-made cover is also helpful in many cases, such as birdhouses, bat boxes, and other protected homes. Be sure that the construction of these houses suits the needs of the animal. For example, different types of birds require different locations for their homes, as well as different shapes and sizes of boxes and their entrances. Even the color of the box can be a factor in its safe use by wildlife. The box should not be attractive or accessible to predators. Height, hole size, and location are key factors in birdhouse safety.

Place to raise the young: Spaces to raise young are often identical to those of cover, but certain additions can ensure a variety of wildlife in the garden. Again, native plants play a key role in provision of these spaces, for many types of native wildlife, such as butterflies, require these plants for laying of eggs.

The key factors in spaces to raise young are safety and proximity to reliable sources of food and water. It is easy and educational to provide such spaces for animals. Wildlife habitats have many benefits, not just for animals, but for children and adults as well. Children can learn about their native environments through observation of wildlife, and feel gratified when their work in the garden calls to animal visitors and inhabitants. There are many solutions to the four requirements for a wildlife habitat, and no matter what the size of a school or home garden may be, it is possible to provide habitat.

All these elements are basic tools from which to construct a landscape. When combining and applying them, it is important to use creativity, and to give the child or children for whom the space is provided a strong voice in its construction. Often, as adults, it is hard to not straighten and enhance the creations of children, but it is important that children feel a sense of ownership for their landscapes. It is also important to be sure that while learning and growing, children develop a lasting love for the act of nurturing life and watching nature give birth to the landscape.

BASE MAP AND SITE INVENTORY

Where Are the Property Lines and What Already Exists on the Site?

Base Map. The next step is obtaining a base map. A base map or property boundary survey map usually comes with the purchase of a land parcel. Typically prepared by a licensed land surveyor, a survey map is drawn to scale, and often shows the relationship between the property boundary lines, topographic contour lines, the location of structures, large trees, easements, and other substantial features (Figure 2-17). A topographic survey locates the

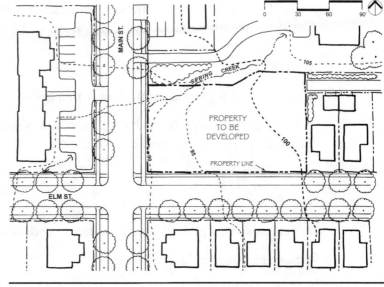

FIG 2-17. Base map. (COURTESY OF BARBARA SIEGEL RYAN.)

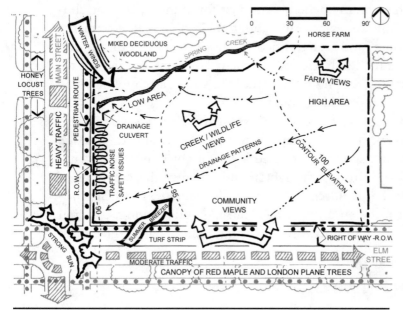

site's elevations. A tree survey inventories the existing trees including type, size, and location. Both can be commissioned through a land surveyor.

Site Inventory. Once a base map has been completed, the existing conditions of the site, referred to as the site inventory, can be documented on the map using text as well as graphics (Figure 2-18). For example, arrows can indicate direction of noise, views, sun orientation, and prevailing winds; large circles or outlines can show the location of a single mature tree or a woodland edge; and outlined areas can delineate flat, low, and high points. The site inventory should note all of the existing conditions of the site. The final graphic plan will help visualize the features of the site with clarity before any work has begun.

The site inventory can include the following information:

- Buildings

- Climate: sun, wind, temperature, precipitation

- Geology and soils (available through the Natural Resources Conservation Service; see http://www.nrcs.usda.gov)

- Hydrology: drainage

- Property lines

- Vehicular and pedestrian circulation: roads and sidewalks

- Special features: lakes, ponds

- Topography (see www.usgs.gov/research/gis/title.html

- Utilities

- Vegetation: trees, shrubs

- Views

- Off-site or adjacent land-use and conditions: noise, views

It is also important to be aware of the laws and regulations affecting the project, such as local zoning regulations and Americans with Disabilities Act (ADA) Design Standards for accessible design (Figure 2-19) (http://www.ada.gov, accessed 2005). Additionally, safety considerations should be addressed.

FIG 2-19. Accessible design should be considered by following American with Disabilities Act (ADA) Design Standards. Raised plant beds accommodate individuals in a wheelchair. (COURTESY OF BARBARA SIEGEL RYAN.)

SITE ANALYSIS

How Do Existing Features of the Site Affect the Design?

Different from the site inventory, the site analysis evaluates and assesses the site conditions for potentials and constraints that may affect the design (Figures 2-20 and 2-21). Ideally, the site analysis can be thought of as a series of keyed map layers. Each layer can be studied individually or layers can be superimposed on one another to show the overall picture. For example, a vegetation analysis map will show the location, type, size, quality, and condition of the trees as

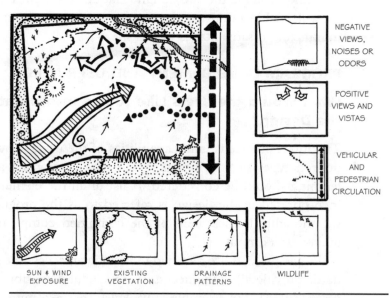

FIG 2-20. The site analysis process is enhanced by making notes about the site conditions using text and graphics. Major trees, elevation changes, drainage patterns, sun and wind orientations are delineated by arrows and outlines. (COURTESY OF BARBARA SIEGEL RYAN.)

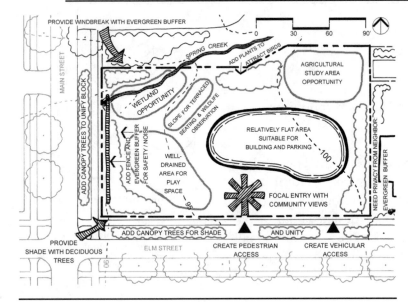

Inside the figure the following labels appear:

PROVIDE WINDBREAK WITH EVERGREEN BUFFER

MAIN STREET

ADD CANOPY TREES TO UNIFY BLOCK

ADD FENCE AND EVERGREEN BUFFER FOR SAFETY / NOISE

WETLAND OPPORTUNITY

SPRING CREEK

ADD PLANTS TO ATTRACT BIRDS

SLOPE FOR TERRACED SEATING & WILDLIFE OBSERVATION

AGRICULTURAL STUDY AREA OPPORTUNITY

RELATIVELY FLAT AREA SUITABLE FOR BUILDING AND PARKING

100

WELL-DRAINED AREA FOR PLAY SPACE

FOCAL ENTRY WITH COMMUNITY VIEWS

NEED PRIVACY FROM NEIGHBOR EVERGREEN BUFFER

0 30 60 90'

PROVIDE SHADE WITH DECIDUOUS TREES

ELM STREET

ADD CANOPY TREES FOR SHADE

AND UNITY

CREATE PEDESTRIAN ACCESS

CREATE VEHICULAR ACCESS

FIG 2-21. Site analysis. (COURTESY OF BARBARA SIEGEL RYAN.)

well as highlight those that need to be protected, saved, or removed. A slope analysis map will show flat, rolling, and steep areas of the site as well as indicate areas that are too low or steep to build without considerable grading either in cut and/or fill (Figure 2-22). The composite layers will clearly show the potential of the site. The analysis may be simple or complex, but it is still helpful to think about the way different kinds of features combine to shape the site design (Haque et al., 2001). Ultimately, the site analysis will enable informed decisions to be made for maximizing advantages and minimizing disadvantages of the site.

PROGRAM DEVELOPMENT AND USER NEEDS

What Would the Users Like to See Incorporated in the Design?

The interests, needs, and capabilities of the users should be determined, and the desired types of activities that will take place such as gardening, playing, and learning should be considered. A list of all the elements and requirements to be incorporated in the design is referred to as the program. This is determined by the thoughtful assessment of the combined composite site analysis and clients and/or users input.

Public projects are required to include an accessible landscape. The ADA Standards provide all of the necessary details for accessibility (http://www.ada.gov, accessed 2005). For example, a walkway that is a minimum of 48 inches (1.2 meters) affords a person in a wheelchair ample space for gardening tools and easy maneuvering while allowing others to pass by. A 6-foot (1.8 meters) walkway

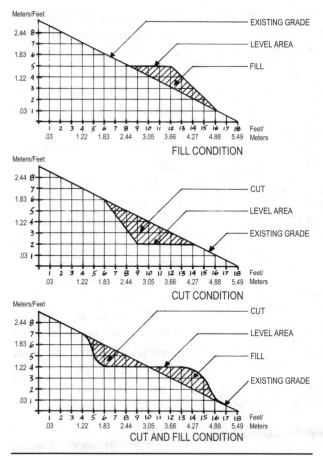

FILL CONDITION

CUT CONDITION

CUT AND FILL CONDITION

FIG 2-22. Various ways to grade a site. (COURTESY OF LOLLY TAI AND BARBARA SIEGEL RYAN.)

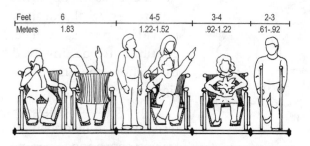

Feet	6	4-5	3-4	2-3
Meters	1.83	1.22-1.52	.92-1.22	.61-.92

FIG 2-23. Dimensions for walkways according to ADA Design Standards. Left to right. (1) path for two wheelchairs, (2) path for a person next to wheelchair, (3) a wheelchair, and (4) a person with crutches. (COURTESY OF BARBARA SIEGEL RYAN.)

accommodates sufficient space for two wheelchairs to pass by each other. Accessible ramps are required to be 8% slope or 1 foot:12 feet (0.3 meter: 3.7 meters) or less (Figure 2-23).

Step 2: Design

How Is the Design Created?

When designing and building a new project, the optimum time to initiate the site design is at the very beginning before any site work has started. Changes can readily be made when the design is on paper rather than after construction has begun. During the design phase, the designer, often a landscape architect, will study the data gathered from the research, site inventory and analysis, program, and client input to shape the design. The design is typically created on trace paper over the "layers" of the base map, site inventory, and site analysis. Colored pencils or markers are applied for visual clarity. Proposed design areas such as buildings, plant beds, play areas, vegetable gardens, walkways, and water fea-

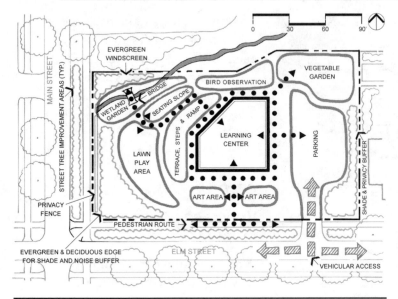

FIG 2-24. Functional diagram. (COURTESY OF BARBARA SIEGEL RYAN.)

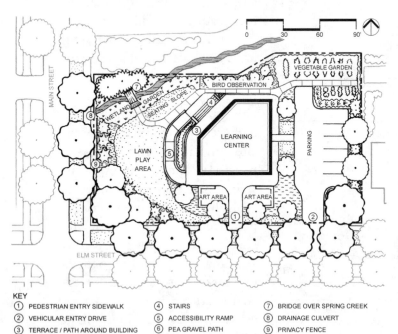

KEY
1. PEDESTRIAN ENTRY SIDEWALK
2. VEHICULAR ENTRY DRIVE
3. TERRACE / PATH AROUND BUILDING
4. STAIRS
5. ACCESSIBILITY RAMP
6. PEA GRAVEL PATH
7. BRIDGE OVER SPRING CREEK
8. DRAINAGE CULVERT
9. PRIVACY FENCE

FIG 2-25. Final design. (COURTESY OF BARBARA SIEGEL RYAN.)

tures should be verified to be sure they respond to the site inventory and site analysis.

Typically within the design phase, three steps are involved: conceptual, preliminary, and final design. The first step, conceptual design, organizes the relationship of the proposed uses on the site plan in a "bubble" diagram, also referred as a functional diagram (Figure 2-24). The second step, preliminary design, transforms the functional diagram into general shapes of the design. The third step, final design, refines the preliminary plan to produce a precise plan for the project (Figure 2-25). During each stage, the client has the opportunity to review the design, provide input, as well as continue to be involved throughout the entire design process.

One or more design alternatives can be drawn on tracing paper and superimposed to evaluate each alternative. Frequently, the best ideas from each of the alternatives can be combined to make up the final design (Figure 2-26).

Step 3: Construction Documentation, Cost Estimating, and Implementation

CONSTRUCTION DOCUMENTATION

What Construction Drawings Are Needed to Build the Job?

The final step of the design process is the construction documentation necessary for contractors to bid the project. The owner may select a contractor directly or through a bidding process.

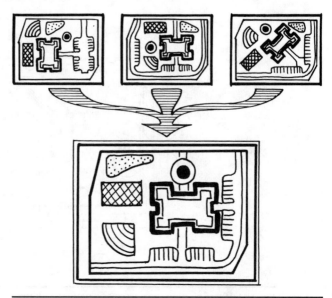

FIG 2-26. Maximum potentials of the site can be determined when multiple layers of the site have been carefully analyzed. Using the strengths of several design alternatives to create the final design solution is the most ideal. (COURTESY OF BARBARA SIEGEL RYAN.)

The bidding process involves invitation of selected firms to submit fees for constructing the project. Once the bids are received, the owner can select the contracting firm based on price quotation and interview. This technical set of drawings typically prepared by a landscape architect comprises the following set of coordinated plans and details:

A. *Layout plan:* denotes the location and dimensions of all existing and proposed site improvements. It is tied to a fixed element on the site such as a building or property line.

B. *Grading plan:* illustrates existing contours and proposed contours manipulated to accommodate appropriate drainage and contouring of the project site.

C. *Planting plan:* shows the individual plant location, name (genus and species), size, height, quantity, spacing, and other notes (i.e., multi-stemmed, single straight trunk, container, balled and burlapped, etc.). In many instances, a project will also call for an irrigation and lighting plan which is typically coordinated with the planting plan (Figure 2-27).

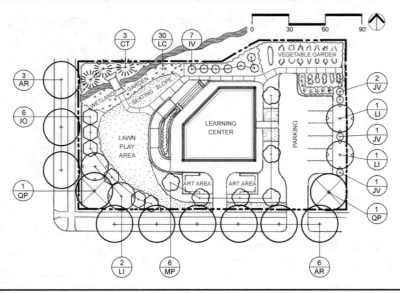

FIG 2-27. Planting plan. (COURTESY OF BARBARA SIEGEL RYAN.)

PLANT LIST

KEY	BOTANICAL NAME	COMMON NAME	QTY.	SIZE	REMARKS
TREES					
AR	*Acer rubrum*	Red Maple	9	8–10′ HT (2.4–3.0 m)	B&B
CT	*Chamaecyparis thyoides* 'Rubicon'	Rubicon Atlantic White Cedar	3	8′ HT (2.4 m)	B&B
IO	*Ilex opaca* 'Nellie R. Stevens'	Nellie R. Stevens Holly	6	5–6′ HT (1.5–1.8 m)	B&B 4 female/2 male
LI	*Lagerstroemia indica* 'Natchez'	Natchez Crapemyrtle	4	3″ Caliper (76 mm)	B&B Tree Form
MP	*Malus* spp. 'Prairiefire'	Prairiefire Crabapple	6	2.5–3″ (64–76 mm) Caliper	B&B
QP	*Quercus phellos*	Willow Oak	2	8–10′ HT (2.4–3.0 m)	B&B
SHRUBS					
IV	*Ilex verticillata*	Winterberry Holly	7	5–6′ HT (1.5 m)	B&B
JV	*Juniperus virginiana* 'Emerald Sentinel'	Emerald Sentinel Eastern Red Cedar	4	5–6′ HT (1.5 m)	B&B
PERENNIALS					
LC	*Lobelia cardinalis*	Cardinal Flower	30	QT pot (.95 L)	15″ O.C. (38 cm)

D. *Planting details:* delineates proper planting methods for trees, shrubs, ground-covers, etc. (Figure 2-28). Plant materials come in different types and sizes, and proper planting details should be followed to ensure successful growth. Instructions regarding soil mixture, mulching, and pruning, should also be followed.

E. *Site details:* delineates proper construction and installation of landscape details such as decks, fences, fountains, paving, patios, rubber surfacing, railings, steps, trellises, walls, and site furnishings (i.e., benches, garden ornaments, planters, signs, etc.).

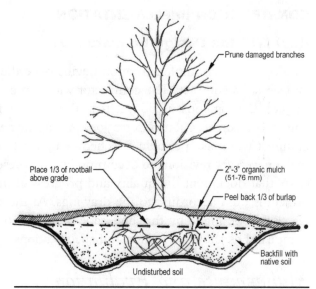

FIG 2-28. Tree planting detail. (COURTESY OF ELLIOT BUFF AND ALBERT LYNN.)

In addition to the construction plans and details, landscape architects also prepare a technical set of written construction specifications, a legal document specifying building or landscape standards and methods of construction. The construction specifications cover quality and testing of materials, installation methods, guarantees, and other factors.

COST ESTIMATE

How Much Will It Cost to Install the Design?

During the design phase, preliminary cost estimates should be generated. A cost estimating firm can be retained for this service. It is ideal to obtain an itemized cost estimate for the project as well as an estimate for each phase of the project if applicable. A cost estimate will not only determine whether the project is on the budget, but will also help identify areas where costs need to be cut or adjusted.

CONSTRUCTION IMPLEMENTATION

How Will the Design be Installed?

The construction implementation begins once the owner has selected a contractor and signed a contract. The contractor will then coordinate, schedule, and build the project. During construction, it is in the owner's interest to retain a landscape architect for construction observation. As the owner's representative, the landscape architect will make periodic or scheduled job site visits to answer questions and to make necessary revisions to accommodate unforeseen circumstances, write field reports that document the quality and progress of the project, and to ensure that the project is built according to the drawings. At the completion of the project, a final check will be made by the landscape architect to ensure that everything has been completed as shown on plans and specifications.

Maintenance and Evaluation

How can the project continue to look good and function efficiently? Once the design is completed, the landscape must be properly maintained for it to live, grow, mature, and acquire the desired appearance and function consistent with the design intent over time. This is sometimes the hardest task. A design may look and function wonderfully when complete, but will quickly deteriorate if not properly maintained. The owner or a landscape contractor should regularly maintain the landscape through mowing, watering/irrigating, fertilizing, weeding, pest and disease control, mulching, as well as plant replacement. The construction items in the design should also follow regularly scheduled maintenance inspections to sustain good condition (i.e., safety repair of loose bolts, etc.) and upkeep (i.e., painting, staining, pressure washing, etc.).

Ideally, the owner or the landscape architect should inspect the project periodically to ensure that it is being properly maintained, is in good working order, is sustaining its original design intent, and/or is in need of improvements. Observations and evaluations of the way children interact and use the space have a great impact on determining the short and long-term improvements needed to enhance and ensure the success of the project for years to come.

CONCLUSION

The key to developing a creative, healthy outdoor space for children is using all the resources available, understanding the needs of the child, and providing nat-

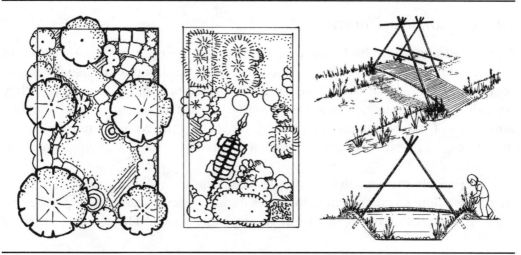

FIG 2-29 (left). A service provided by the American Horticulture Society is a series of 12 demonstration gardens designed for the George Washington River Farm Gardens in Virginia (AHS, 2001). A Grove Garden was designed and installed by DLM Design. Design team: Emily Davidson, Andrea Lybecker, and Emilie McBride. FIG 2-30 (middle). An Imagination Garden incorporates many elements children enjoy with varied plant materials. FIG 2-31 (right). A Ditch Garden is great for small lots and spaces. Designed and installed by Alastair Bolton of Lynn Edward Studio.

ural or naturalized spaces that allow children to engage in play that is not predetermined. It is through the design process that such goals are achieved. The design process is not a simple process. It is ideal to involve professionals throughout the various steps of the project. There are also various national resources such as the National Wildlife Federation (NWF) and the American Horticulture Society (AHS) to call upon for assistance (Figures 2-29 through 2-31). When the project is built, it is never quite finished because on-going evaluation and maintenance are important to sustaining its vibrant life.

The design process cannot be completed without consideration of child safety. In Chapter 4, safety issues are explored. Yet, it is important to consider design principles alongside safety precautions to create successful children's spaces. A design cannot be masterful without meeting the safety needs of children, yet issues of safety and liability cannot overshadow the various desires and needs of the child. The two are not exclusive, and when used successfully in cooperation with one another, provide the best spaces children can have to further their development, happiness, and health.

Installation by Volunteers

Many landscapes for children are being built today as part of schoolyards and various community environments. Because these landscapes are usually grassroots efforts organized by people within the given school or community, they typically have little or no budget for installation. These landscapes rely on various types of fundraising as the primary source of money, and limiting expenditures especially in procedures such as installation is a standard mode of operation.

Using an alternative form of installation in children's landscapes is simply a way of installing an environment that uses nontraditional sources of expertise and labor. It is typically driven by one of several motivations. These are:

1. A need to save money by not incurring conventional types of expenses.

2. The availability of "free" labor in the form of parents, service clubs, or others desiring to perform community service.

3. An opportunity to link the installation with a service learning effort.

The volunteers who make up an installation team consist primarily of parents when a schoolyard is the focus. Parents have a vested interest in developing playgrounds and gardens that will be used by their own children. Civic organizations such as Rotary and Sertoma often seek volunteer roles related to children and their environments. Another excellent source of volunteers is college students who are garnered through classes or clubs (Figure 2-32).

Volunteers have numerous talents and abili-

FIG 2-32. A representative of the playground equipment company guides these volunteers through construction, a process that ensures the correct installation while providing savings of about one-third of the total costs. (COURTESY OF GINA K. MCLELLAN.)

ties to add to any children's environment, but it is important to remember that the process leading to successful installation by volunteers is very different from traditional installations. A three-person leadership team is recommended, which consists of a representative of the recipient school or organization and two volunteers to lead the installation effort. Constant communication between the school or organization representative and the lead volunteers must be maintained. The open communication saves time and assures compliance with requirements of the school or organization.

Many schools and organizations choose to do volunteer installations of such things as playground equipment because it can reduce the cost of the equipment by approximately one-third. When choosing volunteer installation as an approach, it is important to consider bringing the equipment manufacturer's installation professional to the site to guide the volunteers through the process. Usually, it costs a reasonable amount for the professional's time and having this person on site will ensure that the equipment is installed correctly. This can provide legal protection later, and will ensure that the manufacturer's warranty on the equipment is in effect (Figure 2-33).

The two lead volunteers from the leadership team should split the responsibilities into two parts, with each overseeing one part. One school with a highly successful alternative installation involving multiple environments in its school-yard referred to this team as "The Brain and the Brawn." The "Brain" establishes a plan for the installation and identifies specific needs for the process including such things as number of people, equipment, supplies, and materials. The "Brawn" contacts potential volunteers, organizes them into work groups, and is onsite during installation to oversee everything. Usually the two lead volunteers are

FIG 2-33. These parent volunteers consider dozens of nuts, bolts, and pieces to be a giant erector set and enjoy the process of assembling this piece of playground equipment. (COURTESY OF GINA K. MCLELLAN.)

people who were involved in the original ideation phase of the overall project. Most important, they must be able to work well together.

VOLUNTEER INSTALLATION PROCESS

Based on numerous installation projects at schools and communities, a process was developed to help assure the successful installation of projects using nonconventional techniques. These are the most important steps to help assure that volunteers can get the job done (Figure 2-34).

FIG 2-34. This child helps role out fabric in preparation for the playground safety surfacing material. (COURTESY OF GINA K. MCLELLAN.)

1. *Communication is the tie that binds.* Imbed yourself in this concept because literally nothing will get done without it. Communication between volunteer leaders and organizational leaders must begin at the outset and continue throughout the project. With a school project, for example, the principal and the lead parent volunteers would be an excellent communication link. In a government setting, it might be the director of the parks and recreation department and lead members of the citizen's advisory committee. In a church or private garden, the link may be the facility director and the landscape committee chairperson. The important thing is to identify the appropriate person in the organization and the capable volunteer leaders to assure that everything starts and ends with this group.

2. *Follow the yellow brick road.* The master plan is the yellow brick road, and it was developed to provide a roadmap to the finished product. The mas-

ter plan was most likely developed with significant input and ideas from the community that will ultimately use the product and was put together under the direction of someone with expertise in planning and design. If questions arise during installation or an idea surfaces that could simplify or improve installation, they should be brought to the designated volunteer leaders and organization designee. These people can go back to the master planner to determine if changes should be made during installation.

3. *Establish a time line.* Make a list of everything that needs to be done and how long it takes to do each item on the list. Couple this with any built-in limitations such as seasonal weather patterns, recommended planting dates, and construction that must be completed before your project can begin. All of these become considerations in setting the project's time line. Make the time line realistic, and stick to it. When volunteers see that their individual effort is part of the bigger picture, they tend to eagerly work within the established timeline.

4. *Set a work schedule.* This schedule fits hand in hand with the overall time line but provides a specific schedule of days and times for each component to be accomplished. Each member of the leadership trio should have a copy of the schedule in hand throughout the project. The schedule must be realistic, and the person setting the schedule must remember that it usually takes volunteers longer to complete a specific task than if done by professionals. The schedule should also build in additional time between tasks in case of delays.

5. *Identify potential volunteers.* The leadership team can plan for months to do a volunteer built project, but without volunteers, the project just won't happen. Volunteer recruitment is a necessity, and there are many approaches from which to choose. When the first solicitation for volunteers begins, it is important to have a work schedule lined out so the volunteers may choose dates and times to fit their individual schedules. A variety of means of contacting volunteers may be used including e-mails, memorandums sent home from school, phone calls, and media-based requests. The leadership team should decide which methods will work best in their case and then begin the recruitment process. Remember to set aside tasks that can easily be accomplished by the children who will eventually benefit from the environment being constructed. Children take ownership of places they help build

FIG 2-35. Children should be included as volunteers when their safety can be assured, and their tasks should suit their ages. (COURTESY OF GINA K. MCLELLAN.)

FIG 2-36. This child is learning at an early age the importance of helping out. (COURTESY OF GINA K. MCLELLAN.)

and in turn take better care of those places (Figure 2-35).

6. *Protect your volunteers.* Any organization planning to use volunteers to build children's landscapes should check with its own supervisory unit (i.e., school district, city government, association) to determine if and how volunteers are covered in case of accidents. It is always best to seek answers regarding legal liability issues before the installation is underway (Figure 2-36).

7. *Patience is a virtue.* It is important to remember throughout the installation process that volunteers are just that—volunteers. They are not required to help. They may show up when scheduled to—or not. They may be experienced—or not. They may be team players—or not. They may work hard—or not. The "or nots" tend to be few and far between, but the leadership team must be prepared to deal with the situations if they do arise, and a little

patience goes a long way. When you have a leadership team familiar with the variety of personalities in the volunteer corps, it is easier to schedule and place them within groups where conflicts can be kept to a minimum.

8. *Be prepared.* The leadership team with the help of any designees must have on hand all materials and supplies before installation begins. It is easy to overlook or forget something, and it only takes one important item to throw off the entire day's schedule. Have plenty for the volunteers to do. Volunteers are typically busy people, and they will not appreciate waiting around while someone decides what they should be doing. There are two basic approaches to actively engaging volunteers to the fullest. One way is to assign a group of volunteers to a team with a group leader who can provide instructional guidance for that group. Another approach that works well in some circumstances is to give the volunteers a written description of the tasks to be accomplished. They can then team up in their own groups and immediately be underway.

9. *Provide food and drink whenever possible.* This accomplishes two things. One, it eliminates an excuse for your volunteers to slip away and possibly not return. Two, it is one small way to say thank you and let the volunteers know they are truly appreciated. Food and drinks can even be provided by a local restaurant or other sponsor.

10. *Volunteers are like fine wine.* They may be slower to reach their full potential, but they provide so many benefits to the project. Sometimes they seem to take an exceptionally long time to complete a task; sometimes they work at the speed of long-time professionals. Whether they are slower than a herd of turtles in a pond of peanut butter or as fast as a Triple Crown contender on Derby Day, they will do an outstanding job on any project handed to them.

Maintenance by Volunteers

The maintenance aspects of children's gardens, playgrounds, and other environments should be an integral part of the overall planning process. Maintenance is encompassed in the master plan, in specific designs, in grading and engineering, in selection of building materials, and in plant material choices. From this point, three concepts must be kept in mind when deciding who will perform maintenance and how it will be approached. These concepts are:

1. A well-designed project leads to an environment that is easy to maintain.

2. No matter how maintenance free an environment is supposed to be, it will still need to be maintained.

3. If the environment was built by volunteers, chances are it will be maintained by volunteers.

With the above concepts in mind, this section will focus on how to provide maintenance of children's environments by volunteers. The hope is that the environment was well designed with maintenance in mind. The successful maintenance will then depend on organizing the volunteers and assigning duties in a way that leads to success.

MAINTENANCE OF CHILDREN'S ENVIRONMENTS BY VOLUNTEERS

Regardless of the organizational format selected, there are five basic things to keep in mind that will help your volunteer force.

1. *In nearly all situations, volunteers need direction.* This means they need to be assigned to specific locations with specific maintenance tasks identified.

2. *The organization or agency in charge needs to set a base schedule.* A base schedule lists all the tasks that need to be accomplished and a time frame within which the task must be done. This approach gives the volunteers some personal flexibility in the schedule, and can actually increase the volunteer participation because of this flexibility.

3. *If you are serious about using volunteers, they need to be contacted personally.* This gives the volunteer a chance to ask questions and select a time slot. From the organizer's perspective, the personal contact provides greater assurance that the volunteer will actually participate.

4. *Volunteers with a vested interest in the environment to be maintained will be more receptive to donating their time.* Remember there are also service organizations and retirees, for example, with both interest and skills.

5. *It is important for the lead organization or agency to provide equipment and supplies needed by the volunteers.* Most volunteers are amenable to bringing along a few garden tools, but expendable supplies such as fertilizer or weed eradicator should be provided by the organization or agency in charge. Equipment such as mowers and tillers should be provided by the lead organization or agency also.

With the above concepts in mind, the organization or agency that oversees the environment can operate from its predetermined plan for maintenance. One of the most successful formats for maintenance by volunteers is a modification of the way many professionals perform maintenance. This approach entails subdividing the entire environment into subunits that are further divided into either smaller units or into specific maintenance needs. A children's garden in a neighborhood that is overseen by the neighborhood association may break down maintenance tasks by activities such as mowing, planting, weeding, mulching, and so on (Figure 2-37). A school with multiple outdoor environments is better served by subdividing the whole area into separate environments and then tasks within the smaller area. Some tasks such as mowing may exist across the board and may need to be managed through contracted services. The rest will fall to the volunteers (Figure 2-38).

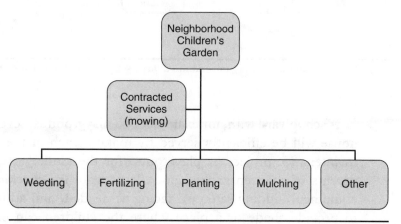

FIG 2-37. Maintenance organization in a small children's environment. (COURTESY OF GINA K. MCLELLAN.)

Although the application of tasks across the entire environment works well in a neighborhood or community garden, larger children's environments such as a schoolyard generally require a slightly different approach. When multiple environments exist at a single location, it is more efficient and effective to divide the maintenance plan into environmental units first and then into tasks.

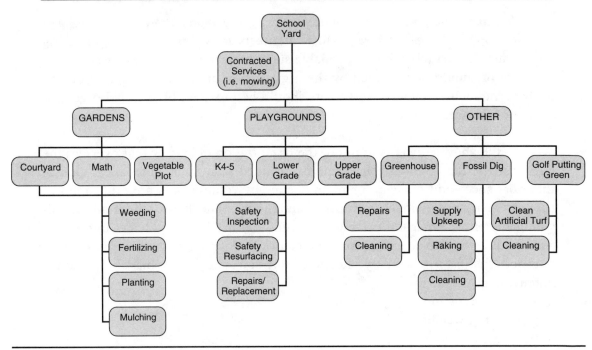

FIG 2-38. Maintenance organization in a large schoolyard. (COURTESY OF GINA K. MCLELLAN.)

A schoolyard with, for example, two playgrounds, several gardens, and a greenhouse will be efficiently served by making each of the individual areas its own maintenance project. A playground for the kindergarteners can be adopted by parents of children at that grade level who like checking and maintaining play equipment, adding safety surfacing as needed, and adding plantings in the area to provide shade or a place where the children can experiment with growing things. Each task such as weeding and planting can be handled by a small group of parents and students. A different group can oversee the playground for the older children, while yet another group maintains a courtyard garden. Any tasks better accomplished by one provider can be arranged as a contract service, which is often the case with mowing. When the latter option is chosen, it is important to communicate directly with the provider to establish any off-limits areas or to discuss special needs in a given area. What you want to avoid is the accidental cutting or removal of special plantings such as native grasses or the herb garden planted by the students.

"We had worked so hard to establish the Serengeti at my child's school. It was a large sand play area with a huge lion in the middle and tall grasses planted in various places to give it the feel of the Serengeti. I was visiting the play area about a month after its opening when the contracted mowing crew arrived. When one worker began cutting the 'weeds' in the sand play area, I bolted to stop him but not before he had cut three beautiful ornamental grasses to the ground with his weed whacker."
—A parent volunteer

GETTING THE MAINTENANCE ORGANIZED WITH VOLUNTEERS

Many schools are at a loss as to how to organize the maintenance of their outdoor areas. In the many schools visited and interviewed during the research for this book, the most effective and most common technique was guidance through an active and involved PTA. The reality of schoolyard environments is that very few are well funded by school districts, and the individual schools are usually fighting to make it through the school year with enough money for materials and supplies. The outdoor environments are not a priority despite their tremendous potential as learning environments. Most schools indicated that beyond mowing and playground safety surfacing, they received no other help or support for the outdoor environments.

When the school or school district does not provide the needed maintenance, the best option reported by schools is coordination of outdoor maintenance through the PTA and a subcommittee focused on that effort. A recommended tool is an overall maintenance manual that breaks the outdoors into individual areas with identifiable tasks for each. There must be a volunteer to oversee the maintenance manual assignments or nothing will ever get done. This could be a parent with particular interest in the outdoors or perhaps the PTA chair of an outdoors committee. Volunteers can then select a task in a specific part of the schoolyard that they want to work on and feel comfortable doing. These tasks are adopted by the volunteer for a year. The chairperson for each environment can encourage the individual volunteers to do the designated job within general time lines, or can opt to have designated work days that can draw additional volunteers to help the designees. When working with volunteers who have families and jobs, it is important to allow as much flexibility as possible within their schedules.

One very important key to maintaining schoolyard environments is involving the students at the school in both the construction of the environments and the maintenance of them. This approach gives the students ownership in the environments, and ownership translates directly into taking care of those environments. The ultimate benefit in involving the students is an educational one. When the students are involved in the planning, building, and maintenance of their schoolyard environments, they are applying concepts learned in the classroom.

CASE STUDIES

The Enchanted Woods™ at Winterthur, Winterthur, DE

Opening date: Father's Day, June 2001
Acres: 3 (1.21 hectares)
Cost: $2 million
Funding: Individuals and foundations

Enchanted Woods™ is a special fairytale children's garden at Winterthur Museum & Country Estate in Delaware. Created to be unique, to fit with the style or "sense of place" of the Winterthur Garden, and to attract families, it includes a charming collection of magical outdoor spaces (Eirhart, Magnani, Smith, personal communication, 2005).

Enchanted Woods™ was designed to be in complete harmony with the Winterthur estate and its mission (Figure 2a-1). It is a unique creation, built under an existing woodland canopy in a style appropriate to the historic Winterthur Garden, with subtle colors in the hardscape and plantings with sweeps of color (Figure 2a-2). The theme developed for the garden was based on the history of Winterthur as well as the

The Faerie Cottage at the Enchanged Woods™ at Winterthur Museum & Country Estate, Winterthur, Delaware. (COURTESY OF LOLLY TAI.)

design team's plans to recycle materials from all areas of the estate (Eirhart, 2003).

THE DESIGN TEAM

The project manager was Denise Magnani, former Curator/Director of the Landscape Division at Winterthur. She assembled a team of horticulturists, arborists, curators, and designers to begin the design process. Preliminary work commenced during the fall of 1998. W. Gary Smith was the landscape architect for the project. A complete list of team members may be found at the end of this case study (Magnani, 2001).

RESEARCH

In preparation for the planning of a children's garden, the design team researched how children learn and play. They visited other children's gardens such as the Children's Garden Project at George Washington's River Farm and interviewed institutions that were planning gardens or play spaces. The team found that

FIG 2a-1. The Enchanted Woods™ was created to fit with the style or "sense of place" of the Winterthur Garden, one of the world's great cultural landscapes. (COURTESY OF W. GARY SMITH.)

FIG 2a-2. The Enchanted Woods™ was built under an existing woodland canopy of plantings with sweeps of color. (COURTESY OF W. GARY SMITH.)

most of those gardens featured large play structures and bright primary colors, with spaces arranged as a series of science exhibits. Although the concepts worked well for those gardens and were visited by many children, they did not fit the Winterthur vocabulary (Magania, 2001).

The design team believed that their new garden needed to complement the existing Winterthur estate, functioning as a unified work of art with a naturalistic, subtle, and sophisticated scheme meant to be experienced as a journey of discovery. It needed to align with the goals of the estate's former owner, Henry Francis du Pont, who wanted visitors to find enjoyment and inspiration in the beauty of the naturalistic garden. The design team's goal was for the new garden to be a place where children would be encouraged to use their imagination and enjoy the beauty of a naturalistic garden (Eirhart, 2003).

The design team studied the historical records and followed present and intended uses. They adhered to the many principles that H.F. du Pont used in creating his garden, one of which was working with the site and its existing plants and landforms. This concept mirrors Winterthur's guidelines to restore and preserve the design intent of Mr. du Pont's garden (Eirhart, 2003).

BASE MAP AND SITE INVENTORY

Being familiar with the physical features and development of the property, the design team chose to create the new garden in a portion of an area referred to as Oak Hill. It is centrally located, fairly level, under mature shade trees of oaks, beeches, and tulip-poplars, and not highly developed (Eirhart, 2003).

One of Winterthur's guidelines is to document the appearance of a garden area, its plants and hardscape, before any major replanting and or other changes take place. Therefore, a local company, Vanedemark & Lynch, was commissioned to survey and map the plants and paths in the area. The design team worked with them to identify the plants. This area was heavily planted with late-flowering azaleas that related to surrounding plantings, which is typical of all du Pont's planting schemes (Eirhart, 2003).

SITE ANALYSIS AND PROGRAM

Although the team was familiar with the site, they each spent time there individually to try to see it with fresh eyes. While on the site, one of the design team members suggested the name "Enchanted Woods" for the new garden. This name set the theme for the project (Magnani, 2001).

The team conducted a thorough site analysis. As part of the vegetation analysis, gaps in the existing tree and shrub layer were identified as potential areas for siting features of the new design. Noted were mature shade trees that would both preserve the historic character of the area and lend to the unique character of the new children's garden. The surrounding ring of mature azaleas was also preserved to maintain continuity as well as a natural screen to the surrounding garden areas. The topographic analysis showed the flat area would require minimal grading and disturbance of the site. Existing features such as the circulation patterns, views, color combinations and time of bloom, soil, sun and light patterns, relationship to other buildings and garden, and rural areas were studied and recorded. Noted also was the importance of retaining existing paths to keep the physical as well as visual connection to the greater garden (Eirhart, 2003).

PROGRAM DEVELOPMENT AND USER NEEDS

Once the site analysis was completed, the program for the project was established. The special features and materials that would be incorporated in the new garden had to be determined. The program was developed keeping in mind that the garden would provide a safe place for children to play and learn about the natural world (Eirhart, 2003).

During program development, the team considered the design for an environment that would be fun, and also (Magnani, 2001):

- Provide opportunities for creative play and contact with nature

- Encourage different experiences in the landscape

- Provide stimulation of all the senses

- Accommodate different ages and activity levels

- Provide space for special programs

- Ensure safety

- Address the needs of parents and guardians.

To fully grasp the needs of the intended users, the team solicited help from parents, teachers, and children, and polled almost every child with whom they came in contact. The Enchanted Woods™ team was also fortunate to have the results of the extensive focus-group discussions conducted by Longwood Gardens concerning their new children's garden (Magnani, 2001).

The Enchanted Woods™ team learned that children wanted three basic elements in the garden (Magnani, 2001): (1) water, (2) places to hide and pretend, and (3) discovery on their own.

FIG 2a-3. The overall site plan, designed by W. Gary Smith, Landscape Architect, is a fairyland of many destinations. (COURTESY OF W. GARY SMITH.)

THE DESIGN

Enchanted Woods™ was designed to be a garden to be enjoyed by adults and children rather than a playground (Figure 2a-3). The project manager, Denise Magnani, commented that different from many high-tech, high-energy, and excitable gardens, this was to be a quiet place where calm children could have refuge and enjoyment (Magnani, personal communication, 2005). W. Gary Smith, the landscape architect, took the lead in developing the atmosphere for the garden by utilizing literary and artistic references to enchantment, fairies, mythology, and history of magical symbols (Figure 2a-4). He also reflected upon his own childhood experiences (Smith, personal communication, 2005).

FIG 2a-4. Smith studied the history of magical symbols and sketched many drawings to immerse himself into the fairy mindset. (COURTESY OF W. GARY SMITH.)

Access from the main garden to Enchanted Woods™ is by way of existing paths. Upon arrival, the paths change from asphalt to cobblestone to alert visitors that they are in a different space. Inspired by Smith's childhood experience and his love of such wildlife, an imprint of a smiling snake on the S-S-Serpentine Path greets visitors. The Faerie Cottage, located at the center of the garden, is nestled among the great oaks and tulip-poplars, and serves as the main unifying element of the area (Smith, personal communication, 2005). Along the Enchanted Woods™ paths, children come upon garden rooms that delight with elements of water, places to hide and pretend, and discovery. The following gardens rooms were especially designed for children's enjoyment (http://www. winterthur.org/for_families/enchanted_woods.asp, accessed 2005)

GARDENS ROOMS

- Acorn Tearoom (Figures 2a-21 and 2a-22)
- Green Man's Lair: The Forbidden Faerie Ring (Figures 2a-11 and 2a-12) and the Green Man's Face (Figures 2a-5 and 2a-6)
- Frog Hollow (Figures 2a-9 and 2a-10)
- Story Stones
- Tulip Tree House (Figure 2a-27)
- Bird's Nest (Figures 2a-19 and 2a-20)
- Fairy Flower Labyrinth (Figures 2a-7 and 2a-08)
- Troll Bridge
- Gathering Green (Figures 2a-23 and 2a-24)
- Water's Edge

The rooms are sited in relationship to one another as well as to the greater Winterthur landscape. The visual connections between the new garden and existing views and vistas were maintained where appropriate. For example, the Flower Fairy Labyrinth was sited within a ring of azaleas on the edge of Enchanted Woods™. It has views to the Sundial Garden, the meadow, and the woodlands beyond. However, it is not visible from a distance and does not impose on the wider Winterthur Garden (Eirhart, 2003).

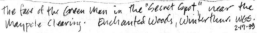
The face of the Green Man in the "Secret Spot" near the Maypole Clearing. Enchanted Woods, Winterthur. WGS. 2-19-99

FIG 2a-5 and FIG 2a-6. The Green Man's Lair is hidden behind a sweeping field of azaleas near the Gathering Green. Visitors of all ages frequently discover surprises within the garden and call out, "Look what I've found!" The Green Man's Lair was designed to appear as if it was emerging from the forest floor. (COURTESY OF W. GARY SMITH.)

COWSLIP	OAK	FOXGLOVE	FERN	LILY-OF-THE-VALLEY	TOADSTOOL

FIG 2a-7 and FIG 2a-8. The labyrinth is supposed to calm the emotions and enhance clear thinking. At The Fairy Flower Labyrinth children skip, dance, and run over the stepping stones, and are exposed to flowers and plants that are engraved on 21 of them. (COURTESY OF W. GARY SMITH.)

Plants are the emphasis of the Winterthur Garden, and they also define the spaces, paths, and views. The seasonal colors direct visitors along different paths during the year. To maintain the garden experience without interruption, it was important to keep as many of the existing plants as possible. For example, the

FIG 2a-9 and FIG 2a-10. Frog Hollow includes a 19th century cast iron watering trough that is wheelchair accessible. In the Frog Hollow, children interact and start the water flow with a hand pump. They are exposed to environmental awareness of water, leaves, and small creatures that inhabit the area. (COURTESY OF W. GARY SMITH.)

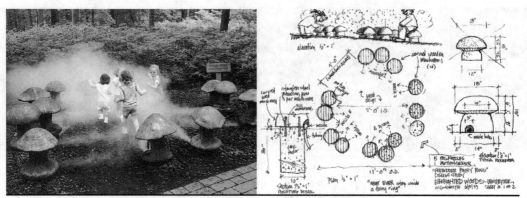

FIG 2a-11 (left). Children discover the Forbidden Faerie Ring and defy the sign, "Never, never step inside a fairy ring!" As they step in, their faces light up as they are engulfed with a cloud of mist. (COURTESY OF W. GARY SMITH.) **FIG 2a-12 (right).** Detail of the Faerie Ring. (COURTESY OF W. GARY SMITH.)

lavender 'Winterthur' azaleas that bloom in mid-May serve as the backdrop for the Forbidden Fairy Ring (Eirhart, 2003) (Figures 2a-11 and 2a-12).

Building upon Mr. du Pont's theme of summer colors and extended season of bloom, broad sweeps of related plants within a select color palette were used. There was a focus on hydrangeas, clethras, and hostas with a white, lavender, and blue theme and a touch of pink. Plants from surrounding garden areas were added to Enchanted Woods™. *Hosta ventricosa,* which blooms in July through-out the garden, was transplanted to the areas along the S-S-Serpentine Path. Sweeps of August-blooming Hosta "Royal Standard" and September-blooming *Aster divaricatus* were duplicated in Enchanted Woods™. In the future, more bulbs will be added to echo the millions of spring bulbs that appear on the March Bank. Every effort was made to retain the integrity of the garden and to main-tain a place that appears as if it has always been there (Eirhart, 2003).

CONSTRUCTION DOCUMENTATION AND IMPLEMENTATION

One of the Winterthur guidelines for installing new features is that they preserve the historic character of the landscape and be compatible in scale, materials, and color. Materials that were used on the estate in H.F. du Pont's day include ex-tensive collections of stones, pillars, fences, and broken and discarded pieces of architecture that were found in the woods or stored in the barns (Figure 2a-13). Details of selected components of the garden are described below (Eirhart, 2003).

The Path: construction drawings for the project were produced by W. Gary Smith. He integrated recycled materials and new materials as appropriate. For

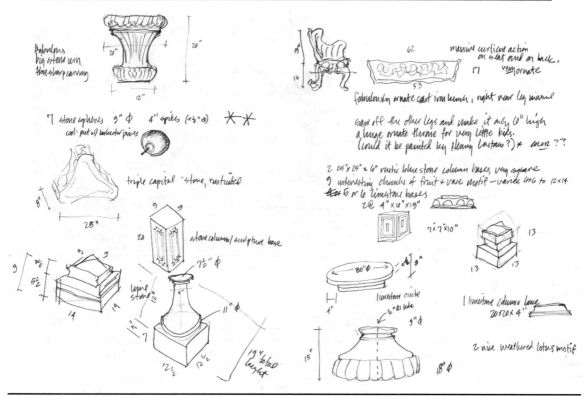

FIG 2a-13. Recycled materials of stones, pillars, fences, and miscellaneous pieces of architecture were used in the construction of the garden. (COURTESY OF W. GARY SMITH.)

example, he used new but compatible paving materials in Enchanted Woods™ to let visitors know they are in a different space (Smith, personal communication, 2005) (Figures 2a-14 and 2a-15). The asphalt and crushed stone paths were replaced with cobblestone pavers, which fit the historic nature of the area as well as the guidelines for accessibility and soft earth colors of browns, reds, and greens. The circulation pattern was maintained; as a result, the spectacular views from the museum into the garden and the great views from the Faerie Cottage to the garden were preserved.

The Faerie Cottage: is constructed of natural materials—stone, wood, and thatch. The colors are soft browns, grays, and blacks. All the unusual stones in the cottage are from the estate. The construction is executed with exemplary craftsmanship, which is in character with the details on the property (Figures 2a-16, 2a-17, and 2a-18).

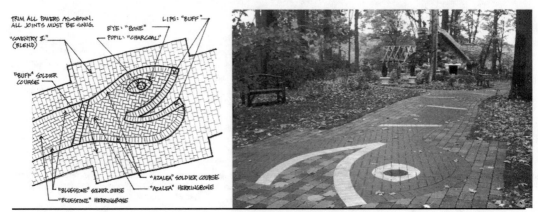

FIG 2a-14. Detail of S-S-serpentine path. (COURTESY OF W. GARY SMITH.) FIG 2a-15. The path was deliberately designed with different paving to delineate the entrance into a different space from the greater Winterthur Garden. The construction materials and colors fit with those of Winterthur. (COURTESY OF W. GARY SMITH.)

Tree protection guidelines were followed by using large stones as the foundation for the house that spans across tree roots. Therefore, as few tree roots as possible were disturbed. After initial holes were dug, the arborist made clean cuts on the roots. One year prior to construction, the trees were verti-mulched to encourage root growth.

The Bird's Nest was also designed to protect and feature the trees. To minimize disturbance, only one center column supports the nest. A ramp constructed of red cedar provides access to the elevated nest through surrounding existing shrubs and trees. It is designed to meet accessibility standards and is low enough not to require a handrail and thereby blends into the site (Figures 2a-19 and 2a-20).

Frog Hollow was the water feature added to the design. It incorporates a recycled 19th century antique cast iron feeding trough from one of the barns. Its height easily accommodates a child in a wheelchair.

The Acorn Tearoom was constructed with columns from the estate's formal perennial and rose garden of the early 20th century (Figures 2a-21 and 2a-22).

The Gathering Green also made use of these columns to support new swinging benches and evoke the memory of swings that were once there (Figures 2a-23 and 2a-24).

The Tulip Tree House was created from a live, but hollow, tree that had been growing on the property and was slowly dying. The base of this tree was trans-

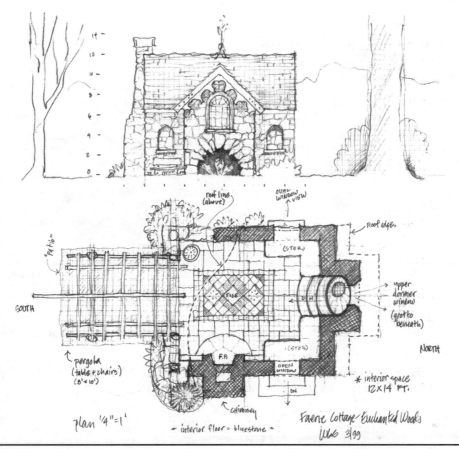

FIG 2a-16. The Faerie Cottage was inspired by 19th century English garden follies. (COURTESY OF W. GARY SMITH.)

FIG 2a-17 and FIG 2a-18. The thatched roof on Faerie Cottage is another architectural feature that reinforces the fairy theme. (COURTESY OF W. GARY SMITH.)

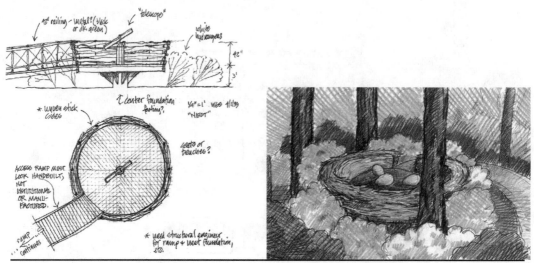

FIG 2a-19 (left). Conceptual sketch of the Bird's Nest. (COURTESY OF W. GARY SMITH.) FIG 2a-20 (right). The Bird's Nest, constructed of beech branches, is accessible via a ramp, and allows children to experience being in a nest atop a cloud of blue and white hydrangeas. (COURTESY OF W. GARY SMITH.)

formed into a tree house; another section is in storage for possible later use (Figures 2a-25, 2a-26, and 2a-27).

New plants that have been added follow Winterthur's guideline of using those that are compatible in form, scale, color, flowering time, and that are disease re-

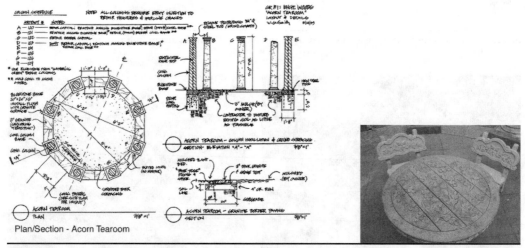

FIG 2a-21 (left). Detail drawings of the Acorn Tearoom. (COURTESY OF W. GARY SMITH.) FIG 2a-22 (right). The children's table and chairs in the Acorn Tearoom are crafted with the finest details. (COURTESY OF W. GARY SMITH.)

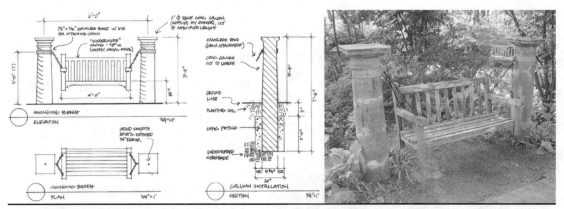

FIG 2a-23. Detail drawings of the swing benches in the Gathering Green. (COURTESY OF W. GARY SMITH.) **FIG 2a-24.** Swing benches are supported by columns from the estate's formal perennial and rose garden of the 20th century. (COURTESY OF LOLLY TAI.)

sistant. For example, *Cercis canadensis alba* has replaced the native dogwood that has suffered from anthracnose. The white Cercis along with *Mertensia virginica* and *Primula elatior,* maintains the late-April and early-May color combination of white, blue, and yellow that was present in the area.

Before the garden was open, the design team reviewed the features with the insurance company, and adjustments were made as necessary. For example, an emergency phone that dials directly into the Winterthur Security Office has been located in the area (Magnani, personal communication, 2005). Ground breaking took place early in the summer of 2000. By the end of 2000, the majority of

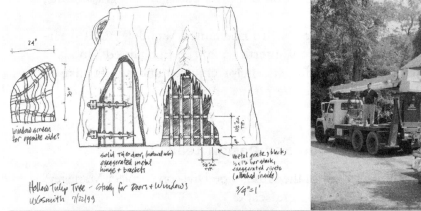

FIG 2a-25. The Tulip Tree House initial concept drawing. (COURTESY OF W. GARY SMITH.) **FIG 2a-26.** The base of a dying tree was preserved to create the Tulip Tree House. (COURTESY OF W. GARY SMITH.)

FIG 2a-27. Inside the Tulip Tree House children experience olfactory sensations. A door and thatched roof were added to it. (COURTESY OF W. GARY SMITH.)

construction was complete. The ceremonial grand opening was on Father's Day, June 2001.

FUNDING AND MAINTENANCE

The Lois F. and Henry S. McNeil Family Trust provided the principal financial support, covering the costs of design, engineering, and infrastructure, as well as a permanent endowment for maintenance. Funds for construction were received from individuals and foundations, many of whom underwrote specific features (Eirhart, 2003; Magnani, 2001).

CONCLUSION AND EVALUATION

By staying true to the history of the estate, the site, and the design style, the design team created a magical space within a magnificent woodland setting. As a result, Winterthur diversified its audience with families, school groups, grandparents, and grandkids, and attendance and membership have increased.

The evaluation of Enchanted Woods™ is ongoing, and suggestions for improvements have been made. A few ideas are for wider paths, sturdier lighting, minor drainage improvements, an evaluation of paved paths versus grass paths, and planned wayfinding.

Children take great pleasure in their visits to Enchanted Woods™. A 10-year-old remarked, "It's cool here. I like it!" (Winterthur, 2001). Enchanted Woods™ stirs the imagination of a new generation and helps children and adults alike to appreciate the beauty, the wonder, and the power of nature.

CREDITS

The Enchanted Woods™ Planning and Design Team

Denise Magnani, Curator/Director of the Landscape Division (Project Manager)
Pam Allenstein, Associate Curator, Landscape
Linda Eirhart, Curator, Plants
Randy Fisher, Arborist Supervisor

Joseph Lazorchak, Associate Curator, Landscape
Laura Payne, Coordinator, Garden Programs and Events
Brian Phiel, Horticulturist II
Jim Smith, Horticulture Supervisor
W. Gary Smith Design Inc., Landscape Architect

Construction Team

Construction Management/Architecture: Buck Simpers Architect & Associates, Inc. David P. Mengers, project architect

General Contractor: Construct Con., Inc., Frank Patille, Jr. and Frank Patille, III, principals

Mechanical/Electrical Engineering: Furlow Associates, Inc

Civil Engineering/Surveying: Apex Engineering, Inc.

The New Indoor Garden at Longwood Gardens, Kennett Square, PA

Opened: Previous Indoor Children's Garden was closed January 2003.
New Indoor Children's Garden is anticipated to be opened in Spring 2007.
Acres: A glass house measuring 4,240 square feet (393.9 square meters)
Cost: Approximately 5 million for the garden/landscape
Funding: Longwood Foundation and Longwood Gardens, Inc.

MISSION AND PURPOSE

The New Indoor Children's Garden is replacing the previous Indoor Children's

The Drooling Dragon at The New Indoor Garden at Longwood Gardens, Kennett Square, Pennsylvania.
(COURTESY OF TRES FROMME @ LONGWOOD GARDENS.)

Garden that was opened to the public in 1987. The new garden will be triple in size (Figure 2b-1). It will celebrate Mr. Pierre S. du Pont's devotion to children, and will focus on plants and water features, which are two of his garden passions. Mr. du Pont (1870–1954) was the industrialist and philanthropist who created Longwood Gardens. His wish was to "exploit the sentiments and ideas associated with plants and flowers in a large way." During his lifetime, he continually improved Longwood with restoration and new construction. The construction of The New Indoor Children's Garden commenced in fall 2003 and is scheduled to open in 2007 (Longwood Gardens, 2003 and http:// http://www.longwoodgardens. org/WhatsNew/Renovations/ChildrensGardenUpdate.htm, accessed 2005).

THE PLANNING AND DESIGN TEAM

The planning and design team consisted of Longwood's design staff (Planning and Design Specialist, Section Gardener, and Visitor Education and Flower Show Specialist) as well as several focus groups. Longwood's design staff met with three groups of adult caregivers and parents, two groups of 11–16 year old teenagers,

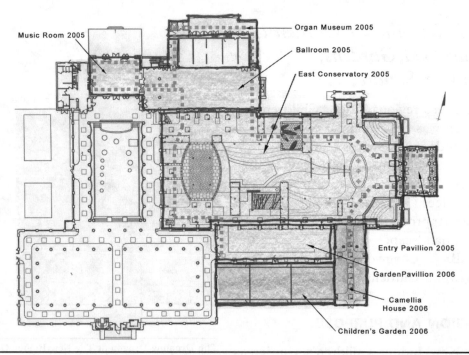

FIG 2b-1. Conservatory key master plan. The New Indoor Children's Garden at Longwood Gardens is located in the southeast corner of the conservatory. (COURTESY OF TRES FROMME.)

and two groups of children ranging from ages 3–5 and 5–10 from a local day care to assemble and analyze issues pertinent to the New Indoor Children's Garden design (Fromme, et al., 1999).

RESEARCH

Longwood's design staff visited and researched case studies of other public gardens such as The Michigan 4-H Children's Garden, The Everett Children's Adventure Garden in the New York Botanical Garden, and the Children's Garden in the Atlanta Botanical Garden. They also visited and studied other influential Gardens including Villa Lante, Villa D'Este, Versailles, and Longwood Gardens itself. In addition, according to Tres Fromme, Longwood's Planning and Design Leader, "We also applied the lessons learned from our previous experience and knowledge about children's gardens." These are described below (Fromme et al., 1999).

1. *Think Holistically:* Look holistically at the entire organization—all the people, skills, gardens, and features. Think in terms of connections and collaborations. Envision every staff person to be a contributing member of the children's experience. Every program and feature should be welcoming to children. Look carefully and discover what children already enjoy (whether intentionally planned for them or not!). Build upon these elements. Opening the "whole" organization to children will expand it to a family experience.

2. *Be Yourself:* Draw from the organization's specific strengths and identity. Create a unique children's experience that visitors could not imagine finding anywhere else. Link the experience back to the organization's mission. Ask how the goals established can be shared with young visitors. Excite them about the goals and perspectives concerning horticulture and public gardens.

3. *Diversify Within Unity:* Create many types of experiential opportunities for children. Offer various levels of interaction and layers of meaning to enrich the visit. Try to appeal to all learning styles, age groups, and abilities. Some elements should completely seduce and delight every visitor.

4. *Collaborate:* Use professionals with a wide variety of backgrounds and perspectives because collaboration generates rich and dynamic experiences. Efforts and resources throughout the organization are better connected when working across departments, job responsibilities, and disciplines. Collaboration invests everyone in the success of the children's experience.

5. *Customize Resource Requirements:* The garden does not need to expend a large amount of money or staff time. Discovering and strengthening children's experiences may not require the huge budget of a major project. Being oneself builds upon existing features and resources. Collaboration extends responsibility and costs throughout the organization.

PROGRAM DEVELOPMENT AND USER NEEDS

The planning and design team determined important considerations or "preliminary big issues" of the project. They identified the essential elements necessary for a creative and unique project to include mood, stimulation, activity and interaction, types of spaces, water and maze, details and materials, and safety (Fromme, 1999).

Mood. The design should integrate a sense of mystery and adventure; exude an atmosphere of magic and enchantment; lend surprises at every turn; and unveil views and experiences from one point at a time.

Stimulation. The garden should actively engage the mind and the body through all the sensory perceptions. It should stir the imagination for creative pretend and role-playing. It should challenge children's minds and motor skills in a nonintimidating and safe environment.

Activity and Interaction. The garden should provide a variety of spaces for visitors to experience and choose from, such as active vs. contemplative, social versus solitary, hands-on versus imaginative participation and manipulation. It should provide opportunities for various spatial interactions such as going under, above, around, through, and within the garden setting.

Types of Spaces. The garden should provide spaces for activities, interactions, and stimulation. Examples are indicated below.

TYPE OF SPACES:	PURPOSES:
Theaters:	For events
Separate areas:	For "kids only" as well as for adults
Elevation changes:	To capture interesting views and spatial perception
Enclosed spaces:	To create nooks for hiding and contemplation
Open surfaces:	To encourage running as well as gathering
Tunnels and overhead walks:	To offer realms for exploration
Easy access:	For emergencies
Selected spaces:	To contain plants and displays to hold the interest of adults

Water and Maze. The garden should incorporate mazes and water features as organizing features. Water should permeate and evoke playful, creative, and safe interaction. The combination of water and maze elements can generate an overall framework from which specific journeys, narratives, and features of the garden are organized.

Details and Materials. The garden should integrate small, unexpected, and unusual features and objects such as serpent-form door handles and animal topiary to intrigue children. Carefully chosen details spur the imagination, support children's stories, and provide opportunities to play pretend. Discovering surprise elements at every corner enlivens the garden journey exploration. Materials used should withstand constant and heavy use or be easily replaced as they deteriorate.

Safety. The garden should be designed for safety and incorporate provisions for surveillance. Adults must be allowed to see and physically access their children. This assures comfort of both. Special features, such as water and elevated areas, must be designed and maintained to avoid psychological and physical discomfort and inconvenience.

THE DESIGN

The New Indoor Children's Garden (Figure 2b-2) is designed with a spatial organization comprised of four key components: main central space, perimeter walkway service areas, and crossover circulation areas (Fromme et al., 1999).

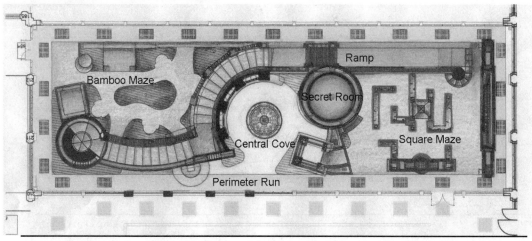

FIG 2b-2. The New Indoor Children's Garden at Longwood Gardens consists of five primary areas. Central Cove, Secret Room, Ramp, Grotto Cave, and Bamboo Maze. (COURTESY OF TRES FROMME.)

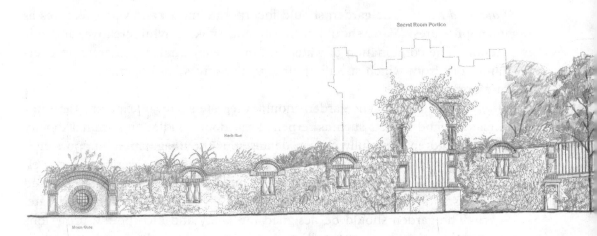

FIG 2b-3. Concept Design. South Elevation. From left to right: Gothic Folly, The Bamboo Maze, The Secret Room Portico, and The Ramp and Herb Run. (COURTESY OF TRES FROMME.)

FOUR KEY COMPONENTS

The main central space is occupied by the children's garden. It is primarily a space designed for children to enjoy their activities and to give the impression that adults are excluded.

The perimeter walkway around the garden is a place for older visitors and adults to enjoy the garden and watch the younger children.

FIG 2b-4 Concept Design. North Elevation. The garden is a series of mazes and engaging experiences enfolded in plants and architectural follies. The design draws upon the tradition of garden design and garden history for its inspiration. Left to right: The Tower and Grotto Cave and Tunnel, The Central Cove, The Secret Room, The Square Maze, and Triumphal Arch. (COURTESY OF TRES FROMME.)

Tower and Grotto Cave

Ramp

Door to Grotto Tunnel (from Bamboo Maze)   Sitting Benches in Grotto Tunnel   Bamboo Maze

Children's Garden
longwood gardens, Inc.

Conceptual Elevations (PS #1)
Fred Priamore, Mary Allinson, Brian Magaraja

October 1998   Scale: ½ inch equals 1 foot

The service areas throughout the garden provide stopping points for stroller parking, water fountain, and seating.

The crossover circulation and visual connection at various intersections across the main garden provide spaces for the adults to interact with children and reach them in case of an emergency.

The garden is designed with five distinct, but integrated theme areas. All spaces are accessible to the physically challenged (Figures 2b-3 and 2b-4).

Secret Room and Balcony

Triumphal Arch

Square Maze

Sitting Niche   Waterfall and Tunnel (to Square Maze)

Children's Garden
longwood gardens, Inc.

Conceptual Elevations (PS #1)
Fred Priamore, Mary Allinson, Brian Magaraja

October 1998   Scale: ½ inch equals 1 foot

FIVE DISTINCT AREAS

The Central Cove features a tree-covered seating area, a central pool with flower-shaped water jets and jewel-like mosaics, and three animal-adorned water pilasters shooting streams of water overhead into the pool.

The Secret Room is home to The Drooling Dragon (Figures 2b-9 through 2b-12). Children will have the chance to move underneath the Rain Pavilion and into the Square Maze of plants accented by story tiles and shooting jets of water.

The Ramp is accented by an ever-changing Water Curtain and animated by the leaping water "glow worm" that leads children to the Tower overlooking the Bamboo Maze.

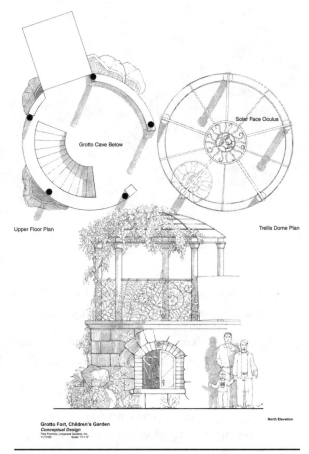

FIG 2b-5. The Grotto Fort. (COURTESY OF TRES FROMME.)

The Grotto Cave and Tunnel is located underneath the Tower and contains a shallow fog-covered pool activated by water dripping from sculpted snakes coiled overhead (Figure 2b-5).

The Bamboo Maze offers a jungle of tree-size bamboos for children to explore. The Maze contains the Gothic Folly, stained glass window, and five visitor-activated water features accented with ornate bird sculptures (Figure 2b-6).

EDUCATIONAL AND PARTICIPATORY ASPECTS

The new garden will be a space where children can immerse themselves in the sensory experience of plants and gardens every day of the year. According to

FIG 2b-6. Five bird-themed sculptural groupings of bronze and cast stone will nestle in the Bamboo Maze groves. Each feature is programmable, and is able to run on a sequenced program or allow for children to activate the water effects. The mother Robin "regurgitates" a "worm" of water into her babies' mouths. The babies then spit upward in various sequences. A water "worm" jumps out of the nest to the paving below in an attempt to "escape." (COURTESY OF TRES FROMME.) **FIG 2b-7.** Carefully designed, detailed and crafted whimsical spitting fish. (COURTESY OF TREES FROMME.)

Fromme, the design team intentionally decided not to emphasize the typical educational approach. For example, a series of specific tasks or information seeking to elicit specific results and/or lessons was not the focus of The New Indoor Children's Garden. Fromme said, "We preferred the over arching goal to be one of enjoyment and exploration in the garden setting."

CONSTRUCTION DOCUMENTATION AND IMPLEMENTATION

Numerous intricate water features have been designed and detailed to engage children throughout the garden. Carefully designed, detailed and crafted "fantastical" animal statues will spit or spray water into pools and lurk in the exuberant plantings (Figure 2b-7). Custom-designed mosaics (Figure 2b-8), painted tiles, and murals will cover the walls and floors. Ornate door handles are detailed in the form of insects and animals such as the snail, lizard, earthworms, scorpion, and beetle. Details and fine crafting is key to the realization of an exquisite project that will leave long-lasting and memorable impressions (Fromme et al., 1999) (Figures 2b-8 through 2b-12).

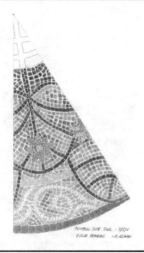

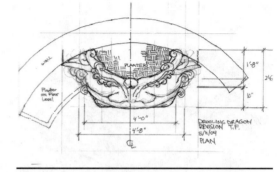

FIG 2b-9. Overhead plan of the Drooling Dragon. (COURTESY OF TRES FROMME.)

FIG 2b-8 (right). Custom-designed colorful (pinks, yellows, blues, and greens) mosaic paving detail in The Central Cove. (COURTESY OF TRES FROMME.)

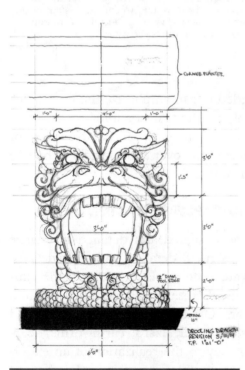

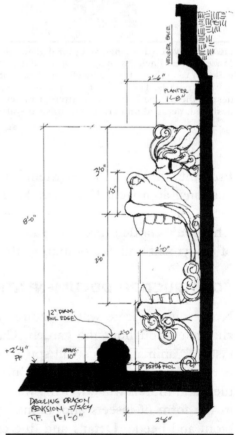

FIG 2b-10. Detail elevation study of the Drooling Dragon. (COURTESY OF TRES FROMME.)

FIG 2b-11. Detail section study of the Drooling Dragon. (COURTESY OF TRES FROMME.)

FIG 2b-12. Study model of the Drooling Dragon. (COURTESY OF TRES FROMME.)

FIG 2b-13 (left). The construction wall informs the public of the upcoming New Indoor Children's Garden. **FIG 2b-14 (right).** The construction wall with an illustrative drawing of the New Indoor Garden excites the public about the forthcoming design. (COURTESY OF MARY TAYLOR HAQUE.)

MAINTENANCE AND EVALUATION

The garden will be maintained in-house with Longwood's horticulture and maintenance staff; Longwood does not traditionally perform formal "evaluations." They observe the built garden for safety, plant selection and culture, patterns of visitor use, and other characteristics. (Fromme et al., 1999).

CREDITS

Longwood Gardens' New Indoor Children's Garden Planning and Design Team:

Tres Fromme, Lead Designer
Mary Allinson, Section Gardener,
   co-developer initial concept design,
   co-designer planting scheme
Fred Roberts, Director
Sharon Loving, Horticulture Department Head, Project Leader
Robert Underwood, Maintenance Department Head, Project Manager
Other Longwood Staff:
   Dave Jones, General Services Forman
   Gregg Erhardt, GIS/CAD Systems Coordinator
   Nick Nelson, Planning and Design Assistant
Leonard Sophrin, Leonard Sophrin Architect, Project Architect
Gary Gabarcik, Gannet Flemming, Structural Engineer
Alan Robinson, Water Feature Consultant
Various artists and artisans

Construction Team:

Contract not yet awarded.

The Children's Healthcare of Atlanta Children's Garden, Atlanta, GA

Opening date: September 17, 1999
Acres: 2 (.19 hectare)
Cost: $2.2 million

Funding: Children's Healthcare of Atlanta and Atlanta Botanical Garden

MISSION AND PURPOSE

Children's Healthcare of Atlanta Children's Garden was built to teach families about how plants keep them healthy and well (Figure 2c-1). Wellness is translated for children in one simple message that plants help us to "live, laugh, learn." This theme is the basis of the fun outdoor environment designed for children ages 4–11 (Laufer, 2001).

The Flower Fountain at the Children's Healthcare of Atlanta Children's Garden, Atlanta, Georgia. (COURTESY OF LOLLY TAI.)

In addition to promoting wellness through learning about plants and horticulture, the goals of the garden are also to (Laufer, 2001):

- ❧ Promote a healthy attitude towards stewardship of our green world

- ❧ Create a "child friendly" and "hands-on" atmosphere

- ❧ Cultivate a love for plants and gardens

- ❧ Develop an understanding of the interdependence of plants and animals

- ❧ Develop a child's imagination and curiosity

THE DESIGN TEAM

The design team was comprised of Atlanta Botanical Garden Board members and staff, the Scottish Rite Medical Center (now Children's Healthcare of Atlanta), educators,

FIG 2c-1. A colorful sign in the Flower Fountain greets visitors with the theme of the Children's Healthcare of Atlanta Children's Garden: "Plants keep us well." (COURTESY OF LOLLY TAI.)

landscape architects, architects, engineers, exhibit designers, local artists, and construction managers. The Children's Healthcare of Atlanta solicited input from their staff child psychologists and color psychologists. Most importantly, children in day camps at the Atlanta Botanical Garden were surveyed to determine what they wanted in "their" garden. Throughout a series of brainstorming sessions, the team developed the concept of how to educate children about the role plants play in their wellness (Tyler, personal communication, 2005).

According to Cindy Tyler, landscape architect, "The designer's job was to listen to the stakeholders and translate their vision into a successful, buildable design, one with both magic and substance. During the concept design stage, we needed to translate the grownup message, "Plants keep us well," into kid language. As adults, we first defined wellness as the balance of body, mind, and spirit. For children, that quickly became, "Plants help us Live, Laugh and Learn." This is the Children's Garden's mantra (Tyler, personal communication, accessed 2005) (Figure 2c-2).

FIG 2c-2. During the design process, the designer's job was to translate "Plants keep us well" into kid's language, which quickly became "Live, Laugh and Learn." (COURTESY OF LOLLY TAI.)

THE DESIGN

The design started in 1996, and continued for two years (Laufer, 2001). Extensive research was conducted and professionals were polled. Because there were not many children's garden models to follow, the design team depended upon the educational staff at the Garden, the donor, the Atlanta Botanical Garden Board, and kids to form the program for the Garden. The site was carefully analyzed, trees inventoried, and garden zones designed (Figure 2c-3). Exhibit designers were interviewed and selected early in the process so that they could help with material selection and value engineering. Color psychologists suggested that a primary color scheme would most appeal to the target audience. The construction managers provided cost estimating and constructability insight. There were many meet-

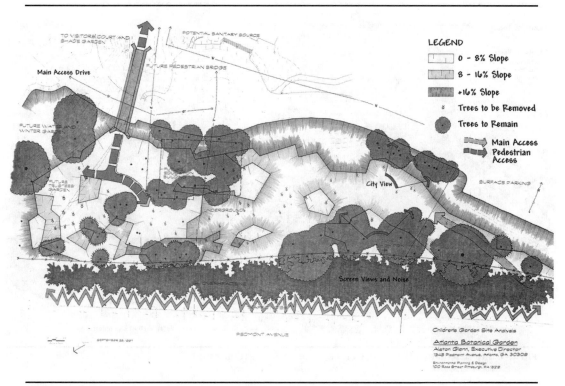

FIG 2c-3. Site analysis by Cindy Tyler, Terra Design Studios, Pittsburgh, Pennsylvania.

ings with the Garden's stakeholders to develop consensus among the group (Tyler, personal communication, 2005).

The 9-month fast-track construction project broke ground on April 6, 1998. The schedule for the various phases of the design process is listed below (Tyler, personal communication, 2005):

PHASES OF THE DESIGN PROCESS	SCHEDULE
Research and Analysis	6–9 months (Figure 2c-3)
Schematic Design	3 months (Figure 2c-4)
Design Development	3 months
Construction Documentation	6 months
Construction	9 months (Figure 2c-5)

According to Tyler, "The garden was designed for high energy, but quiet absorption." The design builds on the concept of three ecosystems: beehive meadow, bog, woodlands and passive woods where plants restore the spirits.

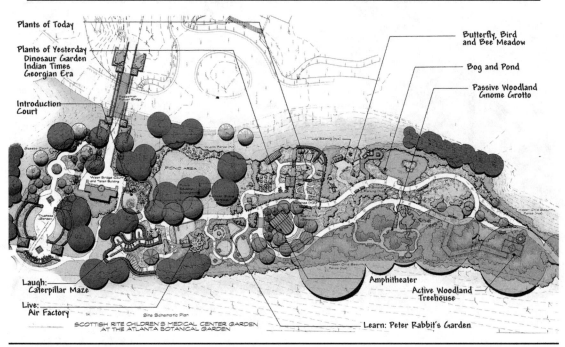

Plants of Today

Plants of Yesterday
Dinosaur Garden
Indian Times
Georgian Era

Introduction
Court

Butterfly, Bird
and Bee Meadow

Bog and Pond

Passive Woodland
Gnome Grotto

Laugh:
Caterpillar Maze

Live:
Air Factory

Amphitheater

Active Woodland
Treehouse

SCOTTISH RITE CHILDREN'S MEDICAL CENTER GARDEN
AT THE ATLANTA BOTANICAL GARDEN

Learn: Peter Rabbit's Garden

FIG 2c-4. Site schematic plan. (CINDY TYLER, TERRA DESIGN STUDIOS.)

The approach to the children's garden is by way of the Flower Bridge decorated with an assortment of color and scented plants and spanning over the main garden drive. A secure environment is provided by the controlled access and the perimeter fence around the entire garden. A Green Man Fountain, a mythical half-man and half-plant sculpted kudzu face greets the visitor at the terminus of the bridge (Figure 2c-6). Upon entering the garden, visitors proceed into the Sunflower Fountain where children delight in getting wet and cooling off during the hot summer months (Figure 2c-7). Visitors then proceed into the Laugh, Live and Learn Garden (Laufer, 2005 and http://www.atlantabotanicalgarden.org/kids/kidsmap.html, accessed 2006). The interpretive garden is guided by many interactive signs. The main paths are 6-foot wide (1.83 m), enough to accommodate strollers and pedestrians, and secondary paths are 3-foot wide (0.91 m) (Laufer, 2001). A centrally located 50-seat amphitheater and stage provide an educational classroom for Saturday classes scheduled from April–October.

FIG 2c-5. Children's Healthcare of Atlanta Children's Garden under construction. (COURTESY OF CINDY TYLER, TERRA DESIGN STUDIOS.)

THEME GARDENS

	EDUCATIONAL FEATURE. CHILDREN LEARN, EXPLORE, AND DISCOVER:	DETAILS IN THE GARDEN INCLUDE:
LAUGH GARDEN:	The process of metamorphosis.	Large stainless steel butterfly with 10-foot (3 meters) span wings (Figure 2c-8); colorful silk-screened Chrysalis Crawlthrough (Figure 2c-9)
LIVE GARDEN:	The role plants play in providing air (Figures 2c-10 and 2c-11).	Sculpture of Tree Tunnel; fiberglass slide.
LEARN GARDEN:	The Peter Rabbit garden story-telling area with laminated copies of the tales (Figure 2c-12).	Sculpture of Peter Rabbit's tree trunk den; MacGregor's wood tool shed and watering can; white wood picket fence; crop rows.

Plants through Time

DINOSAUR GARDEN	The importance of plants throughout history (Figure 2c-13).	Sculpture of a cretaceous era duckbill dinosaur; sand box with fossil dig area; mist sprays.
CREEK INDIAN DWELLING	The dwellings from 200–300 years ago and associated plants used by the natives for food, medicine, and shelter.	Authentic wattle and daub structure.
GRANDMA'S ROOTS	The heritage plants that were introduced by early settlers.	Rocking chairs on Grandma's front porch; a caldron.
EVERYDAY PLANTS	The important role that plants still play in our daily lives.	Barnyard figures (Figure 2c-13); bathtub planted with herbs; mirror that reflects distorted image; measurement wall.

Healthy Earth, Healthy You

BEEHIVE MEADOW	Three of nature's most important pollinators: bees, butterflies, and birds (Figure 2c-15).	Bird sculpture; bee sculpture; beehive display (Figure 2c-14); stepping-stones with inscription of the bee dance (Figure 2c-16).
SOGGY BOG AND BULLFROG POND	Wetland plants and animals. (Figures 2c-17 and 2c-18)	Frog sculptures in water and on banks of water's edge (Figure 2c-19, 2c-20); deck over-looking pond; potted plants.
TREE HOUSE	The transformation of a tree from seed.	Three-story tree house, telescopes; slide; rubberized paving surfacing.
ROCKY POINTE	Woodland stream, bridge, and shady plantings.	Small gnomes; waterfall.

FIG 2c-6 (left). Visitors cross over the Flower Bridge decorated with an assortment of color and scented plants to enter the children's garden. A Green Man Fountain is at the terminus of the bridge. (COURTESY OF LOLLY TAI.) FIG 2c-7 (right). Visitors arrive in the Sunflower Fountain Garden. (COURTESY OF LOLLY TAI.)

FIG 2c-8 and FIG 2c-9. Children learn about the process of metamorphosis as they interact in the Caterpillar Maze and Butterfly Pavilion. (COURTESY OF MARY TAYLOR HAQUE.)

FIG 2c-10 (left). In the Live Garden, children learn about how we breathe in the Air Factory. (COURTESY OF CINDY TYLER, TERRA DESIGN STUDIOS.) FIG 2c-11 (right). Concept sketch of Live Garden sketch by Marshall, Tyler, Rausch, Landscape Architects. (COURTESY OF CINDY TYLER, TERRA DESIGN STUDIOS.)

FIG 2c-12 (left). The outdoor classroom is a terrific place for children to read in the Learn Garden. (COURTESY OF CINDY TYLER, TERRA DESIGN STUDIOS.) FIG 2c-13 (right). Children are engaged in active play as they climb on top of barnyard figures in the Everyday Plants Garden. (COURTESY OF LOLLY TAI.)

FIG 2c-14 (left). Children watch the bees work in the hive with amazement. (COURTESY OF LOLLY TAI.) FIG 2c-15 (right). Children are exposed to bees, butterflies, and birds as pollinators. They run around the stepping-stones to mimic the bee dance. (COURTESY OF LOLLY TAI.) FIG 2c-16 (bottom). Detail of stepping-stones with inscriptions of the bee dance. (COURTESY OF LOLLY TAI.)

FIG 2c-17. Concept sketch of the Bog Garden by Cindy Tyler, Terra Design Studios.

FIG 2c-18. In the Bog and Bullfrog Pond Garden, visitors are exposed to wetland plants and animals. (COURTESY OF MARY TAYLOR HAQUE.)

FIG 2c-19. A whimsical sculpture of two smiling frogs under the waterfall. (COURTESY OF LOLLY TAI.)

FIG 2c-20. Concept sketch of the Bog Garden by Marshall, Tyler, Rausch, Landscape Architects.

FIG 2c-21 (left). A 50-seat amphitheater and stage provide an educational classroom for Saturday classes. (COURTESY OF LOLLY TAI.) FIG 2c-22 (right). Visitors experience how honey is made. (COURTESY OF LOLLY TAI.)

EDUCATIONAL ASPECTS

Through the theme of "Laugh, live, learn," visitors learn how plants keep us healthy and well. Kevin Mercer, Youth Program Manager refers to the garden as "stealth education." He believes children learn, without being aware of it. For instance, as the children are having fun running through the caterpillar maze, they learn about the life cycle of a caterpillar to a butterfly. He remarks that all of the exhibits in the children's garden are designed for self-discovery and learning.

PARTICIPATORY ASPECTS

The children's garden encourages children to explore. Many of the plantings are at "kid level," and are at the appropriate height for maximum exploration.

UNIQUE CHARACTERISTICS OF THE GARDEN

There are small spaces for children to explore, abundant colorful plantings, and themed beds such as the salsa garden, rainbow garden, three sister's garden, giant sunflower plantings, and caterpillar maze.

ACTIVITIES CHILDREN ARE DRAWN TO MOST FREQUENTLY

The Saturday morning amphitheater shows performed by musicians, storytellers, and puppeteers are very popular (Figures 2c-21 and 2-22). The tree house, honeybee observation hive, Bog Garden with Venus Fly Traps are also intriguing to children. Of course, summer visitation would not be the same without the Sunflower Fountain, which is always packed with children (Mercer, personal communication, 2005).

FUNDING, MAINTENANCE, AND EVALUATION

Funding was raised through a joint capital campaign between the Children's Healthcare of Atlanta and the Atlanta Botanical Garden. The annual maintenance is covered by the Atlanta Botanical Garden's operations funds (Mercer, personal communication, 2005).

Since the children's garden opened, visitation and membership enrollment have significantly increased. On busy days, more than 300 children have visited the garden. Evaluation and renovation of the garden spaces have been a continuous process. Safety and sturdy construction are key for long-lasting use. The garden was designed with these thoughts foremost in mind. As children began to use the garden, a few items needed to be adjusted and/or removed, such as a showerhead and a hand pump that did not quite function correctly. The air factory at "Live" and the "Everyday Plants" will soon be renovated. This is normal in the museum and botanic garden world. Tyler said, "The Garden has experienced a new Director and new Education Director since the Garden opened. Often, the garden's program and vision evolve. This is perfectly normal and encouraged. It helps keep things fresh so that visitors want to come back. For example, the crop garden is being redesigned to strengthen the message that food comes from plants. Real chickens may be added to teach children that even our farm animals need plants" (Tyler, personal communication, 2005).

Tracy Barlow McClendon, the current Education Director said, "When the garden was first opened, it was very 'exhibit oriented,' but is less so now because the plants have filled in." Today, the garden continues to carry forward the unique educational theme that plants keep us healthy, but in a very lush landscape (McClendon, 2001).

CREDITS

The Children's Healthcare of Atlanta Children's Garden Planning and Design Team (at the Time of the Project)

Spencer and Lisa Tunnell—Owner's Representatives

Cindy Reittinger—Education Director
Cindy Tyler of Terra Design Studios
Mildred Pinnell, Horticulturist

The Children's Healthcare Of Atlanta Children's Garden Planning and Design Team (Current Staff)

Tracy Barlow McClendon, Education Director
Kevin Mercer, Youth Programs Manager

Construction Team

Architect and Flower Bridge Designer: Jim Winer
Construction Manager: Steve Robinson of Hardin Construction
Sculptor of the Green Man: Christopher Condon
Artist of the large stainless steel butterfly: David Landis

The Tulip Tree House at the Enchanted Woods at Winterthur Museum & Country Estate, Winterthur, Delaware. (COURTESY OF W. GARY SMITH.)

CHAPTER 3

Children's Gardens

Introduction

Children's gardens can be designed to be any size, shape, or theme. As you read about various gardens in this book, take note of the many theme gardens that make a space special. Below is a chart listing a range of ideas for theme gardens. Elaborate on this list by asking your children or classes about their interests, background, and hobbies, and work with them to design their own theme garden.

Develop your child's idea for a theme garden by asking them to research the topic. They will discover interesting facts about plants, fascinating folklore, and relationships between plants, animals, and mankind as they pursue a theme.

At the residential scale, choosing to design a theme garden is a good way to build on your child's personal interests and to narrow the scope of the garden to fit small scale spaces. In larger public gardens, theme gardens give identity to various parts of a larger garden and act as landmarks for children as they move through a large garden via a series of smaller theme gardens.

A series of theme gardens can ensure peaks of interest throughout the year. For example, a Garden for the Seasons might have distinct subgardens that feature spring flowers, summer vegetables, fall fruit, and winter form. A wildlife habitat garden can be designed to attract hummingbirds in the summer and chickadees in the winter.

THEME GARDENS

Pizza garden	Wildlife habitat garden	Herb garden	Fall garden	Bee hive garden	Moonlight garden
Cut flower garden	Ethnobotany garden	Container garden	Winter garden	Xeriscape garden	Annual garden
Rainbow garden	Memorial garden	Rooftop garden	Alpine garden	Carolina Fence garden	White garden
Storybook garden	Edible garden	Plants for pets garden	Bog garden	Organic garden	Artist's garden
Water garden	Heritage garden	Plants for crafts garden	Vegetable garden	Wetland garden	Sculpture garden
Bird garden	Tea garden	Spring garden	Rainbow garden	Rain garden	Vertical garden
Butterfly garden	Ethnic garden	Summer garden	Native plant garden	Desert garden	Sunken garden

Many theme gardens revolve around food. Pizza gardens are popular with children, and they provide opportunities for children to grow their own pizza toppings in a garden shaped like a pizza pie. Tomatoes, onions, peppers, parsley, oregano, garlic, and basil are all easy to grow and fun to harvest from triangular shaped beds (Figure 3-1).

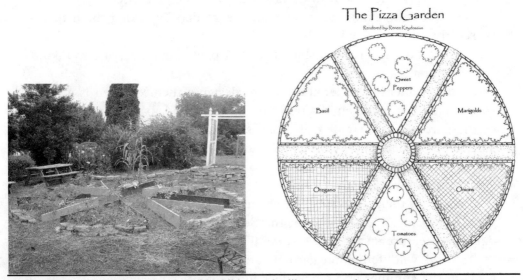

FIG 3-1. "Pizza gardens" are popular with children, who like to grow their own toppings. (DRAWING COURTESY OF RENEE KEYDOSZIUS AND PHOTO COURTESY OF MARY TAYLOR HAQUE.)

In this chapter, concepts and ideas for several garden themes will be discussed. Themes include (1) Storybook gardens, (2) Nature and wildlife gardens, (3) Adventure gardens, (4) Music gardens, (5) Water gardens, and (6) Memorial gardens.

Adventure Gardens

"The formula for adventure playgrounds includes earth, fire, water, and lots of creative materials" (http://adventureplaygrounds.hampshire.edu, accessed 2005).

Most children prefer designing and building their own environment and would much rather make a treehouse than play in one built by adults for them (Figure 3-2).

Children in urban areas often have difficulty finding places where they can create their own fort, dig foxholes, and manipulate their environment. At adventure playgrounds they can envision, plan, and build, using experience-based learning to problem solve with adults and other children. Children get to choose their play; they are not limited by static play equipment or by preplanned activities.

Encouraging community, Adventure Playgrounds are places where children and young people can meet, play, work, and have fun with minimal supervision. They can explore natural materials including earth, water, fire, wood, plants, and animals and can manipulate their environment through building. Animals including chickens, rabbits, and sheep are sometimes found at adventure playgrounds, where children assume responsibility for feeding and caring as well as playing with them (Figure 3-3).

Most Adventure Playgrounds are intended for children five years old and older, but younger children are usually welcome if accompanied by an attentive adult. Older children often walk or

FIG 3-2. Allowing children to get dirty and wet frees them to experiment with natural materials. (COURTESY OF J. C. RAULSTON.)

FIG 3-3. Children participate in the feeding and care of pets at some adventure playgrounds. (COURTESY OF GAGE COUCH AND BARBARA SIEGEL RYAN.)

ride a bike to the playground sites where an appointment is not necessary, but registration is required at some sites, and parents sign their children in and out. Group reservations and parties are sometimes held on playgrounds. Many playgrounds have rules concerning the borrowing of equipment. For example, children may exchange a bicycle key or a playground ID card for a tool. When the tool is returned, they may leave with the ID to return another day.

Fees are charged at some adventure playgrounds to help cover the cost of materials and supervision. Donations of materials and volunteer community members can help reduce fees, but most adventure playgrounds have at least one paid professional with carpentry skills and experience working with children. These "playworkers" encourage children, mediate disputes, and help when needed, but they are careful to maintain a child-centered space. Local businesses are often generous about donating materials for creative play, and contractors can actually save money by contributing left over wood instead of paying to dump it in a landfill.

Although children are taught to pick up nails, sturdy shoes are recommended at adventure playgrounds in case a stray nail goes unobserved. Old clothes are appropriate, because children love to get dirty and wet as they raft on a pond, dig in the sand, slide down a mud bank, construct forts out of scrap materials, or paint the fence surrounding the playground (Figure 3-4).

FIG 3-4. When provided with wood and tools, children can build forts and tree houses of their own. (COURTESY OF MARY TAYLOR HAQUE.)

> *"Children spend a great deal of time building structures, and doing so requires the help of their peers. Children converse to a greater extent with other children at adventure playgrounds than in conventional and contemporary playgrounds [two types of playgrounds with fixed equipment]. At an adventure playground children learn to negotiate their relationships"* (http://adventureplaygrounds.hampshire.edu/essence.html, accessed 2005).

The adventure playground movement, which started in Denmark, grew to include children with disabilities and spread throughout the world. About 1,000 adventure playgrounds currently exist in Europe, with close to 400 adventure playgrounds in Germany alone. Japan also has a significant number of adventure playgrounds. Sadly, the United States has only two adventure playgrounds, one in Berkeley, CA, and one in Huntington Beach, CA. Established in the 1970s, both have survived funding cuts that closed down three adventure playgrounds in Houston, TX, and others in the United States as well. Some communities are incorporating adventure playground concepts into existing playgrounds (http://adventureplaygrounds.hampshire.edu/history.html).

At the Adventure Playgrounds in California, children are encouraged to play and build creatively, and they have designed and built forts, boats, and towers with the tools provided on site. Students from the University of California in Berkeley help manage the construction and distribute tools at the Berkeley Marina playground. (See the following two Web sites for more information about this popular playground: http://www.gocitykids.com/browse/attraction.jsp?id=224, accessed 2005, and http://www.ci.berkeley.ca.us/marina/marinaexp/adventplgd.html, accessed 2005.)

> *"C. Th. Sørensen, a Danish landscape architect, noticed that children preferred to play everywhere but in the playgrounds that he built. In 1931, he imagined 'A junk playground in which children could create and shape, dream and imagine a reality.' Why not give children in the city the same chances for play as those in the country? His initial ideas started the adventure playground movement. The first adventure playground opened in Emdrup, Denmark, in 1943, during World War II. In 1946, Lady Allen of Hurtwood visited Emdrup from England and was impressed with 'junk playgrounds.' She brought the idea to London. These 'junk playgrounds' became known as 'adventure playgrounds'"* (http://adventureplaygrounds.hampshire.edu/history.html, accessed 2005).

When provided with tools, materials, and minimal supervision, children will create and recreate adventure playgrounds of their own (Figure 3-5). The following list of tools and materials can help get them started:

FIG 3-5. Building can include everything from forts to birdhouses at adventure playgrounds. (COURTESY OF GAGE COUCH.)

TOOLS

Hammers—various sizes

Hand saws—shorter is easier to handle

Nails—nongalvanized are easier to put in and take out; include a variety of lengths

Shovels—for children to dig holes and tunnels underground, to redistribute sand in fall areas; and build berms (a man-made mound of earth)

Wheelbarrow—for carrying tools and supplies

Paint brushes—thick and thin

Tool boxes—sized for children to carry tools in

Hose—to water plants or wet down a bare hill and slide down the muddy slope

MATERIALS

Water

Rocks

Sand

Tires

Bricks

Cement blocks

Foam

Textiles—cloth and carpeting

Cardboard

Branches and other plant parts

Paint—permanent, water-based

Furniture

Rope, string, wire

Tile pieces

Wood: 2 × 4 (38 × 89 mm), 4 × 4 (89 × 89 mm), 2 × 6s (38 × 140 mm) are essential; scraps, pallets, plywood are helpful. Note: avoid particleboard, pressure-treated wood, old painted wood, and sharp or splintery wood.

> *"A castle, made of cartons, rocks, and old branches, by a group of children for themselves, is worth a thousand perfectly detailed, exactly finished castles, made for them in a factory."*
> —Christopher Alexander (http://downlode.org/etext/patterns/ptn73.html, accessed 2005).

See the list of resources in the appendix if you want more information on how to start an adventure playground in your community. Although some designers may not want to relinquish the design of playgrounds to children, they should remember that adventure playgrounds are a powerful way to encourage, facilitate, and promote the early education of future designers and contractors.

Edible Gardens

The concept of edible landscapes is as old as the first gardens. Indeed, food for human consumption was one of the first gardening incentives in history. During the Victorian era, gardeners began to separate ornamental gardens from edible gardens, which could consist of herbs, vegetables, small fruits, and tree fruit and nuts. In the late 20th century, authors like Robert Rodale and Rosalind Creasy inspired a renewal of interest in edible landscapes, combining edibles with ornamentals to bring balance back into gardens (Figure 3-6).

FIG 3-6. Edibles such as this grape vine can be both tasty and beautiful. (COURTESY OF MARY TAYLOR HAQUE.)

Plants are vital to our daily lives. Therefore, one cannot underestimate the relationship that exists between humans and the plants we eat, a relationship that has become more complex as new research shifts national attention to health and environmental issues such as safe food sources, nutrition, and sustainable agriculture (Figure 3-7).

As families become further removed from the natural world, their understanding of environmental

FIG 3-7. Issues such as safe food can be addressed by letting children grow their own food organically. (COURTESY OF AMY DABBS.)

FIG 3-8. The satisfaction that comes from a harvest of fresh fruit provides children with physical and emotional well-being. (COURTESY OF KUANG MING TAI AND SALLY HUNT.)

concerns becomes diminished. By exposing children to the physical, mental and emotional well-being that results from growing, harvesting and eating fresh fruits and vegetables, individuals become better connected to the natural world that sustains our lives (Figure 3-8).

Children in the United States are facing increasing rates of obesity and related diseases such as diabetes. Parents, teachers, governments and communities can take action to help children curb this disturbing trend in several ways. (1) Ensure that land use plans promote physical activity including community gardens and parks. (2) Ensure access for children via safe sidewalks and bike paths. (3) School lunch programs and home meals should offer healthier choices (Figure 3-9).

FIG 3-9. Gardening promotes physical activity and healthy living. (COURTESY OF LISA PETTY.)

SCHOOL GARDENS FOR NUTRITIOUS EATING

Many schools around the country and the world are establishing school gardens where children can help grow healthy vegetables to serve as snacks or with meals (Figure 3-10). The National Gardening Association Web site at www.Kids

gardening.com, has excellent information for teachers and parents who plan to garden with children. Texas A&M University also has an informative site at: http://aggiehorticulture. tamu.edu/kindergarden/Child/ cgintro.htm. Featuring resources for school, community, and botanic gardens, this site has many links to individual schools and organizations along with ideas and directions for starting your own garden. Establishing a network with national organizations like The American Community Garden Association is a great way to find tips on starting and maintaining school and community gardens.

Wonderland Gardens in Atlanta, GA, founded by Sheldon Fleming, is committed to stewardship of the earth through gardening, education, and recycling. A community resource connecting people with nature, the garden includes community gardens, an outdoor classroom, an amphitheatre and a pavilion where the principles and practices set forth by Dr. George Washington Carver are taught. Practical, hands-on educational programs in organic gardening and recycling pay tribute to his contributions as a scientist, horticulturist, agriculturalist, and artist (Wonderland Gardens, cited September 18, 2005; available from

FIG 3-10. Cooking what they have grown provides children with healthy snacks and meals. (COURTESY OF AMY DABBS.)

FIG 3-11. Members of the American Horticultural Society network at Wonderland Gardens in Atlanta, Georgia, to learn more about community gardening. (COURTESY OF MARY TAYLOR HAQUE.)

FIG 3-12. Edible gardens can have ornamental value at many scales. (COURTESY OF MARY TAYLOR HAQUE.)

http://www.wonderlandgardens.org/) (Figure 3-11).

The concept of school gardens has expanded to include minifarms in some parts of the world. In addition to growing herbs, vegetables, fruits, and flowers, children at some schools are raising animals such as rabbits, goats, sheep, and chickens. Urban children get to practice animal husbandry and collect and sell eggs. To learn more about minifarms at schools, visit: EcoSchool Design™ www.ecoschools.com.

Edible gardens vary in scale from a small pot of herbs on the windowsill to a network of gardens within a large community (Figure 3-12). Kids' Edible Gardens (KEGs) in New Zealand has attracted positive attention for its work with more than 20 primary schools in Christchurch. Based on permaculture principles focused on design and maintenance of productive ecosystems that have diversity, stability and sustainability, KEGs is teaching children about healthy gardening. (Organic Pathways, http://www.organicpathways.co.nz/garden/index.html, accessed 2005.)

The Organic Garden City Trust has been implementing organic gardening in schools in Christchurch since 1997, so that children can grow their own food. They offer to set up an edible garden in schools assisted by small groups of children and establish ties to curricula in Social Studies, Science, and Health. To achieve this, they provide a garden facilitator, expertise in designing and managing the garden,

FIG 3-13. Potter Children's Garden at the Auckland Botanic Garden, New Zealand, allows children to "feed" this sculpture as they discuss what plants are eaten by native birds and how seed is dispersed. (COURTESY OF SUE WAKE.)

teacher resources including worksheets, and a plan for setting up a school composting system. The program is supported by numerous sponsors to keep school fees low. For more information on this program, visit the Web site at: http://www.organicpathways.co.nz/keg/ (Figure 3-13).

At Clemson University in South Carolina, students in Horticulture, Technical Writing, Geography, and Physical Science have been involved in the development of gardens created specifically to demonstrate sustainable, organic gardening practices such as crop rotation, cover crops, plant selection, vermicomposting, and mulching (Figures 3-14, 3-15, 3-16, and 3-17). Students enrolled in Technical Writing increased their written communication skills through the creation of brochures and case statements for the children's garden. They have assisted in fund raising and educational outreach by creating

FIGS 3-14 through 03-17. Students at Clemson University work with "Sprouting Wings" children at the South Carolina Botanical Garden to design a garden, plant seeds, vermicompost, and market their produce. (COURTESY OF AMY DABBS AND MARY TAYLOR HAQUE.)

The mission of the Calhoun Field Laboratory (CFL) Sustainable Farming Project is exploring more profitable and environmentally friendly farming enterprises through research, education, and public service.

FIG 3-18. Technnical Writing students at Clemson developed brochures to disseminate information on their edible gardens. (COURTESY OF SUMMER TAYLOR.)

FIG 3-19. Save space in an edible garden by espaliering fruit trees or vines against a wall. (COURTESY OF MARY TAYLOR HAQUE.)

educational information sheets on topics such as Kid-friendly Gardening, Gardening for Wildlife, Worm-composting "How To," Composting Basics, Organic Vegetable Gardening, and Environmentally Friendly Gardening (Figure 3-18).

SPACE-SAVING IDEAS

If you're looking for space-saving ideas when designing edible gardens, consider the following.

1. Train fruit trees or vines flat against a fence or wall. This is called an es-palier, and though it takes some pruning to keep them flat, you'll save space for children to play (Figure 3-19).

2. Go vertical. Many vines such as cucumbers and melons sprawl over the ground, eating up space in your garden. Train them up a vertical trellis, or even better, create a simple teepee-shaped structure that will double as a support for your vines and a fort for your kids (Figure 3-20).

3. Experiment with "the three sisters" configuration inspired by Native Americans. Plant corn, pole beans, and squash together to deter insects, and let

the beans climb up the corn stalks to save space. Bacterial colonies on the bean roots capture nitrogen from the air and released it into the soil, nourishing the corn, which needs high nitrogen. Interplanting also allows you to harvest a wide variety of vegetables in a small space, while regaining a healthy diet and exercise habits. If you are interested in experimenting with a variety of recipes using these traditional foods, look for The Three Sisters Cookbook produced by the Oneida Indian Nation Health Department, with funding from the New York State Department of Health, Division of Nutrition. Visit http://www.oneidanation.net/FRAMESfood.html and enjoy the benefits of healthy eating and gardening (Figure 3-21).

FIG 3-20. A teepee of logs covered with vining edible vegetables makes a fun space for children to enjoy at the Atlanta Botanical Garden. (COURTESY OF MARY TAYLOR HAQUE.)

Memorial Gardens

INTRODUCTION

Memorial gardens are intended to commemorate or memorialize a person or event, often through the presence of a monument or other special focal point. When used in association with a religious institution, the term "memorial garden"

FIG 3-21. Harvesting fresh vegetables connects children to the natural world. (COURTESY OF AMY DABBS.)

or "memorial park" often refers to a garden consecrated for the sacred disposition of ashes as a final resting place. Memorial gardens have a quality of recollection and evoke a sense of eternity.

The untimely death of a child is a very tragic event. Not only family and friends, but also often entire communities experience intense grief when a child dies. People feel the need to take action at such times, and memorial gardens can fulfill many needs associated with the death of a child or someone loved by a child.

SCHOOL MEMORIAL GARDENS

The mood at schools where a child has died is often very somber, and teachers and administrators are often at a loss for ways to deal with the collective grief and confusion experienced by an entire student body. One way that school leaders can respond with caring and compassion is to enable mourners to come together to participate in the planning and planting of a memorial garden honoring the deceased. This process involves remembering the loved one and celebrating their life and individuality. Planning the garden provides an outlet for grief. Children can remember fondly the characteristics of the person they are honoring and choose plants to symbolize those characteristics. For example, students at D.W. Daniel High School in Central, SC, chose to plant trumpet daffodils to remember a peer who played trumpet in the high school band.

Because older students are often at risk as they learn to drive and experience peer pressure to experiment with alcohol and drugs, high schools in particular can benefit from a memorial garden. Such gardens provide a tranquil setting where individuals can contemplate and where friends can meet to grieve (Figure 3-22).

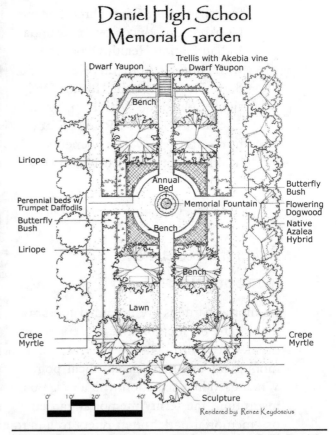

FIG 3-22. This design of a Memorial Courtyard at D.W. Daniel High School honors students who died while attending the school. (COURTESY OF RENEE KEYDOSZIUS.)

MEANINGFUL TRIBUTES

Memorials can be made in many ways. Following is a list of ways to provide tributes in memorial gardens including (1) trees, (2) memorial bricks, (3) plaques, (4) stones, (5) water features, (6) benches, (7) symbolic representations, (8) passage of time, (9) variety of spaces, (10) statues, and (11) labyrinths.

1. A "Tributes through Trees" program can be set up at schools. The cost of purchasing, planting, and maintaining a tree is determined by a knowledgeable committee, and individuals or groups can donate to the program to have a tree planted in memory or in honor of someone. This works best if a planting plan is developed by a professional so that trees are planted in appropriate places on school campuses. Having a plan in place also enables memorials to be planted in a timely manner (Figure 3-23).

FIG 3-23. Children planted an avenue of trees to honor their former principal at Clemson Elementary School. (COURTESY OF MARY TAYLOR HAQUE.)

2. Memorial bricks are often used as fundraisers for institutions. Courtyards or walkways may be constructed in the garden with each brick engraved with a person's name. Family members enjoy searching for "their" brick, and some even donate a brick for every member of the family including those living and deceased (Figure 3-24).

3. Plaques are often used in memorial gardens to commemorate a person or event. Too many plaques can result in a cluttered appearance; so many gardens restrict the use of individual plaques. An attractive and meaningful alternative can be found in an artistically designed group plaque. Placed on a wall, fence, or stone, such plaques be-

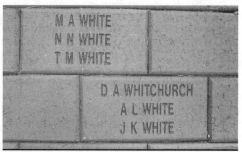

FIG 3-24. Memorial bricks are often used as fundraisers for institutions. (COURTESY OF MARY TAYLOR HAQUE.)

come a focal point, and people find solace in finding the name of their loved one among others. They often take rubbings of the name or run their hand over the name, establishing a tactile connection (Figure 3-25).

FIG 3-25. Artistically designed group plaques make a beautiful focal point. Children like to see their friends' and family's names on the recognition plaque. (COURTESY OF MARY TAYLOR HAQUE.)

4. For some cultures and people, natural materials provide the best memorial. A lichen and moss covered rock or a vertical stone make enduring monuments. If building a natural stonewall, consider asking children and their families to bring stones from places that have meaning for them. The wall becomes a marker rich with significant memories of those who help place the stones.

5. Water features make meaningful focal points in memorial gardens. The sound of flowing water is very soothing, and fountains can introduce a happy note that brings an element of joy to uplift tired spirits. A small birdbath will reflect the sunlight, adding sparkle and attracting birds and other wildlife. People can reconnect with nature and receive solace from the calm waters and living creatures that it attracts (Figure 3-26).

FIG 3-26. The sound of flowing water is very soothing, and fountains can introduce a happy note that brings an element of joy to uplift tired spirits. (COURTESY OF MARY TAYLOR HAQUE.)

6. Benches are also appropriate gifts for memorial gardens. Place them alone and in groups where users can contemplate a distant view, relax in the shade, or gather for songs and stories. A small plaque is often placed on the bench with the name of the person it honors (Figure 3-27).

7. Symbolic representation through icons such as a cross or natural forms including waterfalls, rivers, forests, islands, and seas is sometimes used in memorial gardens. Every tree, stone. shrub, flower, bench, or water feature can be deliberately placed and maintained to create harmony and provide a place of reflection.

8. Memorial gardens are often designed to suggest the passage of time—a day, a month, or a lifetime—with a beginning, center, and ending. The use of deciduous flowering plants that bloom in spring, grow throughout the summer, drop their leaves in fall, and "die" (go dormant) in winter correlates beautifully with the "seasons" of life. These can often be experienced in a walk through the garden along a path with a series of outdoor rooms and plant groupings that peak at different seasons.

FIG 3-27. A bench with a small plaque names the person it honors and provides a place to contemplate and rest. (COURTESY OF MARY TAYLOR HAQUE.)

9. As peaceful, quiet places for mourners with different needs, public memorial gardens are most effective if they include a variety of spaces. Some people prefer a protected spot to sit alone in meditation or prayer. Others need company and seek places where small groups can gather to console each other or recount happy times together. Larger groups often gather for memorial services, and people from many different faiths and backgrounds can come together comfortably for a ceremony in larger gardens. These spaces can be used throughout the year for other purposes, such as meeting places for outdoor classes or for small group discussions about class projects. The variety of different spaces can be connected with pathways, stairways, arbors, or avenues.

10. Statues provide a traditional means of memorializing someone. Artists can be commissioned to work in a variety of materials including metal, stone, or wood, for example. Sculpture is usually most effective if placed in a setting where it can be viewed with the sky as a background. The resulting contrast between dark and light, void and mass can make a very dramatic statement.

11. Labyrinths provide a powerful means of introducing restful movement into children's gardens, faith gardens, community gardens, and into backyards. Unlike mazes, which have dead ends and are therefore challenging and sometimes frustrating, labyrinths are easy to walk. They have only one path, which leads to the center and back out in a symbolic journey that relates to wholeness. Combining the

FIG 3-28. Labyrinths have only one path, which leads to the center and back out in a symbolic journey that relates to wholeness. (COURTESY OF MARY TAYLOR HAQUE.)

imagery of the circle and the spiral, labyrinths have been used for centuries as meditation and prayer tools in many religions. Walking a labyrinth is a right brain activity requiring a passive and relaxing mindset, while walking a maze is a left-brain activity that requires analytical and sequential thinking (Figure 3-28).

Children can help construct a labyrinth by placing stones or plantings to define the paths. Labyrinths make a wonderful community building project, as evidenced by one built for Hospice of the Upstate in South Carolina. Hospice is a volunteer organization that cares for terminally ill patients. Graduating seniors from Clemson University designed and constructed a landscape plan for Hospice, which featured planting for wildlife and a stone labyrinth as its focal points. Community partners included university and high school students and faculty, Sunday school classes, Master Gardeners, garden clubs, landscape professionals, and other community volunteers (Figure 3-29).

FIG 3-29. Clemson University students have designed labyrinths for spiritual sites and for Hospice. The labyrinth path leading to the center and back out again is a metaphor for the spiritual road of life. (COURTESY OF MARY TAYLOR HAQUE.)

The one way path that leads to the center and back out again has become a metaphor for the spiritual road of life, and community groups including children visited Hospice to help build and walk the sacred path. "Finger Labyrinths," beautiful wooden models whose meditative path can be traced with a finger, are a perfect alternative for bedridden patients unable to walk the 60-foot diameter labyrinth outside their room.

The public is invited to walk the path of the labyrinth and enjoy the emerging landscape, which is uniting and uplifting individuals from all stages of life. Candlelight walks scented by wisteria flowers blooming on the pergola adjacent to the labyrinth are scheduled in spring. Followed by a catered dinner in the Hospice dining room, such events double as fundraisers for Hospice and as memorable occasions in the garden.

MEMORIAL GARDENS CAN SERVE MULTIPLE FUNCTIONS

Memorial gardens often serve multiple functions. For example, faculty, staff, and students of the Landscape Architecture Department at the University of Georgia partnered with the Garden Club of Georgia to design and develop a "Founders Memorial Garden" to honor the founders of the first garden club in America. This garden also serves as a laboratory for students interested in botany, forestry, and related disciplines.

Referred to by some as the "Crown Jewel of Duke University," the Sarah P. Duke Gardens occupy 55 acres in the heart of the campus. Recognized both for landscape design and horticulture, the gardens attract visitors from all over the world. Although the garden is a memorial to Sarah Duke, it also provides a place where people of all backgrounds and ages come for beauty, education, horticulture, solitude, discovery, study, renewal, and inspiration.

At Whitehall Elementary School in Anderson, SC, a wide community came together to create an outdoor learning laboratory to memorialize Dennis Hepler, a much loved principal, who was shot and robbed while leaving school one evening. Because successful fund-raising efforts were conducted simultaneously with the design process by school leaders and members of the community, Whitehall Elementary School was able to begin implementing the Memorial Park/Outdoor Learning Lab one month after designs were completed. All of the children submitted landscape ideas in drawing and in writing, and some children were able to practice leadership skills by serving as representatives on the planning, design, fundraising, building, and dedication committees. Such opportunities al-

FIG 3-30. At Whitehall Elementary School, the surrounding community came together to create an outdoor learning laboratory to memorialize Dennis Hepler, a much loved principal. (COURTESY OF MARY TAYLOR HAQUE.)

lowed children to practice graphic, written, and oral communication skills as they presented their ideas to various groups and individuals (Figure 3-30). See Chapter 6 to learn more about how service learning was utilized to create this multi dimensional memorial/outdoor learning laboratory.

HOME MEMORIAL GARDENS

Small memorial gardens can also be created in home gardens to help children work through the grieving process associated with the death of a grandparent or other loved one. These need not be large. Work with your child to choose a spot, place an object such as a birdbath, urn, or statue, and surround it with ferns or flowers to create a "memory garden."

A simple but elegant gesture can be achieved by hanging a cut lead crystal from the limb of a tree. When invisible light rays refract through the crystal, one remembers the invisible soul of the departed with a flash of insight.

> *Memorial Gardens provide places where people can both grieve the death and celebrate the life of their family, friends and pets.*

> *A poignant place of pilgrimage, labyrinths have been used for centuries as meditation and prayer tools in many religions.*

Special occasions such as birthdays and holidays are often emotional days for children after the death of a loved one. Planting a tribute tree or flower can provide a focus for those days, or children can add a new crystal to the tree limb on special occasions. Picking flowers from the garden and placing them on a grave is a very comforting gesture. The fragrance of certain flowers is reputed to have therapeutic properties that can help with depression.

Children who are fortunate enough to experience the special love and trust of a faithful pet are often devastated when their pet dies. Garden burials and memorials can help fill children's need for proper final care associated with pets. Many pets are both devoted to and dependent on children for their needs throughout life. Children value the companionship of these pets, and they have a need to participate in their burial and to create memorials to express grief (Figure 3-31).

FIG 3-31. Statues such as this one at Brookgreen Gardens elicit fond memories of former pets. Statues can serve as poignant memorials and as artistic focal points in a garden. (COURTESY OF MARY TAYLOR HAQUE.)

Music Gardens

The Music Garden at Clemson Elementary School in Clemson, SC, is an example of an environment dreamed up by children and brought to reality by a cross section of expected and unexpected participants. The garden serves both an educational and a recreational function. When Clemson Elementary students identified a music garden as something they wanted in the outdoors at their new school, the planners working on the master plan for the outdoors were not quite sure what the children meant by a music garden. The research process was set in motion, which included interpreting the student's drawings and comments about a music garden. Their general idea was to have a place where they could make music, but no absolute directions were reflected by the children. The next phase of the research was to have a group of students in a Clemson University recreation and leisure environments class develop some conceptual ideas of what a music garden should be.

The concept of a music garden seemed to exude success because it combined two things all children seem to love—music and the outdoors. In addition, increasing numbers of research studies were showing benefits conveyed by music education falling into four categories of success—in society, in school, in developing intelligence, and in life (MENC, 2002). Specific studies refer to gains in standardized test scores including the SAT, improvement in math proficiency, increases in self-esteem and thinking skills, and decreases in disruptive behavior (Catterall, 1999; Graziano et al., 1999). Groundbreaking neurological research using functional magnetic resource imaging shows brains of musicians being more efficient, more organized, and better able to conduct numerous activities at once (Ratey, 2001; Weinberger, 2000). The reasons for including a music garden in a school were easily established; the task at hand was to determine how to do it.

FIG 3-32. Bond Anderson, inventor of Sound Play instruments, instructs volunteers on one of the finishing techniques. (COURTESY OF GINA McLELLAN.)

The University students moved the process from research into program development by linking conceptual ideas with the design process. They first identified the proposed music garden as consisting of musical instruments permanently mounted in a garden setting where students could create musical sounds in an exploratory manner. Then they decided what kinds of instruments might work in such a setting and whether such instruments existed. An exhaustive search of the internet and other sources revealed an individual in a neighboring state who had already invented and built such instruments. The planners made contact with Bond Anderson of Sound Play in Parrot, GA, to gather more information on the instruments and what could potentially work for Clemson Elementary (www.soundplay.com, accessed 2005) (Figure 3-32).

The music garden site was selected and a site inventory and analysis conducted. The site was

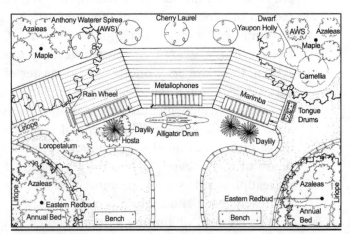

FIG 3-33. The Music Garden site design shows placement of musical instruments on deck and ground. (COURTESY OF GINA McLELLAN.)

a level 25' × 40' (7.6 × 12.2 m) area with no existing vegetation. The location was designated in the Clemson Elementary Outdoors master plan as a music garden, and detailed drawings were done by Clemson University landscape architecture students showing the landscape design with the placement of instruments in the garden.

The landscaping was designed to serve multiple functions. The site was completely open, and needed trees that would eventually provide shade. Other plantings were placed to help control movement on and off the deck and to provide soft backdrops to the rigidity of the instruments. Beds for flowering plants would provide places with visual variation where students could select the plantings. Small grassy areas would provide informal sitting places and visual contrast.

While the above steps were underway, there was a parallel movement by volunteers to secure funding for the garden. Budgets were established ranging from $7500 to $15,000, with the lowest cost consisting of volunteer built instruments and volunteer landscape installation. The highest level was for prebuilt instruments and some paid landscape installation. One volunteer made contact with a foundation whose money originally came from the music industry. A grant was written and submitted that sought funds for the music garden, and the project was funded by the foundation. The funding level then guided the decision to do a community built garden, an alternative installation with volunteers rather than expending money for prebuilt instruments and professional landscape installation. This approach saved approximately one-third of the total cost (Figure 3-34).

The installation of the music garden was a well-orchestrated event with exceptional advance planning. It involved a technique which focused on having a paid professional on-site to lead the volunteers through the building process. In this case, the on-site professional was Bond Anderson, the inventor and builder of the Sound Play instruments. The instruments require specialized equipment to build and are complicated enough that having the professional builder on-site

FIG 3-34. Volunteers work on mounting bracket for a tongue drum. (COURTESY OF GINA McLELLAN.)

assures success and saves time. The model of the three-person leadership team discussed in Chapter 2 was followed and consisted of the school principal and two volunteers, one who worked directly with the instrument designer before and during the building process and one who coordinated the volunteers. While one recruited volunteers and prepared a site for the building of instruments to take place, the other volunteer leader shopped for supplies from the five-page long equipment and materials list. With the site prepared, all materials and supplies on hand, and

FIG 3-35. The prepared deck and grounds are ready for placement of the musical instruments. (COURTESY OF GINA K. McLELLAN.)

Bond Anderson at the school, the building began (Figure 3-35). The 80 volunteers were scheduled in teams of five to six people at a time that provided a small enough group for instruction while providing a large enough group to get the job done. At the end of five and a half days, the six instruments were built and mounted in the garden. One equipment malfunction and one volunteer who never showed up were the extent of the tangible problems during the week and did not affect the overall timeline established for the project. The final installation consisted of the following instruments:

Mounted on main deck:

Tenor-soprano metallophone

Soprano marimba

Base metallophone

Mounted on opposite ends of deck:

Rain wheel

Four-tongue drum

Mounted on ground in front of deck:

Painted raised alligator

The music garden was somewhat different from a volunteer perspective than many of the other play and garden environments built at Clemson Elementary School by volunteers. It drew volunteers with many different talents from throughout the community because this garden provided an opportunity to apply many

FIG 3-36. A volunteer gives the alligator drum a brightly colored whimsical paint job before it takes its place in the music garden. (COURTESY OF GINA K. McLELLAN.)

FIG 3-37. A Clemson Elementary School student tries out the alligator when it's moved into place in the music garden. (COURTESY OF GINA K. McLELLAN.)

different skills. A retired industrial arts teacher and master craftsman, for example, was able to do the skilled woodworking required. The Clemson University band director had the musical ear necessary to craft the instrument pieces to the exact musical tones needed. A local woodcarver donated her time to carve the head of the alligator drum. A local artisan applied her painting talents to creating a whimsical design for the alligator's painted body. At the same time, there were many jobs for volunteers with no building skills and for children who wanted to help develop the music garden at their new school (Figures 3-36 and 3-37).

One major challenge for this type of project was to secure an indoor location necessary for some of the work to be carried out and to provide a protected place for equipment and supplies to be secured overnight. Because Clemson Elementary had just been built and had been planned for future growth, an empty classroom located close to the music garden site was made available. The second major challenge was finding all the materials required for building the instruments. The special types of wood, fasteners, and other specific materials required persistence and time, but the time spent in advance assuring that everything was ready to go made the project flow smoothly during construction.

Although a music garden doesn't have the perception of being a potential safety hazard to the users, safety was a major consideration. The design called for the three major instruments to be mounted on a wood deck. To prevent the necessity of railings around the deck, it was kept no more than a step above the ground. Because the deck was designed to be Americans with Disabilities Act (ADA) accessible, a ramp was installed to ADA slope specifications with a railing. ADA turn dimensions were met so that wheelchairs could be accommodated at the three

FIG 3-38. The ramp and railing help the deck of the music garden meet ADA accessibility standards. (COURTESY OF GINA K. McLELLAN.)

FIG 3-39. Children of all ages enjoy exploring musical sounds in the garden. (COURTESY OF GINA K. McLELLAN.)

instruments played from the deck area. The other key safety consideration was that the mallets used to play the instruments were permanently connected to the instruments by cables and needed to be short enough to prevent entanglement of a child in the cables (Figure 3-38).

Future maintenance was a consideration throughout the entire project. With instruments designed to be permanently placed in the outdoors and extensively tested by the inventor prior to the Clemson installation, the maintenance of the instruments would be minimal for many years. The deck was built with pressure-treated lumber and then protected further with an application of polyurethane. The landscaping followed the minimal maintenance concept with a low growing grass sod, shade trees appropriate to the climate, and shrubs that would not require pruning (Figure 3-39).

The music garden is a unique and well-liked setting at Clemson Elementary School. It is heavily used by children at recess, by after school program participants, by the general community on weekends, and even as an incentive by teachers encouraging their students to work hard. Although numerous opportunities exist in the garden for actually teaching musical concepts, it is the exploration and enjoyment of each visitor that is the ultimate benefit of the garden.

Storybook Gardens

Storybook designs are a powerful way to connect landscape spaces to literature. Children love to read storybooks and then design gardens featuring elements from the story. The American Horticultural Society (AHS) partnered with the Junior Master Gardener program in 2005 to create the "Growing Good Kids—

Excellence in Children's Literature" award program. Honoring outstanding children's gardening and nature books, the award recognizes books that are exceptionally effective at helping children understand and appreciate gardening and the natural environment. Themed books published during the last 100 years were evaluated by a selection committee consisting of both children and adults to identify a one-time "Classics" category. The 40 books receiving this distinction can be found with a synopsis on the AHS Web site at: http://www.k2demo.com/jmg/index.k2?did=11777&sectionID=10398.

To further cultivate the connection between children's garden experiences and reading, the Junior Master Gardener program is developing a curriculum entitled: "Literature in the Garden." Utilizing six of the Growing Good Kids Book Award-winning titles, their goal is to inspire learning by combining outdoor activities and exploration (http://www.jmgkids.us/index.k2?did=11882, accessed 2005). Designing storybook gardens is an activity that will deepen the reader's understanding of the book and inspire creative thinking. Bringing garden design and great books together is a wonderful way to get kids to connect design to both literature and the natural world.

CLEMSON ELEMENTARY SCHOOL STORYBOOK COURTYARDS

When designs for a new elementary school were being drawn up in Clemson, SC, four courtyards were selected to become storybook gardens. The school librarian, teachers, and parents worked with the children to select their favorite story with a strong outdoor theme. They then invited Clemson University landscape architecture students to assist with the development of designs for the following storybook gardens.

Alice In Wonderland Garden

Based on ideas from first and second graders in partnership with college students, the Alice in Wonderland garden features elements from the story. Kids adventure with Alice through the card gates, into the Mad Hatter tea party area, and pretend to shrink as they walk through the forest of bamboo, a tall grass (Figures 3-40, 3-41, 3-42, and 3-43).

> *"Curiouser and curiouser!" cried Alice.*
> —*Alice in Wonderland* by Lewis Carroll

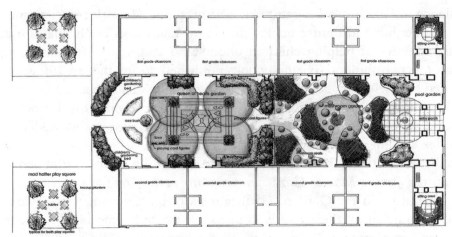

Plan of Alice in Wonderland Courtyard

Section through Courtyard

Mushroom Seating

Rabbit Hole

FIGS 3-40 through 3-43. (Top and middle) Plan and section: Queen of Hearts sunken amphitheater provides an outdoor classroom gathering space, as does the mushroom garden, where seats of various sizes accommodate children of different ages in the Alice in Wonderland storybook courtyard. (Bottom left). Mushroom seating along with tall bamboo makes children feel as small as Alice when she had to make her way through a forest of grass. (Bottom right). Children may choose to walk through the arched doorway or crawl through a conceptualized "Rabbit Hole" to enter the magical Alice in Wonderland storybook courtyard. (COURTESY OF CLEMSON UNIVERSITY LANDSCAPE ARCHITECTURE STUDENTS.)

Peter Rabbit Garden

With input from the kindergarteners and first graders at Clemson Elementary School, the Peter Rabbit Garden is designed to resemble Peter's journey from

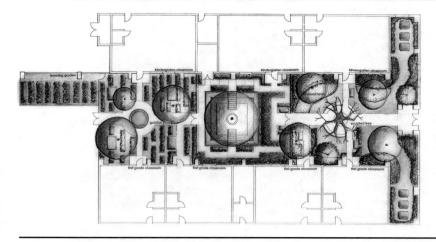

FIGS 3-44 and 3-45. (Left). This plan view of the Peter Rabbit Garden depicts Mr. McGreggor's garden and a variety of outdoor spaces complete with tables, benches, and an amphitheatre. (Right). This artificially sculpted tree provides a "den" where children pretend to be Peter Rabbit. (COURTESY OF CLEMSON UNIVERSITY LANDSCAPE ARCHITECTURE STUDENTS.)

his home to Mr. McGreggor's garden. The cubbyhole of a sculpted tree provides a "rabbit den" where children can pretend to be Peter. Garden plots enable children to be farmers while they grow carrots and cabbages (Figures 3-44 and 3-45).

> *"Once upon a time there were four little Rabbits, and their names were Flopsy, Mopsy, Cotton-tail, and Peter."*
> —*The Tale of Peter Rabbit* by Beatrix Potter

Harry Potter

With help from the fourth and fifth graders, the design for the Harry Potter garden magically materialized. Landmarks from the book include a maze, the whomping willow tree, and a cauldron-like fountain (Figures 3-46 and 3-47).

> *"Summer was creeping over the grounds around the castle; sky and lake alike turned periwinkle blue and flowers large as cabbages burst into bloom in the greenhouses. Too soon, it was time for the journey home on the Hogwarts Express."*
> —*Harry Potter and the Sorcerer's Stone* by J.K. Rowling

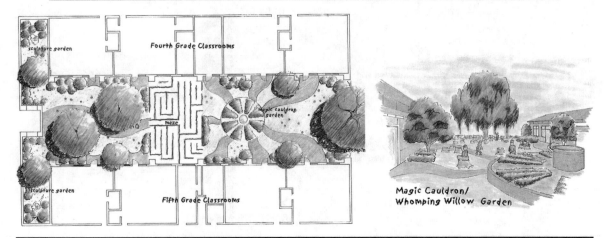

FIGS 3-46 and 3-47. (Left). The maze seen in the center of the Harry Potter Courtyard was the top choice of children when asked what they wanted in the courtyard. (Right). Students clever enough to find their way through the maze are rewarded with the magic cauldron garden.

The Secret Garden

The Secret Garden theme was chosen by the third and fourth graders. The design incorporates storybook elements including: (1) the hidden garden door, (2) an area representing the moor with native grasses and wildflowers, (3) Dickon's enchanted wildlife garden with plants to attract birds and butterflies,

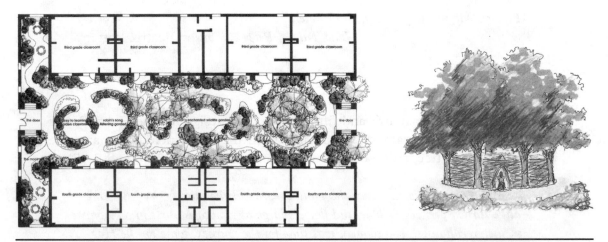

FIGS 3-48 and 3-49. (Left). The themes of discovery, growing, healing, and magic from the story are interpreted into major garden areas in The Secret Garden Courtyard. (Right). A walled garden with gate represents the Secret Garden. (COURTESY OF CLEMSON UNIVERSITY LANDSCAPE ARCHITECTURE STUDENTS.)

(4) the secret garden with footprint impressions of the special robin in the pavement. The footprints lead to an impression of the key, so children can discover the key to the gate. Full of spring bulbs, this garden is designed to inspire Dickon's love of nature in school children (Figures 3-48 and 3-49).

> *"The robin flew from his swinging spray of ivy on to the top of the wall, and he opened his beak and sang a loud, lovely trill, merely to show off. Nothing in the world is quite as adorably lovely as a robin when he shows off—and they are nearly always doing it."*
> —*The Secret Garden* by Frances Hodgson Burnett

Water Gardens

CHILDREN LOVE WATER

Water is the most desired and the least provided element in a child's play world (Figure 3-50). One girl remarked, "If I were blind, I would still come to listen and touch."

Children love water in any form. A dewdrop, birdbath, fountain, creek, river, pool, ocean, or thirst quenching drink each has allure. Even water in its solid state (snow and ice) or its gaseous state (steam, fog, mist) has great appeal (Figure 3-51). Children also love the plant and animal life that is supported by wa-

FIG 3-50. Water is the most desired and the least provided element in a child's play world. (COURTESY OF MARY TAYLOR HAQUE.)

FIG 3-51. Fog units have great appeal for children and help cool an area while misting plants as well. (COURTESY OF MARY TAYLOR HAQUE.)

FIG 3-52. If your school, garden, or playground has a natural water feature nearby, work to make it clean, safe, and accessible. (COURTESY OF MARY TAYLOR HAQUE.)

ter. Housing unusual plants and fish, something as small as a recycled barrel or pot makes a great water garden. If your school, garden, or playground has a natural water feature nearby, work to make it clean, safe, and accessible (Figure 3-52). Where natural features are not available, create your own water feature, large or small.

SAFETY IN WATER GARDENS

When designing a water feature for children, special attention to safety details and health constraints must be given. Approaches to designing participatory water features to minimize the risk of physical injuries and lawsuits may vary. Some designers use exaggerated features to give warning, while others reduce the volume of water and avoid pools. Small volumes of water can appear bigger through aeration, and even fine mist is attractive for small children and their parents. If a deep basin is used where young children have access, a strong wire mesh can be installed just below the surface of the water to prevent a child from falling into the water (Figure 3-53).

There are many problems with allowing people in fountains or pools not designed for participation. Broken statuary, exposed electrical systems, and lights create extremely dangerous situations. Jets are exciting, but exposed holes can cause a twisted ankle or broken leg, so it is desirable to have the source of water covered. Signs give notice of potential danger and of electrical equipment, but young children may not be able to read, and others may choose to ignore them. Both children and dogs sometimes get into the water, causing the health department concern, so maintenance and health constraints are major factors in any water feature. Be sure to check with local officials re-

FIG 3-53. Wire mesh can be installed in deep water trough's such as this one at Winterthur to make them safe for young children. (COURTESY OF MARY TAYLOR HAQUE.)

garding health codes, which are very strict when dealing with public swimming areas and fountains, as well they should be. Recirculated water is often used as a conservation measure, but water treatment is required and can be an expensive factor in the maintenance budgets for larger projects. Young children wearing diapers who get into water features can cause health concerns, so water quality must be monitored regularly.

Health constraints, vandalism, maintenance, safety problems, and the threat of lawsuits all play a part in making a decision about whether or not to include a participatory water feature. But it cannot be emphasized enough that children love to play in water, and participatory projects are not only possible, but practical and enjoyable as well.

In cities where water features are not available, residents desperate for cooling water play have opened fire hydrants to dance and play in the gushing water. Municipalities can avoid this unintended use of hydrants by providing parks where children can gather to play in water features designed for cooling and fun. Many municipalities are showing a renewed interest in preserving or restoring natural water features such as rivers, streams, and lakes. These provide for local sports including boating, swimming, and fishing, encouraging recreation and contributing to physical as well as mental health. When providing access to a body of water, slope the edges so that an abrupt drop doesn't surprise children (Figures 3-54, 3-55, and 3–56). A teacher at one school had to rescue a box turtle that a well-meaning child found and placed in a deep pool. The child had not realized that box turtles are land turtles and cannot survive for long periods in deep water. Allowing fallen logs to extend from land into a water body is another excellent way to provide a sunning spot and safety exit ramp for turtles. Islands in a lake also provide safe havens for birds to nest with protection from fox and other predators.

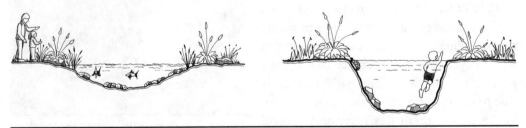

FIGS 3-54 and 3-55. (Left). Gently sloped pool edges allow children to determine water depth and walk back out. Animals like turtles can crawl out of a pool to sun on land. (Right). Pools with steep sides are dangerous. (COURTESY OF GAGE COUCH AND BARBARA SIEGEL RYAN.)

WATER PLAY

Water play can be provided in very simple ways both indoors and out. One Montessori School preschool class had a small plastic basin half full of water accompanied by measuring cups, vessels of different sizes and shapes, and sponges. Teachers observed that children who could not focus on any other activity in the classroom for more than three minutes at a time would play quietly and happily for 20 minutes or more at the water basin. Pouring water from measuring cups into other vessels allowed them to observe liquid volumes in relation to forms. The sponges enabled them to wipe up occasional spills and practice motor skills as they wrung the water from the sponge. Water play at this station had a soothing, relaxing effect on the children, and they rarely got anything wet but their hands and the provided play objects.

Quiet is needed when children live in densely populated noisy areas. Still water can provide quiet places for families to gather and relax. Where walking or biking trails along lakes or rivers are available, families can be found exercising together in a peaceful setting. The relative air temperature is often 5–8 degrees cooler near larger water features, so they are especially valuable on a hot summer day.

The amusing aspects of water are nowhere more apparent than at water parks and fairs where many variations of water games can be seen. Children try to maneuver balls into a basket by means of water guns or play soccer with jets, for example.

One of the few elements not tied down to the concrete, water provides a movable mass, which children can experiment with. Psychologists speculate that a high percentage of vandalism within cities is due to the inflexibility of the environment. Water allows them flexibility and control over their environment, and depending on the form that it takes can facilitate other

FIG 3-56. This pond at the Atlanta Botanical Garden is well designed with gently sloping edges that allow children to closely observe wildlife. (COURTESY OF MARY TAYLOR HAQUE.)

FIG 3-57. This participatory educational exhibit at the EdVenture Children's Museum allows children to guide boats through locks and eddies, simulating a navigable river. (COURTESY OF MARY TAYLOR HAQUE.)

FIG 3-58. Sand and water combine well for creative sculpting and play. (COURTESY OF MARY TAYLOR HAQUE.)

types of experimental play as well (Figure 3-57). A sloping trough with a trickle of water surrounded with sand, for example, enables children to create dams and study the forces associated with water pressure building up behind an earthen structure. Creative sculpting from simple mud pies to complex sand castles will keep children busy for hours. From a small sand box with a pitcher of water in the backyard to a beach with ocean waves, sand and water are excellent natural materials that combine well for children's play (Figure 3-58).

DRINKING WATER

Children need water for physiological reasons, too. They should drink approximately 80 ounces (8–10 glasses) a day to stay fully hydrated, and parks, gardens, schools, and playgrounds should always have functioning drinking fountains available to meet this important need. A fully hydrated child thinks better, is more energetic, less irritable, and has fewer health problems than children who stay dehydrated (Batmanghelidj, 2003) (Figure 3-59).

FIG 3-59. Children should be encouraged to stay well hydrated. Water bottles are an excellent choice when water fountains are not available. (COURTESY OF MARY TAYLOR HAQUE.)

WATER GARDENS AND ENVIRONMENTAL EDUCATION

The sound of water cascading over the terrain along its journey to the sea has the ability to elicit a variety of feelings—peace, serenity, relaxation, vigor, and energy. Something as simple as water is the basis of life and plays a vital role in the health of the environment and in everyday life. Wetland areas carry an especially important responsibility in the environment because they not only host a diverse assortment of plant and animal life, but they act as buffers, filtering out toxic pollutants from runoff and minimizing the effects of flooding. A healthy aquatic ecosystem has the ability to cleanse the water of harmful chemicals and other pollutants as water travels through a watershed. Unfortunately, humans have developed and managed land with little regard to the impact on rivers, streams, lakes, and wetlands, and other bodies of water (Figure 3-60). Poor planning, construction, and management practices result in poor water quality in the nation's water bodies, which directly affects aquatic plant and animal life, wildlife, groundwater quality, and human health. The delicate balance of the aquatic ecosystem is disrupted when the riparian buffer is destroyed or altered and when pollutants enter aquatic systems through excessive runoff and erosion.

FIG 3-60. At the EdVenture Children's Museum in South Carolina, "We all live downstream" exhibits the impact that pollutants have on water as it travels through a watershed. (COURTESY OF MARY TAYLOR HAQUE.)

ENGAGE CHILDREN

Environmental education is vital to protecting and restoring natural water sources. Positive experiences integrating education and the environment may help instill values and stewardship in the public, who need to take action to protect and restore the quality and quantity of the nation's water bodies. Involving communities on a local scale to protect and restore local streams and lakes will create a strong sense of pride and ownership in aquatic ecosystems and bring current water quality issues close to home.

Landscape design projects can creatively educate the public about water quality issues and illustrate methods of restoring local waters. Being involved in these types of projects allows students and community members a first-hand experience with nature and allows them to understand the natural cycle of water and its vital role in the environment. Students around the world are entering outdoor

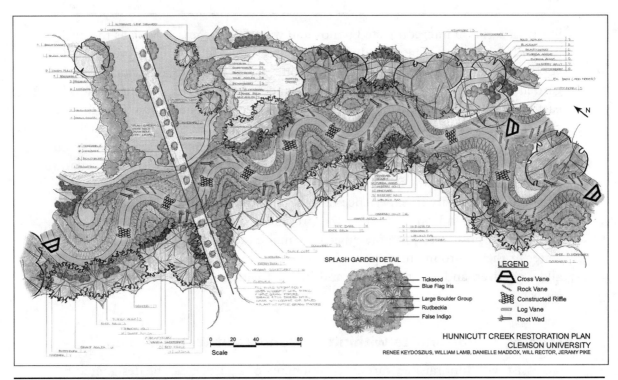

FIG 3-61. This stream restoration project proposes to restore a degraded campus stream with the involvement of students. (COURTESY OF RENEE KEYDOSZIUS.)

classrooms to learn about water quality issues. Children learn how to collect water quality samples at local streams and understand how pollutants affect their health as well as the health of the animal and plant life that depends on the water. By participating in a local stream restoration project (Figure 3-61) students and community members feel a sense of pride for their local waters and learn characteristics of healthy and damaged streams, riparian zones, and watersheds. Designing and installing small constructed wetlands or water gardens in schoolyards also allows students to explore and experience a connection with the natural world at a young age and encourages them to take steps throughout their lives to protect and enhance the environment. Creating a water garden for public use will aid in educating the young and old about how water creates and fuels life on earth.

"THE WONDERS OF WATER GARDEN"

The "Wonders of Water Garden" design serves as a model to guide development of water gardens to suit various sites (Figure 3-62). It consists of a naturalistic, informal series of interconnected ponds and waterfall streams serving as the backbone of the design. The introduction of water into the landscape creates a diverse, ever-changing ecosystem. Many zone seven native plants make up the garden to create a sustainable low-maintenance landscape suitable for the southeastern United States, while different plant selections could fit other climate zones. Native plants are more resistant to pests, are suited to the area's environment, and provide habitat and food for wildlife. The plants chosen are adapted to the moist environment, and will demonstrate various aquatic and wetland species found in natural systems. When built, the entire garden will provide children the opportunity to experience nature and observe how plants, animals, and humans all depend on and enjoy the presence of water in the landscape. The garden's purpose is to promote environmental education focusing on the role of water in the environment as part of an explorative children's garden, which will allow children and adults to learn and interact with nature in a dynamic hands-on way.

Naming Opportunities within the Wonders of Water Garden

To assist with fundraising, various components of a garden can be designated for naming opportunities. These examples from the Wonders of Water Garden illustrate the tremendous variety of settings—and in turn naming opportunities—found in a water garden (see Figures 3-62 to 3-67).

LEARNING OPPORTUNITIES

Construction of a water garden for children will provide many educational opportunities throughout the life of the garden. Seminars and nature walks in the water garden can teach topics such as aquatic plant and animal identification, aquatic ecology, bioremediation characteristics of certain plants, and water quality issues including effects of pollution, sedimentation, and invasive plant species on the natural ecosystem. Children will be able to learn why various plants are needed to support an aquatic ecosystem. They can identify various aquatic plant and animal species and observe life processes, or take water samples and analyze results as they begin to understand the importance of sustainability and the need for water conservation (Figure 3-68). Most importantly, the water garden should help cultivate a sense of respect for the natural environment in children and adults alike. (Figure 3-69).

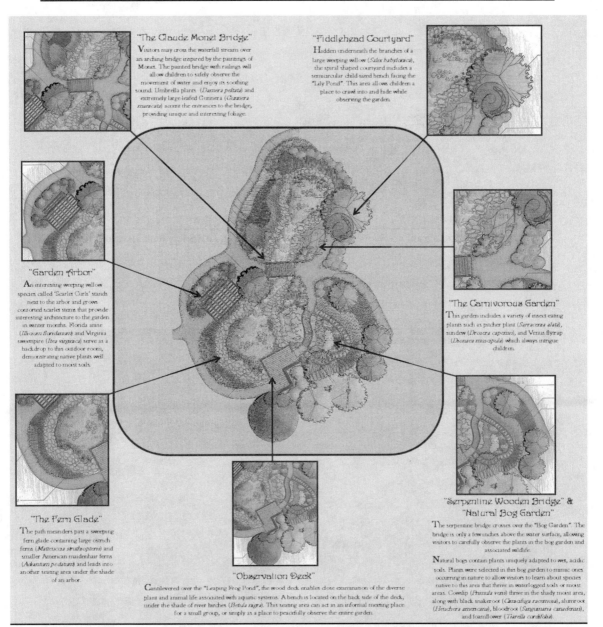

"The Claude Monet Bridge"

Visitors may cross the waterfall stream over an arching bridge inspired by the paintings of Monet. The painted bridge with railings will allow children to safely observe the movement of water and enjoy its soothing sound. Umbrella plants *(Darmera peltata)* and extremely large-leafed Gunnera *(Gunnera manicata)* accent the entrances to the bridge, providing unique and interesting foliage.

"Fiddlehead Courtyard"

Hidden underneath the branches of a large weeping willow *(Salix babylonica)*, the spiral shaped courtyard includes a semicircular child sized bench facing the "Lily Pond". This area allows children a place to crawl into and hide while observing the garden.

"Garden Arbor"

An interesting weeping willow species called 'Scarlet Curls' stands next to the arbor and grows contorted scarlet stems that provide interesting architecture to the garden in winter months. Florida anise *(Illicium floridanum)* and Virginia sweetspire *(Itea virginica)* serve as a backdrop to this outdoor room, demonstrating native plants well adapted to moist soils.

"The Carnivorous Garden"

This garden includes a variety of insect-eating plants such as pitcher plant *(Sarracenia alata)*, sundew *(Drosera capensis)*, and Venus flytrap *(Dionaea muscapula)* which always intrigue children.

"The Fern Glade"

The path meanders past a sweeping fern glade containing large ostrich ferns *(Matteuccia struthiopteris)* and smaller American maidenhair ferns *(Adiantum pedatum)* and leads into another seating area under the shade of an arbor.

"Observation Deck"

Cantilevered over the "Leaping Frog Pond", the wood deck enables close examination of the diverse plant and animal life associated with aquatic systems. A bench is located on the back side of the deck, under the shade of river birches *(Betula nigra)*. This seating area can act as an informal meeting place for a small group, or simply as a place to peacefully observe the entire garden.

"Serpentine Wooden Bridge" & "Natural Bog Garden"

The serpentine bridge crosses over the "Bog Garden". The bridge is only a few inches above the water surface, allowing visitors to carefully observe the plants in the bog garden and associated wildlife.

Natural bogs contain plants uniquely adapted to wet, acidic soils. Plants were selected in this bog garden to mimic ones occurring in nature to allow visitors to learn about species native to this area that thrive in waterlogged soils or moist areas. Cowslip *(Primula veris)* thrive in the shady moist area, along with black snakeroot *(Cimicifuga racemosa)*, alumroot *(Heuchera americana)*, bloodroot *(Sanguinaria canadensis)*, and foamflower *(Tiarella cordifolia)*.

FIG 3-62. Water gardens may be used to create awareness of water quality issues and serve as a model to teach children the importance of water and aquatic plants in the environment. (COURTESY OF RENEE KEYDOSZIUS.)

FIG 3-63. Interesting topographic changes allow ponds to be connected with waterfalls. (COURTESY OF RENEE KEYDOSZIUS.)

FIGS 3-64 and 3-65. (Left). Children are fascinated by carnivorous plants such as these pitcher plants. (Right). The Venus flytraps at the Atlanta Botanical Garden are popular with children. They must be replaced regularly because many children spring the traps. (COURTESY OF MARY TAYLOR HAQUE.)

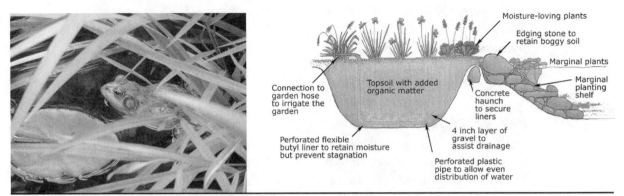

Moisture-loving plants

Edging stone to retain boggy soil

Marginal plants

Marginal planting shelf

Connection to garden hose to irrigate the garden

Topsoil with added organic matter

Concrete haunch to secure liners

4 inch layer of gravel to assist drainage

Perforated flexible butyl liner to retain moisture but prevent stagnation

Perforated plastic pipe to allow even distribution of water

FIGS 3-66 and 3-67. (Left). Boys love to chase bullfrogs and will play in ponds for hours trying to catch tadpoles and bullfrogs. (COURTESY OF MARY TAYLOR HAQUE.) (Right). Bog plants are found beyond the marginal plant zone, where the soil still remains wet. (COURTESY OF RENEE KEYDOSZIUS.)

FIGS 3-68 and 3-69. (Left). Outdoor science labs can be set up next to ponds to encourage students to examine water under a microscope. (Right). A water garden visit can leave children and adults amazed with the lively dynamic nature of a water garden and a realization of how precious and diverse natural aquatic environments are. (COURTESY OF MARY TAYLOR HAQUE.)

> "Often, it takes an initial connection to an orchid, a bird or a plant to inspire a person's appreciation of wetlands. Once appreciated, it's more likely that wetlands will be preserved" (Burrell, C. Colston, Ed. The Natural Water Garden. Brooklyn Botanic Garden, Inc.: Brooklyn, NY. p. 4, 1997).

DaVinci Living Water Garden

An innovative educational project in Portland, Oregon creatively fuses the beauty of art with the fascinating science of water. The DaVinci Living Water Garden resulted from the collaboration between the local DaVinci Arts Middle School and Urban Water Works. The park educates students and visitors about the adverse affects of storm water runoff on water quality while using the arts to illustrate the aesthetic qualities of water. The project reroutes runoff from 15,000 square feet of roofs and parking lots into a 7,200 square foot water garden. Teachers, students, and parents designed the project and constructed it on an abandoned tennis court. A pond, constructed wetland, bioremediation swale, and a system of cisterns collects, cleans and absorbs 100% of captured water. The project serves as an excellent model of storm water collection and diversion for the community while providing recreational and educational opportunities for the students and community (Damon, Betsy. Model Projects: Living Water Garden. Keepers of the Waters; 2001. http://www.wellnessgoods.com/garden.asp, Dec. 5, 2004).

CASE STUDIES

The Children's Garden at Hershey Gardens: Hershey Kisses Garden, Hershey, PA

Opening date: 2003
Acres: 1.5 including Butterfly House and Education Center (.6 hectare)
Cost: $1.8 million
Funding: The M.S. Hershey Foundation and a capital campaign garnered funds from individual, corporate, foundation, and government donors.

Children are greeted by a sweet welcome of giant HERSHEY® KISSES. (COURTESY OF COLLEEN M. SEACE PHOTOGRAPHY AND HERSHEY GARDENS.)

MISSION AND PURPOSE

"The mission of Hershey Gardens is to preserve its heritage and to enrich each visitor's experience through a commitment to horticultural excellence and opportunities for learning." As early as in 1909, Milton S. Hershey acknowledged the importance of agricultural education with the establishment of the Hershey Industrial School for orphan boys. The Deed of Trust states one of the objectives of the School is to teach and instruct in agriculture, horticulture, and gardening (The Children's Garden, n.d., http://www. hersheys.com/discover/milton/hershey_ind_school.asp, 2005).

The Children's Garden at Hershey Gardens was designed as a "Garden to Sweeten the Imagination," where children of all ages discover the wonder of plants through hands-on learning throughout the theme gardens (Figure 3a-1).

FIG 3a-1. Site Plan. The Children's Garden at Hershey Garden provides an educational environment for its visitors within 30 themed gardens. (COURTESY OF HERSHEY GARDENS.).

The interactive curriculum-based programs are conducted throughout the theme gardens including the Education Center, Shaded Classroom, and Amphitheater. Children learn through active rather than passive participation. Educational benefits of hands-on learning are many. Children are more motivated, creative, and perceptive; and they enjoy learning. Children develop increased independent thinking, communication, and reading skills. Through school gardening programs, children exhibit high self-esteem, learn to be responsible, and care for living things (The Children's Garden, n.d.).

More recently, public schools in Pennsylvania have been required by the State Board of Education to provide planned instruction in agriculture or agricultural science annually to every K–12 child. In addition, emphasis is placed on "active learning experiences" or hands-on education. The Children's Garden at Hershey Gardens is an excellent educational resource as their programs fulfill this requirement (The Children's Garden, n.d.).

THE DESIGN TEAM

A committee of 10 people, including community members, advisory board members, and staff, worked with horticulturist Jane L. Taylor and landscape architect Deb Kinney (designers of the Michigan State University 4-H Children's Garden) to create the master plan. The committee believed that the garden should represent Hershey and the central Pennsylvania culture. A brainstorming session was held in November 1999, to determine what should be included in the garden plan. Taylor and Kinney used those ideas together with review and comment from the committee to develop the master plan in April 2001. Derck & Edson Associates, a local landscape architecture firm, created construction drawings followed by project management by The Hershey Trust Company. The construction of The Children's Garden commenced in late 2001, and opened in June 2003 (Huff, personal communication, 2005).

THE DESIGN

The Children's Garden at Hershey Gardens is designed for children to experience plants. Through nearly 30 theme gardens each provides opportunities for hands-on learning, self-discovery, and fun with water features, hideaways (Figure 3a-2), creatures, surprises, and whim-

FIG 3a-2. Children always find surprises such as the hideaway spot under the Weeping Purple Beech. (COURTESY OF CRYSTAL HUFF.).

FIGS 3a-3 and 3a-4. (Left). A little girl finds delight in the whimsical bee garden ornament. (COURTESY OF COLLEEN M. SEACE PHOTOGRAPHY AND HERSHEY GARDENS.). (Right). The garden is planted with unique plants. Top left to right. Chocolate Flower (*Berlandiera lyrata*) and Pretzel Bush Bean (*Phaseolus vulgaris* 'Pretzel'). Bottom left to right. Eyeball Plant (*Spilanthes* 'Peek-A-Boo') and Unicorn Plant (*Proboscidea jussieui*). (COURTESY OF CRYSTAL HUFF.)

sical features (Figure 3a-3). Over 500 plant species are showcased throughout the garden. Many unusual plants delight children (Figure 3a-4) such as the Eyeball Plant (*Spilanthes* 'Peek-A-Boo'), the Chocolate Flower (*Berlandiera lyrata*), the Pretzel Bush Bean (*Phaseolus vulgaris* 'Pretzel'), and Unicorn Plant (*Proboscidea jussieui*) (The Children's Garden, n.d.).

THEME GARDENS	PLANTS AND SPECIAL FEATURES PROVIDED
1 Rose Compass Court:	A colorful entrance with a compass motif in the pavement
2 On-a-Wing Garden:	A vine-covered trellis to feed birds
3 Show-Off Garden:	A display of unusual plants
4 Chocolate Lane:	A path with Hershey's Milk Chocolate Bar pavers (Figure 3a-5)
5 Hugs & Kisses™ Garden:	A circular plaza with a heart-shaped pond and a floating ball fountain modeled after a similar fountain at M.S. Hershey's Lancaster home
6 Boys in the Cannas:	A half moon trellis with cannas and a wall behind

7	Colors Border:	Flowers arranged in the colors of a rainbow
8	Over the Garden Wall:	A limestone wall and gate
9	Pretzel Maze:	A green maze of arborvitae
10	Spa-Tacular Garden:	A living willow curtain
11	Fragrance Garden	A place of fragrant flowers and leaves
12	Chocolate Tropics:	A sidewalk that illustrates the world and chocolate-producing countries
13	Pioneer Patch:	An herb garden
14	Pennsylvania German Four-Court:	A courtyard with four raised planters
15	Treehouse Overlook:	A perch to view the entire garden (Figure 3a-6)
16	Sundial Garden:	A place to tell time by raising one's hand
17	Native American Garden:	A display of native flowers and vegetables
18	Botanical Tunes:	A place to play music
19	River-Banker's Picnic:	A picnic spot that leads to other places
20	Caterpillar Tunnel & Butterfly Garden:	A vine-covered caterpillar tunnel that leads to a butterfly-shaped plant bed
21	ABC Border:	Plants starting with each of the 26 letters of the alphabet
22	Kisses™ Fountain Plaza:	Three water sprays shaped in the form of Hershey's Kisses™ (Figure 3a-7)
23	Derry Hill:	A dairy cow sculpture

Educational aspects: The garden is designed for children to touch, smell, and interact with the plants (Figures 3a-8 and 2-15). In addition, elements such as chocolate bars showing fractions (Figure 3a-5), the human sundial, a pretzel maze, a Native American longhouse and grinding stone, and a globe walkway allow children to learn about math, science, cultures, geography, and history (Huff, personal communication, 2005).

Participatory aspects: All the items mentioned above are interactive. In addition, dance chimes, a xylophone, alligator drum, and misting Kisses™ (Figure 3a-7) provide interactive experiences throughout the garden (Huff, personal communication, 2005).

Unique characteristics of the garden: The entire garden is unique. There are very few elements that could be found anywhere else in the world. The design was meant to fit only Hershey and central Pennsylvania. This garden could not be

FIGS 3a-5 and 3a-6. (Left). Whimsical features surround the garden while providing a rich learning environment. Chocolate Lane gives children the opportunity to learn math. (Right). The elevated Treehouse provides an exciting perspective for children. (COURTESY OF CRYSTAL HUFF.)

FIGS 3a-7 and 3a-8. (Left). Three granite sculptures shaped in the form of HERSHEY'S® KISSES® mist water randomly. (Right.) The garden is designed for children to interact with plants. A little girl finds active play at this tree. (COURTESY OF COLLEEN M. SEACE PHOTOGRAPHY AND HERSHEY GARDENS.)

FIG 3a-9. Housed within the Butterfly House are 300 North American butterflies where children learn about lifecycles. (COURTESY OF COLLEEN M. SEACE PHOTOGRAPHY AND HERSHEY GARDENS.)

picked up and placed in Denver, CO—it just wouldn't make sense (Huff, personal communication, 2005).

Activities children are drawn to most frequently: They are attracted to the water areas including the misting Kisses™ (Figure 3a-7) and Heart pond with a ball that floats on a jet of water (Huff, personal communication, 2005).

Activities most popular with children: They love the dance chimes, longhouse, ABC Border Garden where they spell their names, and the Butterfly House (Huff, personal communication, 2005) (Figure 3a-9).

SAFETY

Because the garden designers, Taylor and Kinney were very experienced with children's garden design, The Children's Garden at Hershey Gardens has experienced few safety issues. They are, however, always alert and are prepared to make corrections if problems arise (Huff, personal communication, 2005).

FUNDING

Hershey Gardens is an operating division of The M.S. Hershey Foundation, a nonprofit organization. The M.S. Hershey Foundation funded the design and a portion of the construction. However, Hershey Gardens conducted a capital campaign to complete the funding needed for construction. Individuals, corporate, grant, and government funds were received to support the construction (Huff, personal communication, 2005).

MAINTENANCE

Funding for maintenance was not reserved as part of the project cost. Maintenance of the entire 23-acre (9.3 hectares) Hershey Gardens including The Children's Garden is supported annually by admissions, gift shop sales, rental and program revenue, and The M.S. Hershey Foundation (Huff, personal communication, 2005).

CREDITS

The Children's Garden At Hershey Gardens Design Team

Crystal Huff, Director of Visitor Services, Hershey Gardens
Deb Kinney, Co-designer and Landscape Architect
Jane L. Taylor, Founding Curator, Michigan 4-H Children's Garden, Michigan State University
Barbara J. Whitcraft, Director of Horticulture, Hershey Gardens
John Hershey, Landscape Architect, Derck & Edson Associates

Construction Team

Bruce Evans, Architect, Cox Evans Architects
Edward Greenebaum, Structural Engineer, Greenebaum Structures Steve Gribb, Electrical Engineer, Consolidated Engineers
Tobie Wolf, Construction Consultant, Strata Development Services
Sue Bingeman, Project Management, The Hershey Trust Company

Camden Children's Garden: Community Based Garden, Camden, NJ

Garden established: July, 1999
Acres: 4.5 (1.8 hectares)
Budget for project: $7.5 million
Funding: Government & Private Partnerships

MISSION AND PURPOSE

The Camden Children's Garden emerged from its roots in the community gardens of the Camden City Garden Club (Cooper's Ferry Development Association, 1999). The Camden Garden Club, established in 1985, was formed to assist Camden city residents with community gardening. Its mission is "to provide horticulture based recreational and educational opportunities for residents of all ages in the City of Camden and the Delaware Valley" (http://www.camden

childrensgarden.org, accessed 2005). The Camden Garden Club has grown in the ensuing years with the addition of new programs including the initiation of Grow Lab in 1989, Summer Job Training program in 1994, garden exhibits at the Philadelphia Flower Show in 1997, the Camden Children's Garden in 1999 (The Camden City Garden Club, 2005).

View of Camden Children's Garden at street level. (COURTESY OF VENTURI, SCOTT, BROWN.)

The mission of the Camden Children's Garden is "to provide stimulating garden environments to engage families in creative and imaginative play. In these thematic and demonstration gardens, visitors discover how plants are important to our everyday lives" (The Camden City Garden Club, 2005).

The Camden Children's Garden provides on-site educational and distance learning programs. All the lessons follow the New Jersey Department of Education Core Curriculum Content Standards and the American Association for the Advancement of Science Benchmarks for Science Literacy. A variety of plant and science classes are offered to children in grades K–12, including customized science lessons and some lessons in Spanish (Camden Educational Program, 2005) (Figure 3b-1).

THE PLANNING AND DESIGN TEAM

The Camden Children's Garden was realized through the leadership and hard work of Mike Devlin, Executive Director, and Val Frick, Director of Education of Camden Children's Garden. They were inspired by a keynote address presented at the first American Horticultural

FIG 3b-1. Children learn about recycling through the educational program offered at the Camden Children's Garden. (COURTESY OF CAMDEN GARDEN.)

Society Youth Gardening Symposium by Jane L. Taylor, Founding Curator of the Michigan 4-H Children's Garden at Michigan State University. They visited the garden, were enthusiastic about what they saw, and were determined to bring a children's garden to their community (Cooper's Ferry Development Association, 1999).

A large group of individuals were recruited for the planning and design team. They included the Camden City Garden Club, teachers, community leaders, architects (led by the late Steve Izenour and Tim Kearney of Venturi, Scott, Brown & Associates), landscape architects (Rodney Robinson), exhibit designers (Dommert Phillips), artists, sculptors, and construction managers (Delaware River Port Authority). The Camden City Garden Club was also an important part of the design team. According to Val Frick, the group met frequently and came up with "primary, secondary and take home messages" for each exhibit. All of the meetings resulted in a design and exhibit document which guided the decisions (Frick, personal communication, 2005).

THE DESIGN

Camden Children's Garden was realized with five years of planning and fund raising. It was designed for children of ages 3–12. The garden features a variety of themed exhibits and demonstration gardens to encourage visitors to use all of their senses to learn about horticulture and the environment and to engage them in creative and imaginative play. Hands-on activities provide the opportunity for visitors to realize that gardening is easy and entertaining (The Camden City Garden Club, 2005).

The project is uniquely sited on the Camden, NJ waterfront across the Delaware River from Philadelphia and adjacent to the Aquarium (Figure 3b-2). It is a part of the revitalized Camden waterfront. According to the late Steve Izenour, of Venturi, Scott, Brown & Associates, Inc., it is a novel idea to juxtapose city scale and distant views with small-scale and

FIG 3b-2. Aerial view of Camden Children's Garden. (COURTESY OF CAMDEN GARDEN.)

FIG 3b-3. Visitors can step into the story book garden of Alice in Wonderland. (COURTESY OF LOLLY TAI.)

low-to-the-ground exhibits. He said, "We're fusing graphics, amusement park, and garden" (Cooper's Ferry Development Association, 1999).

The Garden incorporates educational themes inspired from children's literature, folk tales, local history, and geography (Figure 3b-3). The 4.5-acre (1.8-hectares) interactive garden provides children with the opportunity to explore a variety of indoor and outdoor exhibits as described below (Camden History, Purpose, and Activities, 2005; http://www.camdenchildrensgarden.org, accessed 2005) (Figure 3b-4).

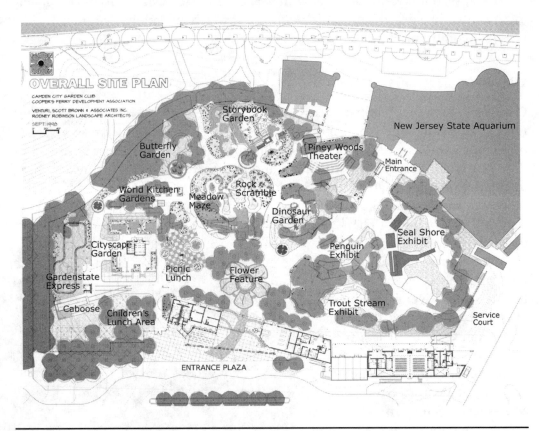

FIG 3b-4. Site Plan. Camden Children's Garden offers a diverse array of indoor and outdoor exhibits. (COURTESY OF CAMDEN GARDEN.)

OUTDOOR EXHIBITS

Violet Fountain Plaza: Visitors can enjoy the themed plaza at the garden's main entry, which focuses on the New Jersey state flower, the Common Violet *(Viola sororia),* and the seasonal water fountains (Figure 3b-5).

Dinosaur Garden: Visitors can learn, dig, explore, run, climb, and sit within a setting of a 35-foot (10.7-meter) Apatosaurus, a Hadrosaurus, a sandy dig pit, giant dinosaur eggs, and fossil imprints (Figure 3b-6).

Storybook Gardens: Visitors can step inside storybooks and play pretend in each of the gardens: Three Little Pigs Garden, The Giant Garden from Jack and the Beanstalk (Figure 3b-7), the Secret Garden, Frog Prince Grotto, and Alice in Wonderland.

The Butterfly Garden: Visitors can learn about the interrelationship between plants and butterflies.

FIG 3b-5. Visitors are greeted with the themed Violet Fountain Plaza at the garden's main entry which focuses on the state flower, the purple violet. (COURTESY OF VENTURI, SCOTT BROWN AND ASSOCIATES, INC.)

FIGS 3b-6 and 3b-7. (Left). Children can explore and have fun in the popular Dinosaur Garden. They can find the state dinosaur, Hadrosaurus here. (COURTESY OF CAMDEN GARDEN.) (RIGHT: COURTESY OF VENTURI, SCOTT BROWN, AND ASSOCIATES, INC.) (Right). Children can step inside a storybook when they enter The Giant Garden and find a larger-than-life size bench and watering can. (COURTESY OF LOLLY TAI.)

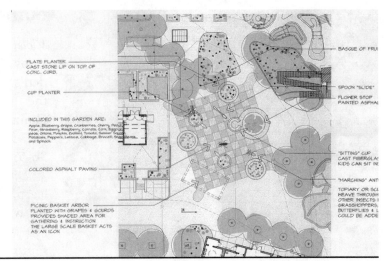

FIG 3b-8. In the Picnic Garden, visitors learn about their favorite foods that are growing in larger-than-life cups and bowls. (COURTESY OF VENTURI, SCOTT BROWN AND ASSOCIATES, INC.)

Picnic Garden: Visitors can learn about some of their favorite foods. The plants are grown in larger-than-life cups and bowls sitting on a pavement of red and white checked picnic blanket. Giant ant sculptures appear to march across the blanket (Figure 3b-8).

Treehouse: Visitors can see the Red Oak Run Maze from above in the Treehouse (Figure 3b-9). Through binoculars they can see wildlife and the Philadelphia skyline. Red Oak Run represents the underground life with plants overhead and life size burrows. Kids can explore the winding burrows, crawl through tunnels, and run through the maze's tall arbors as they mimic animals and insects.

Cityscapes Garden: This garden exhibit represents an urban street façade with two adjacent homes. From season to season, this garden is a continuing display of the potential of the home garden in any environment.

FIG 3b-9. The giant Treehouse overlooks the Oak Red Run maze and kids can explore the winding burrows as they mimic animals and insects. (COURTESY OF CAMDEN GARDEN.)

Piney Woods Amphitheatre: Visitors can find outdoor entertainment and educational presentations developed by the garden staff in this 140-seat amphitheatre.

Railroad Garden: Visitors can ride around miniature landscapes, four "G" scale trains and local landmarks. The historic Camden Caboose can be found here.

Commerce Carousel: Visitors can find delight at this unique carousel made up of a family of a rabbit, a rooster, a pig, a cat, a shark, a sea dragon, a horse, and a hummingbird.

Spring Butterfly Ride: Visitors can ride above the garden for a bird's eye view of the garden. The ride lifts riders to the top of a 40-foot (12.2-meters) column and "springs" down again.

INDOOR EXHIBITS

Philadelphia Eagles Four Seasons Butterfly House and Education Center: Visitors can step into this 1,200 square foot (111.48 square meter) tropical greenhouse and the home to many species of butterflies (Figure 3b-10).

Plaza de Aibonito, Puerto Rico: Visitors can view the orchids, palms, and other flowering plants as they bloom in this space, which resembles the plaza in Aibonito, a beautiful town in Puerto Rico known as "City of Flowers."

Many places within the garden provide opportunities for relaxation, crafts, and special activities. Interpretive signs are located throughout the garden to inform children as well as adults about plants and home gardening ideas. All aspects of the garden were especially designed and/or crafted with the consideration of children. For example, Fred Kreitchet, sculptor of the Hadrosaurus dinosaur, knew that he had to use strong materials if

FIG 3b-10. Children and adult observe butterflies in the Philadelphia Eagles Four Seasons Butterfly House and Education Center. (COURTESY OF CAMDEN GARDEN.)

FIG 3b-11. Signs of various shape and color identify each garden area. (COURTESY OF LOLLY TAI.)

children were going to be playing and crawling around it (Cooper's Ferry Development Association, 1999). The signs were designed to appear whimsical and kid friendly. Virginia Gehshan, sign designer, intentionally had fasteners on the signs in odd places so it looked as if a kid put it together (Figure 3b-11). Signs acknowledging funders were designed in a shape reminiscent of a popsicle stick, holding a seed packet, and placed slightly askew (Wieber, 2001).

Alice Dommert, exhibit designer noted, "During the exhibit development, you think about how to make the exhibit content and experience relevant to your audience." Many examples relevant to the "Garden State" of New Jersey can be found in the Camden Children's Garden. For example, *Hadrosaurus foulkii*, featured in the dinosaur garden, is based on the discovery of this dinosaur less than 10 miles away (Wieber, 2001). The state tree (Northern Red Oak, *Quercus rubra*) (Figure 3b-12) is the motif used for the Treehouse and the name given to Red Oak Run Garden. The state flower, the Common Violet (*Viola sororia*), is painted on the paving of the Violet Fountain Plaza (Figure 3b-5).

FIG 3b-12. The state tree, Northern Red Oak (*Quercus rubra*), is the motif used for the Treehouse. (COURTESY OF CAMDEN GARDEN.)

EDUCATIONAL AND PARTICIPATORY ASPECTS

The Camden Children's Garden has a series of family festivals on the second and fourth Saturday of each month from April through November, ranging from "Dino Day" to "Goblins in the Garden" to "Chocolate and Vanilla Flavor Festival." The festivals include arts & crafts, performers, and special hands-on activities alluding to the festival's theme. The annual "Holiday Festival of Lights" is a great culmination for the end of the year. Thousands of lights decorate the Garden during the month of December on Friday and Saturday evenings. Santa Claus is available for pictures, various Christmas trees are decorated with whimsical themes, and the Winter Wonderland exhibit is a great place to bring the family. On-site lessons are available for students of all ages. Some of the over 30 available lessons include *Hungry Caterpillar, Tree Homes, Seed Detectives, Let it Rot!,* and *Weird Weather,* among others. Lessons are available by reservation. For those who cannot make it to the Garden, the lessons are also available through Distance Learning. "Garden Festivals for School" are special activities available for schools during springtime. These festivals include hands-on activities for students, centered on Garden themes.

The Garden offers a unique and whimsical setting for birthday parties and other family functions (Frick, personal communication, 2005).

ACTIVITIES CHILDREN ARE DRAWN TO MOST FREQUENTLY

Children love to explore the different areas of the Garden. "Storybook Garden" always seems to have kids pretending to be the Three Little Pigs or Jack in the Giant's garden. The Dinosaur Garden's sand pit is a magnet for would-be anthropologists (Figure 3b-13). The giant ants in the Picnic Garden are also a major draw, as is the seasonal water feature in the Violet Plaza. The Red Oak Maze is a playground for the imagination as children run through the exhibit pretending to be their favorite animal or insect. But

FIG 3b-13. Children can find the state dinosaur, Hadrosaurus in the Dinosaur Garden.

the Philadelphia Eagles Four Seasons Butterfly House seems to be the favorite spot in the Garden (Frick, personal communication, 2005).

FUNDING

Funding for the Camden Children's Garden was provided by the State of New Jersey, Delaware River Port Authority, and Camden County, as well as, foundations, corporations, sponsors, individual contributors, membership, and earned income, such as from the rides and Ginkgo's Gift Shop (Frick personal communication, 2005).

PROJECT EVALUATION AND CONCLUSION

Camden Children's Garden has added new features each year since its inception (Figure 3b-14). The "Ben Franklin's Secret Garden" will be featured in 2006 (Frick, personal communication, 2005). When it opened its doors in 1999, more than half a million visitors came to visit the Garden and the adjacent Aquarium (Cooper's Ferry Development Association, 1999). The Children's Garden has hosted up to 625,000 visitors annually. According to Frick, "Visitor surveys and increased participation in our programming have shown a need for expanded activities and additional garden features. This feedback has been included in the Garden's plans, and has resulted in the addition of a new ride, increased educational programs and festivals added in 2005" (Frick, personal communication, 2005).

FIG 3b-14. The Camden Children's Garden has evolved and grown each year with the addition of a new exhibit. (COURTESY OF CAMDEN GARDEN.)

Mike Devlin believes, "The major legacy is that the garden provides a soft green place where children can come and be inspired about the environment, gardening, horticulture and that they can take the ideas home with them" (Cooper's Ferry Development Association, 1999).

> *"There was a child went forth every day; And the first object he look'd upon, that object he became; And that object became part of him for the day, or a certain part of the day, or for many years, or stretching cycles of years"*
>
> —Walt Whitman (Figure 3b-15).

CREDITS

The Camden Children's Garden Planning and Design Team

Client: Mike Devlin, Executive Director of the Camden Children's Garden and President of Camden Garden Club

Client: Val Frick, Director of Education of the Camden Children's Garden

Architect: Steve Izenour at Venturi, Scott Brown and Associates, Inc., and Tim Kearney of Cueto Kearney design, llc

Landscape Architect: Rodney Robinson Landscape Architects

FIG 3b-15. Statue of Walt Whitman by sculptor John Gionotti. (COURTESY OF VENTURI, SCOTT BROWN AND ASSOCIATES, INC.)

Exhibit Developer and Designer: Alice Dommert of Dommert Phillips Architects

Industrial and Graphic Designer: Cloud Gehshan Associates

Illustrators: Stacey Lewis, Chris Reed

Artist: Cara Flint

Fabricator of giant bench: Sam Gilmar of Declan Weir Productions

Sculptor of Hadrosaurus: Fred Kreitchet

Sculptor of Apatosaurus (made from recycled car parts): Jim Gary

Sculptor of Walt Whitman Statue: John Gionotti

Sculptor of Frog Prince: Gary Lee Price

Construction Team

Construction Manager: Delaware River Port Authority

Carpenter of Treehouse: David Robinson

Entry Sign: Capital manufacturing, Landsdale, PA

Printed Sign Graphics: Visual Impressions, Inc., Charlotte, NC

Longwwod Gardens Bee-aMazed Garden, Kennett Square, PA

Opened: Previous indoor children's garden was closed January 2003.

Bee-aMazed Garden opened May 8, 2004, Mother's Day
Acres: 0.2 acre or 8,500 square foot (798.68 square meters)
Cost: $50,000 (for materials only)
Funding: Longwood

The Bee-aMazed Children's Garden is comprised of Honeycomb Maze, Flower Fountain, and Buzz Trail. The Flower Fountain contains five basic parts of a flower. The petals, pistil and stamens, and stem and leaves are represented by a fountain basin, water jets, and colored pavement, respectively. (COURTESY OF LONGWOOD GARDENS.)

MISSION AND PURPOSE

Longwood's Bee-aMazed Children's Garden (Figure 3c-1) opened in 2004 as an interim outdoor garden while a large new indoor garden was being constructed. This garden is located near Longwood's Idea Garden and was inspired by honeybees. The goal is to teach children about how bees and plants depend upon each other (Shearer, 2004).

Longwood Gardens was created by the industrialist and philanthropist, Pierre S. du Pont (1870–1954) to "exploit the sentiments and ideas associated with plants and flowers in a large way." During his lifetime, he continually improved Longwood with restoration and new construction (Longwood Gardens, 2003).

The history of the children's garden can be traced to 1987,

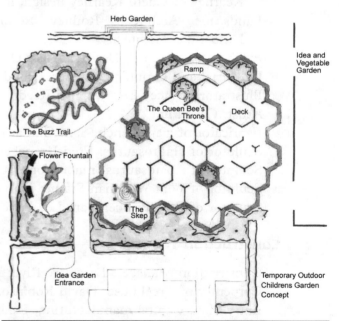

FIG 3c-1. Site plan. (COURTESY OF LONGWOOD GARDENS.)

when Longwood built its first indoor children's garden, as a temporary three-month display (Longwood Gardens, 2003). Mary Allinson, Section Gardener, recalls, "Kids grew up with the first interior garden." It was designed by Catherine Eberbach, former graduate student at Longwood. Since then, this garden had undergone several redesigns (Allinson, personal communication, 2005). Recognizing the importance of the Children's Garden, Longwood closed this garden in January 2003, to make way for a new indoor garden, triple in size. This garden is taking several years to construct and is anticipated to open in 2007. While waiting for its completion, the Bee-aMazed Garden was installed for the young visitors to continue to find enjoyment at Longwood (Shearer, 2004).

THE PLANNING AND DESIGN TEAM

Longwood recognized how precious the Children's Garden was to young visitors, and already had in progress a new outdoor garden design. During the fall of 2001, the Outdoor Children's Garden Task Force was formed by Longwood staff members (Shearer, 2004). They researched Camden Garden, Michigan 4-H Garden and Children's Museum at the Brooklyn Botanical Gardens and used them as case studies (Allinson, personal communication, 2004). One of the initial design concepts was to build the garden with modular components. Jennifer Pennington, the lead designer and Longwood's Display Specialist said, "Thinking of the garden as a collection of units immediately brought to mind honeybees, who are natural modular architects. Over the course of two years, the task force refined the design and implemented ideas gathered from discussions with local elementary school students." Construction began in fall 2003, and the garden opened on May 8, 2004. To date, everything has been approved by an Advisory and a Landscape Committee (Shearer, 2004).

THE DESIGN

The Bee-aMazed Garden features three main areas as described below (Shearer, 2004; http://www.longwoodgardens.org/WhatsNew/Renovations/BeeaMazed ChildrensGarden.htm, accessed 2005).

Honeycomb Maze "is composed of hexagonal rooms that resemble the cells of a honeycomb. The rooms are delineated with 3.5-foot (1.1 meter) yew hedges and vine covered wire mesh and masonry panels." According to Allinson, "The fence is high enough to grow vines. It's low enough to jump over, and low enough for adults to be able see their children."

> *"The Honeycomb Maze is designed with a variety of interesting elements such as tunnels, a beehive arbor, and a gently sloping ramp leading to an elevated deck approximately 2' high"* (0.61 meter). *The ramp, and the brick and mulch paths in the garden are wheelchair accessible. Nearly the entire garden is planned under an existing large mature tree (Zelkova serrata cv. Village Green), which provides comfortable shade for the young visitors.*

The Queen Bee's Throne, a colorful oversized chair, is a popular spot for kids to pretend to be a queen bee (Figure 3c-3). It was designed in playful tribute to the regal name of the Crown Imperial Fritillary, *Frittilaria imperialis*. The throne is surrounded by fritillaries for children to see the real plant in bloom. Apparently, the foliage of Frittilaria smells like a skunk, and children find this to be cool.

Flower Fountain is a concrete fountain that represents the five basic parts of a flower. "The petals form the fountain basin, the pistil and stamens are the water jets, and the stem and leaves are two dimensionally represented in the surrounding pavement" (Figure 3c-4). To maintain a shallow level

FIG 3c-3. Children pretend to be queen bee for the day. (COURTESY OF MARY TAYLOR HAQUE.)

FIG 3c-4. The Flower Fountain represents five basic parts of a flower. (COURTESY OF LOLLY TAI.)

FIG 3c-5. Children cannot keep their hands out of the Flower Fountain. A raised platform inside the pool maintains a shallow pool depth for safety. (COURTESY OF LONGWOOD.)

of water, a platform is built in the fountain. Children can reach the water and splash their hands in the moving water without the fear of falling in (Allinson, personal communication, 2005) (Figure 3c-5). Colorful seasonal beds around the fountain provide a jovial and lush setting for children and parents to enjoy.

Buzz Trail was planned for very young children. It's brick "ribbon" pattern or curvilinear path follows the imagined flight path of a honeybee and is set within a field of grass (Figure 3c-6 and 3c-7). Adirondack chairs sized for kids provide a place of respite for kids (Figure 3c-8).

FIGS 3c-6 and 3c-7. (Left). Adjacent to the Buzz Trail is the skep in the Honeycomb Maze (COURTESY OF LOLLY TAI.) (Right). Children love to run around the Buzz Trail. (COURTESY OF MARY TAYLOR HAQUE.)

FIG 3c-8. Adirondack chairs in the Buzz Trail are sized for kids and provide a place of respite for them. (COURTESY OF LONGWOOD GARDENS AND RONDEL PEIRSON.)

EDUCATIONAL AND PARTICIPATORY ASPECTS

Signs throughout the garden provide educational opportunities for children about the relationship and important role of bees and plants in nature (Figure 3c-9). In addition, volunteer-led programming enhances these concepts through kinesthetic play and hands-on exploration.

ACTIVITIES CHILDREN ARE DRAWN TO MOST FREQUENTLY

"Children love to run in the Buzz Trail, hide in the Honeycomb Maze, play in the water at the Flower Fountain and experience heights on the elevated deck," said Allinson. Younger children are particularly attracted to the Buzz Trail as they are less intimidated in this space (Allinson, personal communication, 2005) (Figure 3c-7).

FIG 3c-9. Signs throughout the maze provide an educational opportunity for children to learn about the life of a bee and the honeycomb. (COURTESY OF LONGWOOD GARDENS AND RONDEL PEIRSON.)

FIG 3c-10. It's not necessary to install the most expensive or high-maintenance plants in the children's garden. One large plant can give a fabulous show. (COURTESY OF LONGWOOD GARDENS AND RONDEL PEIRSON.)

FUNDING AND MAINTENANCE

Longwood funds the project. Staff maintain the display. The garden is evaluated by gardening staff as well as the Landscape Committee. Maintenance is by Longwood's grounds crew for this area (Allinson, personal communication, 2005).

EVALUATION

Allinson remarked that it is not necessary to install the most expensive or high-maintenance plants in the children's garden. It is more effective to incorporate "one big show, with one big plant instead of annuals and perennials" (Figure 3c-10). Children have a tendency to unintentionally walk over and destroy fragile plants. Although parents enjoy flowers and are interested in learning about plants, there are no plant labels in the children's garden thus eliminating a tripping hazard. Parents and seniors visit the garden with a lot of gear. It is important to accommodate them with shade, tables, chairs, and bathrooms within close proximity (Allinson, personal communication, 2005) (Figures 3c-11 and 3c-12).

FIGS 3c-11 and 3c-12. (Left). Parents and seniors with a lot of gear appreciate the provision of shade, tables, chairs, and bathrooms within close proximity. (COURTESY OF LOLLY TAI.) (Right). Nearly the entire garden is planned under an existing large mature tree (*Zelkova serrata* Village Green), which provides comfortable shade for the young visitors. (COURTESY OF LONGWOOD GARDENS AND RONDEL PEIRSON.)

The Bee-aMazed Garden is a good example of how Longwood continues to preserve the past and build the future of du Pont's internationally renowned horticultural legacy.

CREDITS

The Longwood Gardens' Bee-aMazed Children's Garden Planning and Design Team

Jennifer Pennington, Longwood Display Specialist
Kirk Himelick, Visitor Education Specialist
Harold Taylor, Longwood Section Gardener
Bob Scanzaroli, Longwood Senior Gardener
Iris Gestram, Education Department Head
Julie Schwartz, Education Intern
Resa Hoffman, Display Intern
Mary Allinson, Longwood Section Gardener

Construction Team

Construction of the garden: Longwood craftsmen
Woodworking (of the queen bee chair): Michael Zuba of Kinlock Woodworking
Longwood Painters (of queen bee chair): Longwood painters

Michigan 4-H Children's Garden: The Health, Heart, Hands, & Head Garden, East Lansing, MI

Opening Date: August 11, 1993
Acres: 3/4 (.3 hectare)
Cost: $700,000, raised over $2.4 million to date
Funding: All gardens are privately funded through gifts and grants made to the Michigan 4-H Foundation.

MISSION AND PURPOSE

The Michigan 4-H Children's Garden at Michigan State University in East Lansing has over 60 theme gardens in only 3/4 acre. This award-winning garden has been called the "most creative half-acre in America" (Maziak, 2005) (Figure 3d-1).

FIG 3d-1. The Monet Bridge allows visitors to cross the Pond and Water Garden and view its many interactive features. (COURTESY OF ERIN JORDAN KNIGHT.)

The need for such a garden was discovered after a study in Michigan showed that although 50% of garden visitors are children, little of the typical garden is to a child's scale or designed for a child's preferences. The garden's mission is "To promote an understanding of plants and the role they play in our environment and our daily lives; to nurture the wonder in a child's imagination and curiosity; and to provide a place for the enrichment and delight of all children" (Maziak, 2005).

THE DESIGN TEAM

Much of this garden's success is attributed to the involvement of children in the initial stages of design and throughout the development process. Kids were asked what they would like to see in the garden, and even the ideas that seemed fantastic were not dismissed, but were instead adapted by the design team so that the spirit of children's desires were represented in innovative and exciting new

FIG 3d-2. The Pizza Garden helps children understand where the food they eat comes from. (COURTESY OF ERIN JORDAN KNIGHT.)

ways. For example, the request for a pizza stand in the garden led to the incorporation of the pizza garden, a circular plot cut into "slices" that grow the ingredients of that popular food (Figure 3d-2). The intent of the Michigan 4-H Children's Garden designers is creation of space scaled and designed with sensitivity to children's needs, providing these most important garden visitors with a rich, multilayered experience that invites discovery, interaction, learning, and wonder. Jane Taylor, Founding Curator, interpreted the input of children and others, adding her own ideas, then Landscape architects Jeff Kacos and Deb Kinney, of the Michigan State University Division of Campus Parks and Planning, adapted all these creative concepts into a theme and detail-rich space full of discoveries.

THE DESIGN

The garden is divided into the Sunburst, Amphitheater, Rainbow, Treehouse, Butterfly, Pond, Maze, and Chimes Areas, each of which contains many theme areas. A few of the themes within each are listed below.

Theme Gardens: Plants and Special Features Provided

SUNBURST AREA (FIGURE 3D-3)

FIG 3d-3. The Sunburst Area welcomes visitors to the Michigan 4-H Children's Garden. (COURTESY OF ERIN JORDAN KNIGHT.)

1. *Imagination Grows Garden:* Entry garden near parking lot

2. *Storybook Garden:* A colorful entrance with a compass motif in the pavement

3. *Teddy Bears and Animal Garden:* Topiary bears sit in front of and among plants with animal names

4. *Crayon Color Garden:* A crayon fence is fronted by plants named for crayon colors

5. *Sunburst Terrace Garden:* A colorful terrace surrounded by vibrant flower and vegetable beds

6. *Imagination Arbor:* Arbor inspired by "In a child's garden—imagination grows."

7. *ABC Kinder-Garten:* Grows plants from Alyssum to Zinnia

8. *Dwarfed Fruit Trees:* These trees represent the Michigan fruit industry

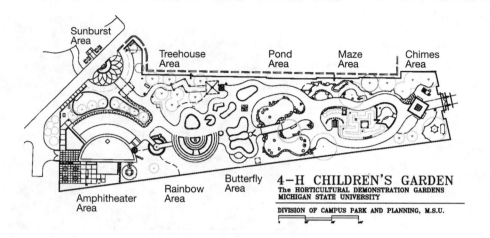

FIG 3d-4. Site plan for the Michigan 4-H Children's Garden designed by Landscape architects Jeff Kacos and Deb Kinney of the Michigan State University Division of Campus Parks and Planning. (COURTESY OF JEFF KACOS, DEB KINNEY, AND JANE TAYLOR.)

9. *Train Garden:* A miniature train set speeds by to the delight of visitors (Figure 3d-4)

AMPHITHEATER AREA

10. *Enchanted Garden:* A garden of fairies, gnomes, and other magic

11. *Health for Better Living:* Vegetables rated top 10 for health by the USDA

12. *Creation Station:* Seating area for hands-on projects

13. *Kitchen Garden:* Minivegetables and culinary herbs

14. *Amphitheater:* Demonstration plaza and seating area

15. *Cottage Garden:* Old-fashioned plants as in Mother Goose poems (Figure 3d-5)

FIG 3d-5. The Cottage Garden provides opportunities for children to seek enclosure behind a veil of hanging flowers. (COURTESY OF ERIN JORDAN KNIGHT.)

RAINBOW AREA (FIGURE 3d–6)

16. *Cereal Bowl Garden:* Grows cereal grains like corn, oats, rice, and rye

17. *Meat, Milk, and Wool:* Plants grown provide feed for animals

18. *Pioneer Garden:* Based on *Little House* books by Laura Ingalls Wilder

19. *International Garden:* Plants from a different nation each year are on display (Figure 3d-6)

FIG 3d-6. The Rainbow Garden helps children learn about plants from other cultures. (COURTESY OF ERIN JORDAN KNIGHT.)

20. *African-American Garden:* Plants introduced to the Americas by African-Americans

21. *Hispanic-American Garden:* Plants introduced to the Americas by Hispanic-Americans

22. *North American Indian Garden:* Plants introduced to the Americas by North American Indians

23. *Asian-American Garden:* Plants introduced to the Americas by Asian-Americans

24. *Small World Globe:* A globe on which to find the nations represented

TREEHOUSE AREA

25. *Perfume Garden:* Fragrant plants

26. *Peter Rabbit Garden:* Plants and statue inspired by Beatrix Potter's stories (Figure 3d-7)

FIG 3d-7. The Peter Rabbit Garden reminds children of a favorite character from the stories of Beatrix Potter. (COURTESY OF ERIN JORDAN KNIGHT.)

27. *Little Prairie Garden:* Plants of the Great Lakes region and from the *Anne of Green Gables* book series

28. *Sense-Sational Herb Garden:* A rich variety of herbs to touch and smell

29. *Pizza Garden:* The "slices" of the garden grow ingredients for this favorite food

30. *Special Child's Garden:* Raised beds for handicap accessible gardening

31. *Treehouse:* Handicap-accessible treehouse (Figure 3d-8)

BUTTERFLY AREA

32. *Pharmacy Garden:* Plants that have healing properties

33. *Science Discovery Garden:* Experiments and innovative cultivars are demonstrated

34. *4-H Granite Diamond:* The 4-H symbol and motto embedded in the pavement

35. *Cloth and Color Garden:* Plants used to make dye and cloth and a weaving loom for grasses (Figure 3d-9)

36. *Pot O' Gold:* At the end of the rainbow grows a pot of marigolds and pyrite in the pavement

37. *Butterfly Garden:* Nectar-rich plants grow in a bed the shape of a butterfly (Figure 3d-10)

38. *Scarecrow Garden:* A scarecrow and *Wizard of Oz*-themed plants

FIG 3d-8. The Treehouse overlooks the garden and is handicap accessible. (COURTESY OF ERIN JORDAN KNIGHT.)

FIG 3d-9. The Cloth and Color Garden teaches children how important plants are in the making and dyeing of textiles. (COURTESY OF ERIN JORDAN KNIGHT.)

POND AREA

39. *Monet Bridge:* A green bridge like the artist's at Giverny

40. *Bog Garden:* A garden of plants that grow in moist places

41. *Merry-Go-Round Fountains:* When a child turns the swinging gate, it powers the spitting frogs in the pond (Figure 3d-11)

42. *Magic Bubble Fountains:* These bubbling fountains are close enough to touch

FIG 3d-10. The butterfly-shaped beds of this garden draws children as well as winged visitors. (COURTESY OF ERIN JORDAN KNIGHT.)

43. *Pond and Water Garden:* The pond is full of plants, fish, and frogs

44. *Performing Plants Garden:* These plants do special things

MAZE AREA

45. *Rock Garden:* Displays of rocks and minerals of Michigan

46. *Dinosaur Garden:* Dinosaur-era plants, a large rib cage to crawl through, and a sandbox "dig" (Figure 3d-12)

FIG 3d-11. When the Merry-Go-Round gate is turned, water spits from this frog's mouth. (COURTESY OF ERIN JORDAN KNIGHT.)

47. *Maze Overlook:* Great views of the garden from above, especially the maze

48. *Sundial Garden:* Children can tell the time by the cast of their own shadows

49. *Wild Garden:* A wildflower garden

50. *Alice In Wonderland Maze:* This maze has characters from Wonderland along it

FIG 3d-12. Under these metal ribs, children can go on a "dig" in the sandbox. (COURTESY OF ERIN JORDAN KNIGHT.)

FIG 3d-13. Beyond this gate, children will discover the Secret Garden. (COURTESY OF ERIN JORDAN KNIGHT.)

51. *The Secret Garden:* Peek into this garden and discover Mary Lennox and blooming flowers (Figure 3d-13)

52. *Garden of Delight:* A medieval garden display

UNIQUE CHARACTERISTICS

Perhaps one of the most intriguing aspects of the garden, for children and adults alike, is the incredible attention to detail. Within the paving throughout the garden are impressions of children's hands, as well as elements symbolic of the different themes. For example, beside the Cereal Bowl Garden (Figure 3d-14), an observant child will find the impression of a variety of grains impressed in the pavement surrounding an embedded mill wheel, while tiny butterflies dance around the Butterfly Garden's border, which is itself shaped like the insect its plants attract. These minute discoveries surround all of the theme areas and encourage visitors to look closely and care-

FIG 3d-14. The Cereal Bowl Garden uses a mill wheel embedded in the path and grains impressed into the pavement to add interest to plantings. (COURTESY OF ERIN JORDAN KNIGHT.)

FIG 3d-15. The discovery of intimate details that accompany every theme area is one of the most enjoyable aspects of the Michigan 4-H Children's Garden, such as this impression in the pavement encircling the Butterfly Garden. (COURTESY OF ERIN JORDAN KNIGHT.)

fully and experience the garden on an intimate level (Figure 3d-15).

The significance of the plant material selected for the garden is more than what is seen at a glance as well. The names of the plants are also related to the themes of the areas, and all are marked for the enjoyment of the visitor. For example, in the Pot O' Gold Garden area, the marigolds are "Gold Nugget" variety.

Children love great detail and the small, thoughtful elements that give their spaces wonder and discovery. In the garden Web site's Teacher and Parent sections, the first suggestion made is for adults to experience the garden as a child would, and the very design of the space encourages this approach; adults are drawn into the space just as the children are, and find themselves seeking wonder and making connections between themes with childlike delight.

"What you need to do in a garden is people watch," says Taylor. "Find out what people respond to" (Taylor, 2001). Taylor has observed many visitors to the garden and feels that the responses she sees prove the effectiveness of the garden. She

FIG 3d-16. People often feel a deep and personal connection to plants, and in this plant-rich garden, sharing of stories and multigenerational bonding is inspired by the Rainbow Garden and other areas. (COURTESY OF ERIN JORDAN KNIGHT.)

once watched as a multigenerational Asian family explored the Rainbow Garden Area, which includes plantings representative of several cultures, and the grandmother fell to her knees and called out in delight for her family to come see what she discovered. There, in the Asian-American plot she saw the plants of her home and childhood, and she delighted in teaching her grandchildren about them and sharing her memories (Figure 3d-16).

As the above story illustrates, Taylor says that next to children, no one enjoys the garden more than the elderly. "The two groups look for some of the same things in a space," she says. "Color, a happy place, places to sit, and not too far to walk. The needs are the same at both ends of the spectrum."

For young and old, the garden is fully handicap accessible and even has a Special Child's Garden with raised beds and windows into the root system of a plant for children to explore, designed at a comfortable eye level for a child in a wheelchair.

Making the garden accessible for the play and discovery of all children was an important consideration at the Michigan 4-H Children's Garden, as it should be in any public space. The resulting design challenge of doing so, however, was the need to address the paved areas, which became an extensive feature within the 3/4 acre (.3 hectare) space. However, with the addition of vibrant colors, textures, and impressions, and occasional changes in material to beautify and create patterns, the pavement is not only softened and made more dynamic, it becomes yet another opportunity for discovery (Figure 3d-17).

PARTICIPATORY ASPECTS

In the 4-H Children's Garden, theme beds are designed to encourage curiosity and wonder about plants. Children are drawn into beds by stepping stones and plant-covered tunnels and teepees. Taylor says children often have strong responses to the discoveries they make in the garden, often feeling compelled to touch and interact with the many features that intrigue them. This is encouraged, for one of the principles the garden was founded on was not telling kids "no," but letting them feel free to become intimate with their surroundings.

FIG 3d-17. Pavement details abound in this garden, such as the handprints of children and those related to garden themes. These add interest and discovery to the garden. (COURTESY OF ERIN JORDAN KNIGHT.)

Children hug the statue of Mary Lennox in the Secret Garden, and make her wreaths of flowers to wear as crowns and necklaces (Figure 3d-18). The Dance Chimes call to children, and are often faintly marked by impressions of small, muddy tennis shoes or bare footprints. Even the Small World Globe encourages children to touch while they learn, as is evidenced by a large, worn, shiny spot over the state of Michigan, where children have so often rubbed their home state over the years (Taylor, 2001).

EDUCATIONAL ASPECTS

The emphasis of the 60+ theme areas is on plants and the important part plants play in a child's everyday life. The areas are small enough that their designs can be "taken away" and inspire ideas for families to apply in their own backyards.

ACTIVITIES CHILDREN ARE DRAWN TO MOST FREQUENTLY

Touching, smelling, looking . . . being free to explore from one theme planting to another. It's all about self-discovery and then showing others what they see, and then making the connection about how important plants are to them.

FIG 3d-18. Children clearly feel an intimate connection to this garden and its many features. Here, an offering of a flower wreath has been left at the feet of the Mary Lennox statue in The Secret Garden. (COURTESY OF ERIN JORDAN KNIGHT.)

UNIQUE CHARACTERISTICS OF THE GARDEN

"The emphasis is on plants in a garden-like setting with small theme or specialty gardens that relate to children, as opposed to an "adventure playground" with some plantings," says Taylor.

SAFETY

The property is American Disabilities Act accessible, water features are minimal, and a fence encircles the entire garden.

MAINTENANCE

The garden is maintained by the Gardens Manager, Curator, Education Coordinator, and two student interns. Volunteers also help with planting and spring and fall maintenance.

CREDITS

The Michigan 4-H Children's Garden Design Team

Michigan State University Child Development Laboratory School: Children, Dr. Alice Whiren, Director, and Staff

Landscape architects: Jeff Kacos and Deb Kinney of the Michigan State University Division of Campus Parks and Planning

Jane L. Taylor, Curator and Horticulturist at MSU

With input from many 4-H horticulture leaders and 4-H members statewide

Construction Team

Dennis Hansen of CPP, Superintendent of Site Construction

Brooklyn Botanic Garden: Edible Garden, Brooklyn, NY

Opening date: 1914 (The Oldest Children's Garden in Continuous Use in the World)

Acres: 1 (.4 hectare) Children's Garden

Cost: Not available—The Garden was designed and made long ago.

Funding: Because BBG has a strong record of success, they have received grants to help support programming and

The Brooklyn Botanic Garden, established in 1914, is the oldest children's garden in continuous use in the world. (COURTESY OF LOUIS BUHLE.)

renewal of the Children's Garden. Projects are typically funded from government grants, membership funds, foundations, and individuals at approximately 25% each.

MISSION AND PURPOSE

Education is a primary mission at Brooklyn Botanic Garden (BBG). Since its founding in 1910, BBG has been an internationally recognized leader and innovator in environmental education programs, teaching that plants are essential to life. Brooklyn Botanic Garden teaches children and adults about plants at a popular level, and offers instruction in the exacting skills required to grow plants and make beautiful gardens. Educational programs enable young people and adults alike to acquire a broader sense of the natural world and to understand the responsibility individuals assume in preserving and improving the quality of our environment. Brooklyn Botanic Garden serves more than 150,000 children annually through a wide range of on-site, in-school, and community-based initiatives.

THE DESIGN TEAM

Ellen Eddy Shaw led the design team in 1914.

THE DESIGN

The 1 acre (.4 hectare) Children's Garden is subdivided into 4 × 15′ (1.2 × 4.6 meters) beds easily gardened by teams of two children with an instructor. They are connected by pathways and surrounded by a fence that defines the space designated for children (Figure 3e-1) Children dig in the soil to plant lettuce,

FIG 3e-1. A fence with roofed seating rooms encloses the space designated for the BBG Children's Garden. (COURTESY OF MARY TAYLOR HAQUE.)

tomatoes, squash, onions, peppers, along with other vegetables and companion plants such as herbs and flowers.

EDUCATIONAL ASPECTS

BBG's award-winning Children's Garden Program includes an array of classes, workshops, internships, teacher training, and guided tours of the Garden. Educational programs also reach beyond the garden walls to involve more than 37,000 adults and children in neighborhood conservation efforts by partnering with schools, libraries, block associations, and other community organizations to create and sustain gardens as well as an awareness of the importance of preserving green spaces and sustainable landscapes in communities.

Issues like organic waste disposal, for example, are addressed at both the garden and the community level. Within BBG, a Home Composting Demonstration showcases compost piles and compost bins and provides instruction on how to compost successfully. On a larger scale, BBG conducts an Urban Composting Project. Supported by the New York City Department of Sanitation, BBG provides technical assistance and resources for community gardens and institutions, as well as information on residential composting.

In addition to working with children, vermicomposting programs are also available for teachers. Ideas and activities for incorporating worm composting into science, math, and language arts for students of all ages are discussed (Figure 3e-2).

PARTICIPATORY ASPECTS

Children plant, grow, harvest, cook (including bread and pies!) and create crafts in the Children's Garden. Very young children (four- and five-year-olds) are called "Seeds" at BBG, and they learn basic gardening skills such as planting and maintain-

FIG 3e-2. Children compost weeds and organic waste as part of their gardening activities at BBG. (COURTESY OF BROOKLYN BOTANICAL GARDEN.)

ing communal plots. They proudly take home flowers and vegetables they have tended and harvested themselves (Figure 3e-3). Seeds get to hear garden stories, play games, and construct crafts with natural materials as they learn the fundamentals of gardening.

Five- and six-year-olds are called "Seedlings," and they work in pairs to learn more advanced gardening skills. Seven to 13-year-olds, "City Farmers," also grow food and flowers from seed to supplement their family table. These programs provide a wonderful setting for meeting new friends, acquiring new skills, and having a

FIG 3e-3. Children plant, grow, harvest, and take home food from the BBG in this 1930 photo. (COURTESY OF LOUIS BUHLE.)

good time in the garden. During summer, young gardeners might dig, plant, weed, cultivate, and harvest a variety of crops including radishes, carrots, lettuce, scallions, squash, eggplants, cucumbers, tomatoes, beans, and other plants of their own choosing.

Through programs like "Summer Science Adventures" children can follow-up morning gardening sessions in the Children's Garden with afternoon explorations of theme-related topics such as plants from around the world, wildlife in the city, and nature-inspired arts and crafts. Children are encouraged to follow their curiosity, pose questions, and use the entire Garden for individual and team explorations. These include "Ecological Explorations," where children investigate the complex and essential relationships between plants, animals, and their environment. From walking the Native Flora Garden to creating a wetland environment, participants explore different habitats and the plants and animals that inhabit them. Environmental stewardship is encouraged by discussing current environmental problems and figuring out how to be an active part of the solution.

Brooklyn Botanic Garden offers many seasonal programs, and caregivers are often encouraged to learn along side three- or four-year-olds to enhance their youngster's experience at Brooklyn Botanic Garden. Even during the winter, opportunities are provided to grow plants indoors and in cold frames.

UNIQUE CHARACTERISTICS OF THE GARDEN

As the oldest children's garden in continual use in the world, the Children's Garden at BBG is an excellent model for growing vegetable gardens as well as for

COLLECTIONS & HIGHLIGHTS

1) Magnolia Plaza/
   Visitor Center Entrance
2) Daffodil Hill
3) Alice Recknagel Ireys
   Fragrance Garden
4) Shakespeare Garden
5) Celebrity Path
6) Alfred T. White Memorial
7) Japanese Hill and Pond Garden

8) Herb Garden
9) Cherry Walk
10) Cherry Esplanade
11) Louisa Clark Spencer
    Lilac Collection
12) Osborne Garden
13) Overlook
14) Native Flora Garden
15) Home Composting Exhibit
16) Cranford Rose Garden

17) Bluebell Wood
18) Conifers
19) Monocot Border
20) Butterfly Bushes
21) Rock Garden
22) Steinhardt Conservatory
23) Lily Pool Terrace
24) Mixed Perennial Border
25) Annual Border
26) Children's Garden
27) Discovery Garden

FIG 3e-4. The Children's Garden is a small part of the larger Brooklyn Botanic Garden (numbers 26 and 27 on map), which hosts a wide variety of garden spaces and programs for children and adults. (COURTESY OF BBG.)

growing leadership skills in youth (Figure 3e-4). The Garden Apprentice Program (GAP) provides students with opportunities for personal growth and career development.

ACTIVITIES MOST POPULAR WITH CHILDREN

Authentic activities like planting seeds, cultivating, harvesting, and cooking are very popular. Children prefer growing familiar plants like tomatoes, peppers, potatoes, and radishes, but are also interested in unusual plants like Devil's Claw, an unusual ornamental. They like pepper plants because they produce for a long time. Children like to work. Hence, the BBG staff motto, "Let kids do it themselves!" Plants are most popular when in season, that is, grapes and blueberries when fruiting, and sunflowers when in full flower.

MAINTENANCE

Ten percent of the Children's Garden budget is reserved for maintenance. The garden is plowed with a tractor each spring, and organic cover crops like rye, clover, and vetch are established in the fall.

THE BROOKLYN BOTANIC GARDEN DISCOVERY GARDEN: A RECENT ADDITION FOR CHILDREN

Adjacent to the Children's Garden is The Discovery Garden, a more recent addition to the children's garden experience at BBG. Designed smaller in scale especially for toddlers, the garden includes plants that are stimulating to all the senses, a pump with a bamboo water channel, a stream, and a diminutive nature trail connecting a variety of surprises including a giant green spider. This garden is designed for small groups as opposed to large classes, and paths are narrow and twisting to slow children down so they can enjoy the plantings alongside the walkway (Figure 3e-5).

In the Discovery Garden, children can hike a nature trail to explore, or participate in special programs. On "Thirsty Thursdays," for example, they can water thirsty plants in the discovery garden and learn about water and aquatic plants at the "wet water table." Discovery Carts full of games, puzzles, and natural objects are available for children and families to learn more about plants and science through sensory experiences (Figure 3e-6).

FIG 3e-5. The Discovery Garden at BBG is designed with small-scale features especially for young children. (COURTESY OF MARY TAYLOR HAQUE.)

FIG 3e-6. Plants are trained on low arbors and sculptural topiaries to create landmarks along the path through the BBG Discovery Garden. (COURTESY OF MARY TAYLOR HAQUE.)

Alice in Wonderland Courtyard Design for Clemson Elementary School, Clemson, SC. (COURTESY OF JASON SMIT AND BARBARA SIEGEL RYAN.)

CHAPTER 4

Schoolyards, Playgrounds, and Backyards

Historical Development of Playgrounds

Playgrounds and play yards have been fixtures of the American landscape since the 1800s in settings ranging from schoolyards to backyards. The first playground venture began with outdoor gymnasiums of the early 1800s, which focused on exercise for older children and never garnered any degree of popularity. By the end of the 1800s, the playground movement in the United States began a continuing period of development with the initiation of the Boston sand gardens to provide play activity for poor children living in slum conditions.

As the playground movement continued to grow, more credence was given to the benefits of play in general through the work of people such as John Dewey. Dewey reported that play and playground experiences of young children helped their cognitive skills and social development. Others expounded on play as a means to coordinate the psychological and physical aspects of child behavior.

World War I was a motivator to shift playgrounds from parks and neighborhoods to schools due to the unavailability of materials to build them. The early schoolyard environments usually consisted of swings, slides, merry-go-rounds, seesaws, and climbers mounted on asphalt, concrete, dirt, or other hard surfaces. These traditional playgrounds eventually led the way to the development of adventure, designer, creative, and vest-pocket play areas.

Adventure playgrounds require the presence of play leaders or supervisors because children playing in them can do activities they often cannot do in other play environments. This would include building things such as forts and tree houses and playing in ways that are creative and reflective of day-to-day life. Adventure playgrounds, with a few exceptions, never caught on in the United States because they require trained staff, are unsightly, and are perceived to be unsafe.

Designer play areas of the 1950s and 1960s incorporated metal and concrete into play sculptures and used wood and rope to establish creations of boats, trains, spaceships, and cars, and thus encouraged children to use their imaginations. Playground equipment manufacturers then began providing modular equipment that could be purchased and easily erected on chosen sites. Building playgrounds became easy because of the commercial equipment available, and playgrounds were visible almost everywhere—in parks, fast-food restaurants, schools, day care facilities, airports, resorts. and back yards.

Although play areas of the 1950s and 1960s were numerous and did provide a place for children to expend energy, the ability to play creatively seemed lost. The advent of creative playgrounds was an effort to reignite creative play by merging elements of traditional playgrounds with acceptable elements of adventure playgrounds such as loose parts like tires, building materials, and large wooden spools. These playgrounds required more maintenance than those consisting of permanently placed equipment, making it difficult for schools and recreation departments to maintain them.

Trends in Playground Design

One important result of the creative playground era was the gradual awareness that nature could provide the loose parts on a playground in the form of twigs, pinecones, rocks, leaves, roly-polys, lizards, and much more. With this concept providing the lead, a new type of playground has become a 21st century trend as play areas go through remarkable growth and transformations. Playgrounds today are moving beyond the long established parameter of a single large piece of equipment in a park or schoolyard to a mix of commercially manufactured equipment and natural elements of sand, water and plantings (Figure 4-1).

FIG 4-1. This child is captivated by her find of a horned lizard at this play site, an opportunity that can be built into the play area design (COURTESY OF GINA K. MCLELLAN.)

As the naturalistic approach to playgrounds grows, the realization that outdoor play environments are good learning environments also grows. The benefits of outdoor environments in the learning process are discussed in more detail in Chapter 6. Natural elements in play areas can be indigenous to the site or can be added to the site. This design concept is providing a new level of excitement in the planning and design of play areas. Schoolyards are a primary focus with the addition of environments extending well beyond the playground to include nature trails, outdoor classrooms, and gardens of many kinds. Public

FIG 4-2. Loose parts in a play area like seeds and stones give these children a chance to explore and observe a part of nature. (COURTESY OF GINA K. MCLLELLAN.)

parks, neighborhoods, child care centers, and even hospitals are examining and implementing naturalistic and sustainable approaches to play areas with the realization that these play areas offer a well-balanced approach to play (Figure 4-2).

Residential gardens and the typical back yard are perfect places for a natural approach to children's play areas. The back yard is probably the cradle of natural play areas going back to times when children roamed the woods and fields behind their homes with more freedom than is permitted today. Minimal play equipment and extensive opportunity to explore natural surroundings are not only

FIG 4-3. A backyard is a perfect place for a child to develop a special garden and play area. (COURTESY OF GINA K. MCLELLAN.)

less expensive to build and maintain, but provide endless opportunities for play through exploration and for learning through observation (Figure 4-3).

Role of Municipal and County Park and Recreation Departments in Providing Play Places for Children

The role of city and county park and recreation departments in providing play spaces for children is a long-established and very important one. These public entities have been advocating, building, and maintaining public play areas for well over 100 years.

Like schools, they are challenged by health and safety regulations, heavy use, and sometimes vandalism. Although it is desirable to see creative and unique play places developed, playground safety standards are so complex and stringent that few public agencies are willing or able to take on the risks and costs of custom design and maintenance. Playground safety is essential, but the safety standards have narrowed the options, especially in terms of equipment that spins, swivels, or moves. The end result is that public playgrounds are built to be safe and durable, but are sometimes static, dull, and repetitive depending on the selection and limitations of commercial playground equipment. With a little input from children in the community and creative input from designers, public playgrounds can move from dull to delightful.

Plantings that help give a naturalistic feel to play places also encounter hurdles. Public landscapes take a beating through wear and tear from many users. Plantings are sometimes stolen; flowers are often picked; young trees are climbed; and other unintentional damage occurs from activity uses such as skateboarding or biking. As natural as bees are to the outdoors, blooming shrubs and plants near play areas are often removed or avoided to reduce the risk of bee stings.

Julie McQuary, the Parks Project Coordinator for the Olympia, Washington Parks, Arts and Recreation Department and a Certified Playground Safety Inspector, shares some creative successes in that community. A thematic approach to playgrounds is drawing much attention and lots of children. Olympia's Priest Point Park Playground reflects the coastal natural history of the area with the SS Fun Ship, a nautical link to Budd Inlet in a playground that has been in existence for 100 years. An early toy boat playground steered community allegiance to another play boat when the area was upgraded. In addition to the SS Fun Ship, children also delight in the safety surface

FIG 4-4. Olympia's Priest Point Park Playground reflects the coastal natural history with Budd Inlet themes including a sailing ship, sailboat, whales, and salmon. Note the safety surface graphics depicting salmon swimming along the edge of the bay. (COURTESY OF JULIE MCQUARY.)

graphics where salmon swim near the shore of the bay. The sense of place at the playground prompts a father to sit below deck playing sea chanties on the guitar while his children play all over the ship while singing along with him. Rubberized poured-in-place safety surfacing lends itself to thematic support and is easier and less expensive to maintain than most safety surfaces, but the initial cost is much higher (Figure 4-4).

With the success of Priest Point Park Playground, Olympia Parks, Arts and Recreation Department is building other themed play areas. One is a frog theme tied to its wet, forested site, while a second playground has a sunny day theme with a huge sun, puffy clouds, and birds to provide a sunny atmosphere even on a cloudy day. Olympia also plans to continue with its approach to integrate public art and custom design into their parks such as artist designed seating areas, stepping stones, and wall imprints that relate to the playground themes.

Public park and recreation agencies have an important role to serve in the provision of quality children's play places. It will take some creative thinking, a lot of involvement of children in the communities, and a philosophical willingness to break away from the recent staid playgrounds. Equipment manufacturing companies are willing and able to work with unique concepts and ideas to build what a community really wants.

Safety in Play Area Design

Other chapters in this book examine how and why children play and focus on design processes that lead to the provision of play environments that fit well with children's needs. Regardless of the specific environment developed for children, an overriding concern is safety. This section will address the safety issues that must be addressed when planning, designing and building children's play environments.

When designing outdoor spaces for the enjoyment of children, safety and liability issues are of paramount importance. Children learn and develop through experimentation and by challenging themselves through play, but safe spaces must be provided for this exploration. According to the United States Consumer Product Safety Commission (CPSC), there has been a dramatic increase in playground injuries over the past 2 decades (CPSC, 2001). It is estimated by the CPSC that nearly 200,000 accidents in playgrounds send children to hospital emergency rooms each year. An estimated 40% are related in some way to inadequate supervision, and nearly 70% are caused by falls from equipment.

There are many ways to make a playground area or outdoor play space safer for children, but the first steps are learning about practices that promote safety and identifying unsafe play areas (NPPS, 2001). There are many good resources for such study mentioned throughout this chapter. However, the key to responsible landscape design for children is designing with safety issues in mind and supervising proper use of equipment.

PLANNING SAFE PLAY AREAS

Planning for safety means anticipating as many situations in which a child may be injured as possible and then taking steps to prevent such injuries. Also, consider age appropriateness and design for the various children who may use the site (Sawyers, 1994). For example, an elementary school space may use equipment that requires significant coordination and strength, such as climbing structures, but such equipment may not be appropriate for a preschool or kindergarten playground design. In fact, many states require separate play areas for kindergarten, and equipment manufacturers oblige with structures designed for the preschool-aged child. Also, ensure that the spaces you provide intrigue the children who will play there. Safety is important, but so is the discovery experience of play. This can be achieved with great care for child safety, but it takes creative thought and variety.

"You really need to look at how many different play opportunities you can provide," says Pat Plocek, special services manager for the Tampa Parks Department (American City and County, 1999). The question lies in how to create spaces that provide adventure and safety, discovery, and security. Landscape architects and other professional landscape designers are rarely involved in the design of such spaces, and it is crucial for those developing the space without formal training to familiarize themselves with all the issues faced in playground safety. These include equipment selection, height of equipment, maintenance, fall surfaces, supervision, age-appropriateness, and site and situation specific factors (Figure 4-5) (NPPS, 2001).

FIG 4-5. Playgrounds which will have large numbers of children using them at one time should be designed with open areas and multiple play elements to enhance safe use of the area. (COURTESY OF GINA K. MCLELLAN.)

DESIGNING SAFE PLAYGROUNDS

The Consumer Product Safety Commission (CPSC) is a valuable resource with a 25-step plan to designing safe playgrounds that can be accessed on their Web site at http://www.uni.edu/playground/tips/general/planning.html (CPSC, 2001). Some of these suggestions are summarized below, and considered along with other safety resources and studies.

The CPSC suggests the design process begin with the development of a committee consisting of 3–10 people, led by a chairman, where ideas are recorded by a secretary at each meeting. These members could include many people, including teachers, administrators, parents, support staff, and others who are interested. A certified playground safety consultant can be contacted for preliminary design advice. There are several associations that deal with playground safety issues, such as the American Alliance for Health, Physical Education, Recreation, and Dance (AAHPERD), the National Program for Playground Safety (NPPS), and the National Recreation and Park Association. Such professional advice may incur fees and expenses, but the advice and expertise they provide should save money over the long term of the project. Also, written guidelines or standards should be obtained on program safety. Some resources for playground safety information include:

1. Guidelines: United States Consumer Product Safety Commission (CPSC) Handbook for Public Playground Safety (http://www.cpsc.gov)

2. ASTM International Standards: F-1487 for Public Use Playground Equipment; and F-1292 for surfacing (http://www.astm.org/international)

3. National Recreation and Park Association (http://www.nrpa.org)

Next, evaluation of resources and existing features to determine whether to retain or remove them is important, as well as identification of elements to repair and materials and equipment to purchase (NPPS, 2001). Keep in mind the needs of children, including children of different ages and those with disabilities.

Consider site hazards, and how to deal with them for child safety. Also, check insurance company requirements and other legal issues to know the costs and guidelines as well as risks involved. Decide who will be in charge of site supervision; and be sure that in structured play environments such as schools, supervisors are well trained in child safety (CPSC, 2001). Programs for training as well as training videos are available through the CPSC and others.

Next, develop ideas about what those who use the site want to incorporate. Ask children, teachers, supervisors, youth leaders, and others what they want to see. Set goals for the site, and keep them in mind throughout development. Then order at least 10 catalogs from various playground companies and compare styles of equipment as well as prices and other factors. You do not have to choose all your equipment from one company, but physically connecting different companies' equipment invalidates the warranty and raises safety questions. If you mix equipment from different companies, be sure each piece stands independently from the others.

Consider the various surfaces that go under the equipment as well. Again, send for at least 10 catalogs that represent the safety surfacing in which you are interested.

The next step is to create a budget based on catalog prices for desired equipment, safety surfaces, installation, and maintenance costs. Then request information from the companies of interest and ask for plans and quotes. If a design plan was developed in a previous step, ask the manufacturer to fit equipment to that plan and provide quotes for that plan. Most companies are willing to provide two or three levels of pricing if a range of costs is desired.

This is a good time to verify the knowledge of the company in regard to children's safety. Ask for information on the safety of their products and recommendations for installation. Compare this information to knowledge gained through the research process to ascertain each company's reputation and reliability.

The next step consists of gathering information about installation and maintenance from involved companies. It is possible to reduce the total cost of playground equipment by one-third by using volunteers to install it. If this method meets your organization's requirements in terms of its volunteer program (liability, safety), then hire the equipment company's installation supervisor to lead the volunteers through the process. Installation will be better and quicker, and the manufacturer's warranty will be in effect due to the professional leadership. This method also offers more legal protection because correct installation has been verified. A payment method should be developed and a file system created and maintained throughout the process to ensure clear documentation of all decisions.

FIG 4-6. Moving parts such as these skywheels are not inherently dangerous but require supervision and the safe use as shown by these children waiting their turn. (COURTESY OF GINA K. MCLELLAN.)

Once equipment is installed, instruct teachers and supervisors about safety precautions for the equipment and require them to teach the children how to use the equipment. These lessons should be taught yearly to reinforce the information. Accident report summaries reflect that the most likely occurrence of accidents is at the start of the school year when children are not yet used to the equipment, so additional supervision at the start of the year is a good idea (Figure 4-6).

TEN STEPS TO SAFER PLAY AREAS

The following guidelines from the CPSC cannot prevent all playground injuries, but these safety guidelines will protect children from unnecessary risk in their play environments (CPSC, 2001).

1. Make sure adult supervision is present at the playground
   a. Children should never play on equipment with out supervision.
   b. Adults need to watch for potential hazards, observe children playing, intercede and facilitate play, when necessary, and be available in case of injury.

2. Guide children to play on age-appropriate equipment
    a. Children are developmentally different. Younger children tend to be weaker and less coordinated than older children.
    b. Playgrounds should be divided into age-appropriate areas, 0–2 years, 2–5 years, and 5–12.
    c. Children should only play on age-appropriate equipment. Older children using younger children's equipment tend to become bored quickly and use it in inappropriate ways. This can include climbing over equipment, hanging from it, sitting (or standing) inappropriately on it, and other uses never intended by the manufacturer or designer.

3. Survey the play area and make sure it is free of apparent hazards
    a. First, visually survey the area for immediate hazards. This could include broken glass and metal pieces, or poor arrangement of equipment that could create congestion and cause children moving through the space to collide with each other or equipment.
    b. If the area is near a street or parking lot, fencing is essential to keep children out of these areas.
    c. Look for signs designating appropriate ages of children for play in various areas. Also, look for any signboards stating the rules of the playground.
    d. Be sure metal equipment is shaded or has a protective surface to prevent burns.

4. Check the playground surface for cushioned surfacing beneath equipment and its fall areas
    a. Falls from equipment to surfaces below account for over 70% of playground injuries.
    b. Improper surfacing is the leading cause of many of those injuries.
    c. Hard surfaces such as asphalt, blacktop, concrete, grass, packed dirt, or rocks should not be used.
    d. Surfaces such as hardwood fiber/mulch, pea gravel, and sand are good organic materials. Synthetic surfaces that are good options include rubber tiles, mats, or poured surfaces.
    e. Surfaces should be maintained at a depth proportionate to the height of equipment. A standard rule is to use 12″ (.3 meters) of loose fill for equipment up to 8 feet (2.4 meters) in height. For synthetic surfaces, check the manufacturer's guidelines (Figure 4-7).

f. Maintenance of surfaces is important. Loose-fill surfaces may need to be pushed back under equipment if the material moves, slides, or spreads. Cushioning material should be provided under all equipment and in its fall zones. Each type of equipment has its own standards for fall zones, but a general rule is at least 6 feet (1.8 meters) to every side of the equipment's perimeter. It may be more for elements such as swings and slides where children will be propelled farther due to the downhill momentum (Figure 4-8).

FIG 4-7. Playground equipment must meet required distances between equipment and edging materials to assure that children will not tumble off the safety surfacing if they fall. (COURTESY OF GINA K. MCLELLAN.)

5. Examine equipment such as ladders, platforms, and steps
   a. Climbers and monkey bars have the highest incidence of injury on public playgrounds and require intense supervision. To prevent injury on such equipment, there are several safety practices to follow.
   b. Be sure steps are in good condition and that handrails are the appropriate size for a child's hand to grip.
   c. If a platform is off the ground, a guardrail or protective barrier is essential.

6. Examine types and quality of swings
   a. Swings are the pieces of moving equipment that are most likely to cause injury to children. Preventive measures include removal of animal swings, replacement of wooden and metal seats with soft seats, and removal of the swing framework from any adjacent equipment. For example, do not purchase swings

FIG 4-8. Rubber mats placed under swings help to hold loose fill safety surfacing in place and therefore at the proper depth. (COURTESY OF GINA K. MCLELLAN.)

attached to slides, platforms, monkey bars, and other devices, as this increases chance of injury.
  b. Place only two swings in each support bay.
  c. Position swings at least 24" (7.3 meters) apart at the base of seats and 30" (9.1 meters) from any supports.
  d. Swings should have a fall zone twice the height of the pivot or swing hanger in the front and back of the swing sets. The fall zone should also extend 6 feet (1.8 meters) to each side of the support structure.

7. Check the slides
  a. Slides should be well anchored, have firm handrails for gripping, and have steps with good traction.
  b. Steps should have drainage holes to make them less slippery.
  c. There should be no spaces between the slide platform and the slide bed where strings from clothing could catch and cause strangulation.
  d. Make sure metal slides are shaded or covered to prevent burns in hot sun.

8. Review the seesaw area
  a. Make sure the handles of the seesaw are secure and of a size and design that children can grip easily.
  b. Check to see if there is a soft bumper under the bottom of the seat to cushion the hit at the ground.
  c. Make sure that all pivot points are covered to prevent pinched fingers.

9. Inspect merry-go-rounds
  a. Merry-go-rounds should be firmly anchored into the ground and have handles for children to grasp easily.
  b. The surface under the bed of the merry-go-round should be positioned so that children cannot slide underneath.
  c. The gear box should be covered so fingers cannot get caught.
  d. A governor should be attached to control the ultimate speed of the unit.

10. Take care of the spaces children enjoy
  a. Leave the space in a condition as good as or better than you found it.
  b. Redistribute any loose surfacing that may have been pushed aside by play.
  c. Close all opened gates.

d. If you found any problems that need immediate attention, contact the administrator and report relevant facts.

e. Call the CPSC at 800-638-2772 to report any product hazards or product-related injuries. This could prevent the injury of other children in the future.

SAFETY SURFACES IN PLAYGROUNDS

Safety surfaces are essential for playground safety, particularly considering that approximately 70% of injuries are fall related (NPPS, 2001). Appropriate surfacing can disperse the momentum of a falling child, reducing the risk of life threatening injuries and preventing some fractures (JOPERD, 1994). There are many aspects to consider when choosing surface material; and while there are many treatments, each with particular benefits, no surface can prevent all injuries. The two basic types of surface treatment are organic and inorganic, and within these types are various alternatives (Wade, 1999).

Loose Fill Surfaces

Loose fill materials include shredded rubber, wood chips, wood fiber, bark mulch, sand, and pea gravel. Grass and turf, as well as other earth surfaces, are not sufficient cover because their ability to absorb shock is directly related to wear and climactic conditions, according to the Sawyers. Many recycled materials such as shredded tires can become safety surfacing, thus providing two beneficial services of safety and recycling. Loose fill should be carefully considered relative to the play site. Pea gravel can stick to soles of tennis shoes and be carried into a building's interior when it is located near the play area and young children love to fill their pockets with it (Figure 4-9).

FIG 4-9. This playground uses engineered wood fiber as a safety surface which drains well, is inexpensive, meets depth requirements, and is ADA accessible. (COURTESY OF GINA K. MCLELLAN.)

Synthetic Surfaces

There are many man-made surfaces that absorb the shock of a child's fall, and some tests suggest that some of these surfaces are safer than others (Lancet, 1997). Rubber tiles, rubber mats, and pour-in-place rubberized surfaces are a few of the products available for a number of years, and granular rubber is a newer alternative in the synthetic surfaces array (Figure 4-10).

FIG 4-10. Poured in place rubberized surfacing is ADA accessible, easy to maintain and has multiple creative design options but is more expensive to install initially than other safety surfaces.

Surface Selection

There are several questions the CPSC recommends a designer or playground developer ask before selecting the best surface for that project (CPSC, 2001). First, be sure it meets American Society for Testing and Materials standards and CPSC guidelines. These guidelines will lead the purchaser to select surfaces that best protect a child from head and body injuries.

Next, consider climactic effects on the surface, and research each product to see if it is successful in the type of climate where it will be used. Pick a surface that is readily available with reasonable initial costs and maintenance costs. Finally, think of the playground's needs for durability, drainage, and accessibility, and decide if that surface will meet those particular needs.

Cushioning Fall Zones

The area under and around playground equipment where children may fall is called the fall zone, and it is these areas that must be covered by safety surfaces. The total area of such spaces is dependent on the type of equipment it surrounds (NPPS, 2001). A general guideline of the CPSC is that the surface should extend a minimum of 6 feet (1.8 meters) in all directions from the stationary playground equipment (CPSC, 2001). Fall zones around slides and swings are calculated differently, as the movement of children on them extends the danger zones.

For slides higher than 4' (1.2 meters), add 4' (1.2 meters) to the height of the slide to determine the extension of the fall zone from the exit of the slide, with a maximum of 14 feet (4.3 meters). So, a 5' (1.5 meters) slide has a 9' (2.7 meters) fall zone from its end.

For swings, the fall zone is twice the height of the pivot or swing hanger in front and in back of the swing seats. If the hanger pivot height is 10' (3.0 meters), the fall zone must be 20' (6.1 meters) on either side of the swing seat, totaling 40' (12.2 meters) in overall depth. Surfacing should also extend 6' (1.8 meters) to either side of the swing's support structures.

Maintenance

Proper maintenance is essential to the safety of any surface. Loose fill surfacing has a lower initial cost but greater maintenance demands than installed synthetic materials (Sawyers, 1994). In areas with high play loads, these materials may need daily raking or periodic tilling to loosen their compaction. Materials may need to be periodically replaced due to spread or movement during play. Additional loose fill may need to be added annually or semi-annually to maintain depths. Also, it is an important safety measure to inspect loose fill, looking for any foreign objects such as glass or metal that could cause harm.

For synthetic materials, maintenance is not as taxing but is just as important. Repairs to gouges, burns, and loose areas must be prompt and thorough. Frequent sweeping to prevent sand, dirt, rocks, and other loose materials from becoming a slipping hazard may be required. Both loose fill and synthetic materials must have good drainage, or slipping hazards can develop.

Safety Surfaces for Handicap Accessibility

The most generally accepted materials for safety and handicap accessibility are uniform wood chips, also known as engineered wood fiber, synthetic products such as rubber mats or tiles, and poured-in-place surfaces (CPSC, 2001). However, new surfaces for these needs are developed frequently. Such surfaces may not be necessary over the entire playground, but it is important to assure that all children can reach equipment for equal play opportunities.

Accessible paths should be 60" (1.5 meters) wide, slip resistant, and have a slope of no greater than 1:12 (.3m:3.7m). The CPSC also recommends transfer stations on equipment and parking areas for wheelchairs to improve a playground's accessibility.

AGE-APPROPRIATE PLAY AREAS

As mentioned above, creating the right space for a child's age and development level is crucial to safety (Sawyers, 1994). If the play equipment is too challenging, the child will lack the coordination and strength to meet the physical challenges it holds, therefore risking injury. If the child is too old and mature for the play area, rough and creative play will result, and equipment will be used in ways it was not intended. Examples include going down slides headfirst or backward, standing in or jumping from swings, and many other dangerous activities. Therefore, during the design process, be aware of the age of the child who will use the space, and put appropriate signage in the playground to show parents which areas are designed for their child's age and ability level (CPSC, 2001).

Different types of play are pursued by children of different ages. Young children often engage in functional play in which simple repetitive activities stimulate a child's senses. Examples are filling a bucket with sand to pour in another bucket and then pouring it back again or walking around the sandbox frame again and again while trying not to fall off.

Constructive play develops later, in which intentional building or creating with objects or materials occurs. It is the most frequently observed type of play among three- and four-year-olds.

Fantasy play, in which a child's imagination plays a vital role, is common at ages three–five years. Children can imagine themselves to be other people or use imaginary objects as playthings.

At about age 5, children begin to play games with rules. At first, the rules may be made up by the child and changed throughout the course of play. This is most effective when the rules are few and simple and the game is not competitive.

As children get older, play within groups and social interaction becomes important. Yet sometimes children may still wish to play independently, and a landscape should meet all these needs with different spaces. It is therefore important that "loose" or "transportable" play equipment be provided to make play more adaptable to the desires of the child and his or her creativity.

Finally, the challenge level should be age-appropriate to encourage the child to learn and experiment. Failure is often devastating to development, as children are not likely to repeat unsuccessful experiences. Again, different play spaces for different age groups is the answer to this problem.

It is important to remember that play becomes destructive and unsatisfying when the same materials and experiences are offered over and over again (American City and County, 1999). Children need variety and spaces designed for their level of competence. If these are provided, children will grow into the new spaces and continually have the variety and competency level needed for happy and productive play.

ALTERNATIVE DESIGNS FOR SAFE PLAY

The above guidelines describe play in traditional equipment-based play yards, but there are many solutions that eliminate dangerous climbing structures and other equipment in favor of more creative play in natural environments. This may be particularly appropriate in school environments where nature can educate as well as entertain children. Although this approach is rare and unique, it will allow for children's various needs for active play, mental stimulation, variety, and interaction.

One such outdoor play space at Jack Fisher Park in Campbell, CA, incorporates dynamic elements and interactive stations to entertain and educate (Hamilton, 1999, student project). This playground, featured in Newsweek in an article entitled, "Playgrounds for the Future: they ain't got swing" by Kendall Hamilton and Patricia King, is innovative and creative in its approach to play and safety (Hamilton, 1997). One structure allows children to build wet sand dams then press a button to flood the concrete channel and test the strength of the structures. Slides are plastic, with special wood chip cushioned impact zones. There are no monkey bars or jungle gyms. The article predicts that such structures with their known and perceived safety risks will be hard to find in California in the future. California is the first state to mandate compliance to federal safety recommendations, which the Jack Fischer Park meets in a creative way. This approach will require the modification of swings, slides, and seesaws, as well as the elimination of jungle gyms and monkey bars.

Some question the changes and innovations facing safe play spaces of the future and fear that in this effort to protect children, important needs and desires of childhood may not be met (White, 1998). However, safety activists estimate that 200,000 children end up in the hospital each year due to playground injuries, and approximately 15 die each year (NPPS, 2001). According to Seymour Cold, professor of environmental planning at the University of California-Davis, playgrounds are among the five greatest hazards for children in the United States. It is clear that change is needed, but sensitivity to the needs of children is also crucial.

FIG 4-11. The mallets attached to this alligator drum are attached with cables short enough to prevent entanglement of the child in the cable. (COURTESY OF GINA K. MCLELLAN.)

Future playgrounds may house equipment lower to the ground. They may have no merry-go-rounds, and may be limited to spring-loading see-saws in place of traditional designs that allow children to jump off while in motion. Animal-shaped swings, notorious for hitting nearby toddlers with great impact, are unsafe for playground inclusion. Even normal swings are expected to become scarce, and those that are high will be eliminated completely. It is estimated that falls from swings, slides, and climbers account for 87% of all injuries, according to the Journal of Physical Education, Recreation, and Dance (Sawyers, 1994). With such statistics, it is reasonable to assume that with the modification or elimination of these most dangerous elements, children at play will be safer, and fewer injuries will occur (Figure 4-11).

These safety steps are controversial, as some proponents of traditional play still cling to the playgrounds of their own childhood. Even with these safety measures, children will still be hurt during play in such spaces every year. Some planners and even parents believe that we are a society too quick to protect everyone from everything and that in the case of playgrounds, children need to be challenged by the variety and demands of play equipment. It is part of what teaches them developmentally to minimize risks, an important lesson to learn for later life. "The new rules are aimed at eliminating deaths, not minor injuries," says Susan Coltsman, a playground designer in Berkeley, CA.

EVALUATING TREE HAZARDS IN CHILDREN'S LANDSCAPES

Although trees are essential to beautiful outdoor spaces for children, there are related risk and liability issues. In most cases, tree failures can be predicted and proper precautionary measures can be taken before damage is done to property or people (Matheny, 1994).

Determining the hazard risk of a tree is a subjective process, and anyone who attempts to assess their site without the help of a professional should study all the complex issues that can play a role in tree safety. When liability issues are also present, as in a school situation, an arborist should evaluate the site and return every one to two years to monitor changes in site conditions and tree development (Barrows, 1988).

Some basic guidelines are discussed here to help with risk assessment and to create a better understanding of a tree's typical structural behavior. Trees typically grow in a predictable manner with recurring themes and patterns. Understanding these patterns is important to help identify unusual events that could lead to the failure of the tree's structure (Matheny, 1994). Some defects result from natural developmental events, such as resprouting from stumps, poor branch spacing, or wound response (Figure 4-12).

FIG 4-12. Trees that are located in play areas must be assessed for hazardous tree conditions. The agency or school responsible for the play area must also weigh the naturalistic attributes it provides to the site versus the liability risk should a child climb it. (COURTESY OF BILL JORDAN.)

The most likely situation for tree failure combines structural defects with severe or unusual weather. Identifying structural defects such as the presence of decay or weak branch attachments is the first step in recognizing failure patterns.

Branch and trunk failures occur when unusual stress exceeds the strength of the wood or that strength is compromised by the presence of defects such as decay or disease. Roots are also potential failure sites on trees. They typically fail when root strength is reduced due to decay, disease, or injury.

Ground structure is another source of failure, and should be evaluated for site conditions that restrict root growth or have insufficient soil strength to anchor the tree. Ground failures are usually related to severe weather conditions and are typically more difficult to identify than branch, trunk, and root failures because they are not evidenced by specific and visible structural defects.

When examining the entire tree, there are several specific elements to evaluate. Overall form and symmetry should be examined, focusing on the balance and form of the crown, evidence of past pruning, spacing of scaffold branches, degree of lean, live crown ratio, number of trunks, crown class, age class, and special values associated with the tree.

Vigor and health of the tree should also be evaluated. Examine foliage color and density, as well as the color of bark in growth cracks. Look at woundwood development over past wounds and pruning cuts. Also, look for epicormic shoots and determine if they are typical for the species.

Once all these elements are examined, it is important for the layperson evaluating the tree to do further study to determine if the tree characteristics seem likely to cause failure. When the evaluation does not result in conclusive identification of hazard elements or healthy trees, a professional arborist should be called to answer questions.

Trees can show many clues to their health in their overall appearance and the conditions of their site. When evaluating a site, the key is to identify any behavior that is unusual or detrimental to the tree.

Most people can easily identify these clues to disease and decay when looking carefully, but it is extremely important that an expert be consulted when there is any doubt in the health of the tree. When children are involved, their safety is too important to allow any avoidable risk to go undetected.

MONITORING AND PROMOTING SAFETY

The National Program for Playground Safety in 1995 created the *National Action Plan for the Prevention of Playground Injuries*. This program is designed to help communities examine critical issues surrounding playground safety (NPPS, 2001). This provides a blueprint of playground safety designed to be used by adults who care about children. The program is based on four goals:

1. Design age-appropriate playgrounds

2. Provide proper surfacing under and around playgrounds

3. Provide proper supervision of children on playgrounds

4. Properly maintain playgrounds

The plan outlines the action to be taken by professional organizations, such as the American Alliance of Health, Physical Education, Recreation, and Dance, Association for Childhood Education International, National Association for Education of Young Children, National Recreation and Park Association, National Safety Council, and National Safe Kids Campaign.

This plan also applies to state and local governments and organizations. These groups, working together on all levels, strive to create safer play areas for all children.

Easy viewing of play areas is an important safety concern but one that can easily become a detriment to happy, safe play when care is not taken in its provision. Although easy viewing is important, often schools and public playgrounds facilitate this by removing all plant material that could block views so a single adult can supervise the entire play area. While facilitating supervision, this is detrimental to the character of the space and the experience children will have there.

In *The Experience of Nature,* similar perceptions toward the environment exist among people throughout the world based on research of different cultures, demographics, and gender (Kaplan, 1989). It was found that spaces in which nature is dominant and aspects of the environment favor outdoor survival are the most popular environments among all types of people. Three major desires dominated, one of which is a desire for mystery. Mystery stimulates curiosity, which leads to learning, and yet it is this quality that is so often stripped from schoolyards in the name of safety. Although safety issues are of paramount importance, safe principles can be implemented without taking the essence of mystery and beauty from children's landscapes.

CONCLUSION

It is important to balance safe spaces for children with stimulating nature-based playscapes. Safety can be provided through an understanding of potential dangers of a site, and even a novice designer can confidently create spaces for children that are safe and exciting. The National Program for Playground Safety teaches the principles of designing safe places, supervision guidelines for safe play, and how to meet high safety standards in children's play areas. Through such resources and with a firm understanding of the basic principles of playground safety, children's play areas can be safe.

Many of these national programs for children's safety focus on play structures and equipment of the schoolyard and public playground environment. Although these are the most common environment for children, it is important to remember that children need all types of stimulation through their play.

When providing natural environments, safety is an issue as well. Heights must be considered carefully, just as for built equipment, and other threats of nature must be recognized and addressed. Teaching rules of the outdoors to children as well as removing unsafe elements will improve safety in the outdoors. Every outdoor play area is different and decisions regarding each area must be made specific to that place.

Safety is a duty of designers, parents, and those who care for children. Not even the most carefully considered and well-designed play area or garden will be free of hazard, but caregivers can try to prevent as many injuries as possible and minimize their severity. Children's safety is crucial, and careful planning assures that their explorative and developmental play is safe and healthy.

CASE STUDIES

Clemson Elementary Outdoors, Clemson, SC

Date: Spring 1999 to present
Acres: 36 (14.6 hectares)
Cost: $174,800
Funding: PTA, grants, community donations, focused fundraisers

Clemson Elementary Outdoors is one of the most extensive developments in this country of children's outdoor environments within a schoolyard context. Outdoor gardens and play areas were implemented as extensions of the traditional classroom learning spaces at Clemson Elementary School in South Carolina. The vision for the Clemson Elementary Outdoors project was that it would be a multifaceted effort to assure that the new Clemson Elementary School had outdoor environments to help provide interdisciplinary, experiential, and environmental play and learning. This vision was predicated on research, observations, and experiences that tell us that children who are able to interact with peers and teachers in changeable and ecologically diverse settings expand their learning and social interaction skills to a greater degree than those in traditional and confined settings. The school's outdoor environments would be a vehicle for teaching all subjects and for motivating children to learn through their play and instinctive curiosity.

BACKGROUND

The Clemson community had waited a long time for a new elementary school to be built to replace the two old and inadequate schools which for 40 years had housed the elementary grades. When the site was selected and building plans announced, it was truly a cause for celebration and a call for community involvement. The 36-acre (14.6 hectares) site was recognized from the beginning as not only a place for a school building but also a place for an extensive outdoor learning laboratory. Approximately 25 acres (10.1 hectares) of the site had been open pasture, unused for the last 50 years. The remaining acreage consisted of a deciduous forest with a beautiful rocky stream running through the woods.

An architecture firm was hired and a building task force appointed to work directly with the project architect. The building task force consisted of school administrators, teachers, parents, community representatives, and Clemson University faculty. From the outset, the "three Clemsons"—Clemson Elementary, City of Clemson and Clemson University—worked as a team to make this school a true community school.

The idea for Clemson Elementary Outdoors began to gel when several of the task force members walked the site for the first time with school principal Dr. Paul Prichard, whose support and encouragement paved the way for the project's ultimate success. It quickly became obvious that there was much more potential for the site than a playground and ball field, and that the architect would need to understand the importance of the outdoor environment when designing the indoor environment.

The first step taken by the task force subcommittee for the outdoors was to write a vision statement for the school's outdoor environment including belief statements and specific recommendations regarding existing features of the site. This simple document became the basis for the architect and the task force to work from, and all the recommendations were accepted with minor alterations to only two. The philosophical forethought given to the site turned out to be critical to the preservation of existing desirable elements.

The belief statements in the task force document included the beliefs that:

- The pedagogical basis of the school's outdoor environments are the development of an interdisciplinary, experiential, and environmental thrust.

- Children learn best through the environment when they are able to interact with peers and teachers in diverse, changeable, ecologically valid settings.

- The school's outdoor environment should be a vehicle for teaching all subjects and for motivating children to learn through their play and instinctive curiosity.

❧ The experiential focus of the school's outdoor environments will help the children understand the environment as a human artifact—an economic, social, scientific, and cultural resource.

❧ Children will develop respect for themselves, for the people around them, and for their world as they come to understand the interactional support systems that thrive in the outdoors.

The task force subcommittee outlined specific recommendations to guide protection of the site, which included:

❧ Leave untouched from any kind of development or encroachment the wooded land at the east end of the property that bounds both sides of the stream running north to south across the property.

❧ Leave standing the single 100-year-old hickory tree at the east end of the property situated prior to the onset of the wooded area.

❧ Leave standing the circle of oak trees located at the southwest corner of the parcel and fronting on Berkeley Drive.

❧ Leave natural buffers between school grounds and the surrounding neighborhoods and highways as visual and sound buffers.

❧ Leave standing the forest of bamboo at the west end of the property along Berkeley Drive.

❧ Have the selected architectural firm work closely with members of the Building Task Force to assure that the placement of the school itself meets the physical requirements for effective school operation and allows for the following types of outdoor environments:

-natural areas	-nature trails
-gardens/compost bins/potting sheds	-meeting places
-age appropriate play areas	-amphitheater/stage
-adventure play areas	-athletic play areas
-animal habitats	-outdoor study areas

Although the written vision statement, beliefs, and recommendations provided direction for the project architect, there were numerous conflicts that arose during the planning stages. Months of discussions and decisions ensued, interspersed with compromise. The new school and the concept of Clemson Elementary Outdoors were linked from this point forward. Those planning for the school's outdoors, while hopeful of developing a unique and effective outdoor environment that fit the ecology of the place, knew the reality of the engineering and architectural design process. In a public school setting with limited construction funds and preset expectations of a school district relative to new construction, some approaches to construction would be unchangeable. For example, an 80-foot (24.4 meters) change in elevation from the front of the school to the back could have been accentuated with tiered development or placing wings of the building at differing elevations connected by ramps and steps. A two-story building that could reduce the footprint on the land in size and future resource consumption was also negated. A better ecological fit to the land and the more interesting visual presentation of multiple levels was lost. The design team had to pick up and accept some of these givens as a design challenge.

THE DESIGN TEAM

The design team for Clemson Elementary Outdoors did not fit the traditional model of design teams. Located in a university town, the planning and design involved many different individuals and groups. University professors and their classes in landscape architecture, horticulture, parks, recreation and tourism management, and architecture were all part of the design team contributing conceptual designs and layouts to the overall plan. The appointed building task force was part of the design team. These were people with various kinds of expertise to contribute to the development of the school and its outdoor environment, and of course teachers and administrators provided input throughout the design process.

Perhaps the most important members of the design team were the children who attended the school. These students were asked in an open ended format to share their visions of what the outdoors at their new school should look like. These visions were the starting point of the master plan for Clemson Elementary Outdoors. The drawings and letters of several hundred students were categorized and tallied by students in a recreation and leisure environments class at Clemson University.

The initial requests of the students could best be described as creative, diverse, and often hilarious. The expected groupings of playground equipment and athletic fields were included, and the design team wasn't especially surprised to see the students ask for a nature trail, greenhouse, and outdoor classroom. The team was pleasantly surprised to see numerous requests for gardens, ponds, and bird-watching areas, but was unprepared for requests such as a barn, pizza stand, helicopter landing pad, and horse racing track. The starting list of requests is found in Figure 4a-1.

The long list of students' dreams was reviewed by the design team and ultimately reduced to a list of ten planning areas that became the basis for the Clemson Elementary Outdoors master plan. This consolidated list drew from student ideas, the school's outdoor needs, and a healthy dose of creative thinking on the part of the design team and others. The initial working list included:

1. Playgrounds

2. Athletic fields

3. Courtyard gardens

4. Special interest gardens

5. Barn

6. Greenhouse

7. Nature areas

8. Outdoor classrooms

9. Amphitheater

10. Other significant areas

BASE MAP AND SITE INVENTORY

With 10 planning areas and a long list of children's ideas, students from Clemson University in landscape architecture and park and recreation planning began to map potential locations for the desired areas. This effort was paralleled with the architect's design and location of the school. It was important from the start that the outdoor environments fit with the school design and be located where the physical features of the site could accommodate the recommended environments. The architect provided grading and topographic maps to the design team during the planning process. The matching of planned outdoor environments with potential locations around the school was done by Clemson University students working closely with the design team.

PLAYGROUND AMENITIES

swings
sandbox
slides
climbers
4-square
hopscotch
sand box

CREATIVE BOX AMENITIES

fort
treehouse
climbing wall
tires
castle
clubhouse
pyramid

GARDEN AND LEARNING AREAS

nature trail
outdoor exploration area
outdoor museum
outdoor classroom
greenhouse
flower and vegetable gardens
pond
story gardens
music garden
art garden
fountains

TRACKS

horse racing track
dog racing track
go-cart track

ANIMAL RELATED AMENITIES

animal habitats
dog walking area
barn
petting zoo
fake spiders
bird watching area

SPORTS AREAS

skating rink
bowling
swimming pool
soccer/football field
kickball/baseball
basketball
batting cage
boxing ring
tennis courts
volleyball
running track

OTHER MISCELLANEOUS IDEAS

roller coaster
water park
pizza stand
sauna
laser tag
secret garden
golf putting green
boats
Pokemon room
fake school bus
mile long arcade
space station
helicopter landing pad
trampolines

FIG 4a-1: List of responses from children when asked "What do you want to see outdoors at your new school?" (COURTESY OF GINA K. MCLELLAN.)

SITE ANALYSIS AND PROGRAM

The Clemson Elementary School site offered many opportunities for outdoor environments, and its students had offered many ideas to fit those spaces. The site analysis and program step was an opportunity to fit the site, the ideas, and the learning and play needs into a master plan for the outdoors that would provide the guidance for implementation.

FIG 4a-2: A door from every classroom to the outdoors provides teachers and students with quick access to outdoor learning environments. (COURTESY OF GINA K. MCLELLAN.)

The importance of a great working relationship with the architect and the school principal cannot be emphasized enough. Early in the planning of this school, the design team realized that for teachers and students to maximize use of the outdoor environments, they needed easy access to those environments. The recommendation was made for each classroom to have a door providing direct access to the outdoors. The principal agreed, and the architect made that adaptation in the design (Figure 4a-2).

A second example of a good working relationship also came early in the planning process. The school site was home to a 100-year-old hickory tree that a certified arborist declared to be robust with no sign of disease—definitely a specimen worth saving. The tree seemed safe at first based on its location towards the back of the property. Then two things arose that threatened its life. First, the planned placement of the building on the property would necessitate the removal of the tree because of the school cafeteria abutting it. Second, the Department of Transportation (DOT) wanted the school driveway moved further from the road in front of the school because of traffic and safety.

The design team members who also served on the building task force went quickly back to the drawing board. They came up with a plan that shifted the school slightly in its placement on the site and altered the driveway to meet the specifications requested by the DOT, which would work because the school had been shifted on the site enough to accommodate the driveway redesign. The architect revised the location of the school and then worked to get DOT to accept the driveway redesign. The tree was saved!

A third example of the necessity of a good relationship arose when the school district requested that all trees and vegetation along the two roads bounding the property be totally removed. Visibility seemed to be favored so a new school could be seen by passersby. The design team again approached the architect to explain to the school district that leaving trees between the school site and the highway would be a good noise buffer, and that the lower visibility of the school from the highway might be a benefit in terms of safety. The architect was also able to transmit to the school district that the circle of large mature oak trees near the front corner of the property and totally out of the way of any proposed development was actually a historical tie to the earlier use of the property as a farm.

Learning Standards

As the design team continued to mesh the ideas for the outdoors into the master plan, the members continually aligned the desired environments with their learning potential. Each was analyzed in terms of its potential contribution to the pedagogical goals of the school and the physical, mental, and social development of the students. If the environment could contribute to these goals, it would become part of the Clemson Elementary Outdoors master plan (Figure 4a-3). Fol-

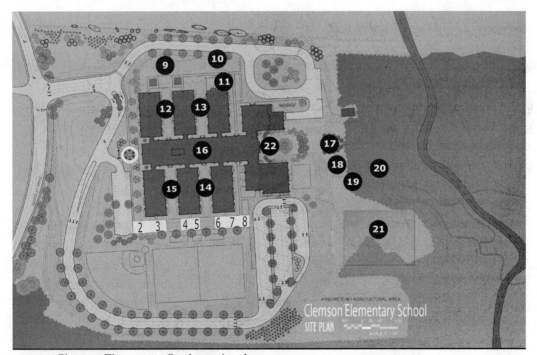

FIG 4a-3: Clemson Elementary Outdoors site plan. (COURTESY OF GINA K. MCLELLAN.)

lowing this procedure, considering the design of the school, and merging the ideas of the students, a master plan was formulated that included:

1. Entrance plaza garden
2. Golf putting green
3. Carolina Fence Garden
4. Fossil dig
5. Music exploration garden
6. Environmental exploration area
7. Arbor sitting garden
8. Art garden
9. Playground for first and second grade
10. Playground for K–4 and K–5
11. Kindergarten covered play area
12. Alice in Wonderland courtyard garden
13. Peter Rabbit courtyard garden
14. The Secret Garden courtyard garden
15. Harry Potter courtyard garden
16. Interior courtyard for native plants
17. Barn
18. Greenhouse and experimental gardens
19. Nature trail
20. Outdoor classroom
21. Adventure play area
22. Amphitheater

Sustainability

The design team considered sustainable development to be a necessity for Clemson Elementary Outdoors. The sustainable approaches used in the outdoors would align with the concepts applied in the design of the building itself such as the geothermal heating and air conditioning system and the gym floor made from recycled athletic shoe soles.

The sustainable focus in the outdoor project planning was conservation of resources. Native plant materials requiring little or no watering beyond rainfall to hardscapes made from local natural materials to addition of plantings that would ultimately help shield the building from natural elements such as sun were all sustainable approaches.

Flexibility

Flexibility is a key word in teaching and education, and the Clemson Elementary Outdoors project is no different. The master plan for the outdoors was a plan designed to guide, but to also be amenable to change based on need or simply a better idea. There were also places throughout the schoolyard where teachers and classes could establish whatever kind of outdoor environment suited their needs.

The flexibility of the plan was tested only a month after the new school opened its doors, and it came in the wake of 9/11. The fifth-grade classes wanted a way to externalize what they felt about 9/11, to honor those who died in the attacks, and to promote peace. These students adapted what was in the master plan as an art garden and turned it into a beautifully designed and landscaped peace garden. The art focus was represented in the hand-made messages and sculptures interspersed in the garden.

A second special area was built during the first year the school opened. It was a reading garden dedicated to the teenage daughter of the school's principal who died following a brief illness. The America Reads program, operated through Clemson University and conducted at Clemson Elementary, served as the catalyst for this garden and planned, funded, and built it with the help of the America Reads children. The Chrissy Prichard Reading Garden is a tranquil place where many children enjoy reading.

A third example is a small area outside a kindergarten classroom that does not open into one of the storybook courtyard gardens. With the help of parents, this teacher built a small garden with a pond and bridge crossing over the pond. The children monitor the tadpole development and check on the goldfish as they feed them. With butterfly bushes, there is always an element of excitement as the children identify what kind are coming to visit. Birds are welcome, too (Figure 4a-4).

FIG 4a-4: This pocket garden outside a kindergarten classroom was added to *Clemson Elementary Outdoors* by the teacher and her students with help from parents. (COURTESY OF GINA K. MCLELLAN.)

DESIGN AND IMPLEMENTATION

The Clemson Elementary Outdoors (CEO) schoolyard was designed to be a multifaceted environment that would provide interdisciplinary, experiential, and environmental play and learning. It was designed to provide learning and play environments, and to add a comfortable and sustainable aesthetic quality to the school's outdoors. A project of this size and diversity in a school setting should be expected to take a long time, so the speed at which the CEO developed was surprising. Within the first four years of opening, 16 of the 22 originally planned environments were in place.

As with many children's environments, there are a number of key reasons that the environments become reality. In the case of Clemson Elementary Outdoors, the success has been a combination of enthusiastic support of the school, an extraordinary group of parent volunteers, the City of Clemson, Clemson University, and other members of the surrounding community.

Conceptual designs were completed before the school opened, with several hundred students involved from across the University campus. Landscape architecture and horticulture students translated conceptual designs and children's ideas into landscape and planting designs. The following breakouts by CEO environments will provide a general idea of how the designs and accompanying implementations were approached.

Front Entrance Plaza Garden and Sculpture

The circular garden at the front of the school was initially designed and planted by a horticulture class at Clemson University. Particular attention was paid to soil preparation, because red clay is dominant on the school site. The extra care in preparing the soil is still paying off today. The garden boasts some evergreen shrubs to maintain foliage throughout the winter, with the remaining plantings a mixture of perennials. Winter color is added with winter flowering annuals. First- and fifth-grade students are often spotted weeding, fertilizing, and generally caring for the garden (Figure 4a-5).

FIG 4a-5: First graders help to weed and plant this entrance plaza garden before a creative writing session that will connect back to their garden experience. (COURTESY OF GINA K. MCLELLAN.)

A second element in the entrance plaza is a beautifully detailed bronze sculpture of a little girl sitting on a bench reading Charlotte's Web. The idea of bronze sculptures was conceived by a group of Clemson University students during a CEO conceptual planning session. *Wildlife Bronzes by Carl McCleskey* in Cloudland, GA, was identified as a desired source, and the process of securing the bronze sculpture began. A parent volunteer coordinated the writing of an accommodation's tax grant through the City of Clemson and coordinated an art festival to bring visitors to the community as the grant required. A sculpture class at the University poured the bronze in the molds provided by the artist to help us reduce the cost of the sculpture overall. The artist then put the molded pieces together and did all the finishing work. This entire process covered a period of more than two years (Figure 4a-6).

FIG 4a-6: Carl McClesky's *Wondrous World* sculpture welcomes children to sit and read. (COURTESY OF GINA K. MCLELLAN.)

Carolina Fence Garden

A Carolina Fence Garden is a reflection of the natural and cultural elements of the State of South Carolina and features the state's official bird, flower, stone, grass, butterfly, and wildflower. In addition, a Carolina Fence Garden incorporates a split-rail fence as a reflection of the early farming and livestock practices.

The 25 × 25-foot (7.6 × 7.6 meters) area designated for the Carolina Fence Garden was adopted by a landscape implementation class at Clemson University. They coordinated the design of the garden and the selection of plant materials. This group of students also installed the garden using locally harvested black locust for the split-rail fence, a species that is very durable for this type of use (Figures 4a-7 and 4a-8).

FIG 4a-7: The Carolina Fence Garden is a reflection of the natural and cultural elements of South Carolina. (PHOTO CREDIT: GINA K. MCLELLAN.)

FIG 4a-8: The arbor provides a cozy social spot where children can visit. (COURTESY OF GINA K. MCLELLAN.)

The garden has filled in quickly, is beautiful, and in addition to attracting the targeted wildlife species also attracts many children who find numerous play and socialization opportunities in it. The funding for this garden was provided by Duke Power Company and the Landscapes for Learning program at Clemson University.

Music Garden

The details of the music garden design and installation are presented in detail in Chapter 3. The music garden is an excellent example of a community built environment from start to finish.

Arbor Sitting Garden

This garden is a lush setting designed and installed by fifth-grade students at the school. Led by a teacher with both interest and talent in gardening, they planned a garden with a variety of plantings liked by children. In the 25 × 25-foot (7.6 × 7.6 meters) area, paths traverse it with benches for sitting, reading, talking or just watching butterflies. The students added numerous functional and decorative elements to the garden such as bird feeders and rain gauges. Funding for this area came from gardening grants secured by a teacher.

Peace Garden

Originally planned to be an art garden, 9/11 changed the focus. Children in the school wanted to transfer their personal grief to a symbol of peace. The garden was designed by students and planted by students. River rocks are scattered throughout the garden with the word peace painted on each rock in a different language, reflecting not only the call for peace but also the international diversity of students in this school. First graders placed white paper doves that they made in the garden at its opening. Plant materials for this garden were donated by people and businesses in the community.

Playground for K–4 and K–5

South Carolina, like many states, requires a separate playground for kindergarten. This is an excellent requirement, particularly in terms of safety and socialization. Both teachers and students had extensive input into the design and development of their playground in the CEO project. With those ideas, the design team made up of school representatives, CEO planners, and parents juggled the benefits of play and movement for 4- and 5-year-olds with the types of environments and equipment that would provide those benefits. It was decided that a variety of areas would serve the children

FIG 4a-9: Friends! (COURTESY OF GINA K. MCLELLAN.)

better than the playground of the past with one major piece of playground equipment. The design team recognized the need for developing the proprioceptive sense, or movement in space, and the vestibular, or equilibrium, sense. Swings and slides promote both. Climbing and balancing apparatus were included in the playground design to encourage kinesthetic development, or how bones and joints work relative to each other. A sand play area provides a tactile environment for play. A large panda and a turtle made concrete accentuate the play area and can be climbed on or under (Figures 4a-9, 4a-10, and 4a-11).

Funding for this play area came from PTA fundraisers over several years in anticipation of a new school being built. The equipment was purchased from a playground equipment manufacturing company, and was installed by parent volunteers.

FIG 4a-10: These children are pretending to be turtles and are hiding in their shells. (COURTESY OF GINA K. MCLELLAN.)

Playground for First and Second Grade

FIG 4a-11: Kindergartners help their principal cut the ribbon to their new playground. They were involved in the process from planning through construction and with the official opening. (COURTESY OF GINA K. MCLELLAN.)

The design team took a new approach with the first- and second-grade play area. Rather than follow the current trend of placing one big piece of playground equipment in the designated area, the team used a multienvironment approach. Each of the six environments found in this playground has a different focus and look from each of the other environments. The river is filled with blue shredded rubber that the children cross by jumping from one stepping stone to another as two big alligators look on from the river banks. Another journey finds children running through the savanna or hiding behind tall grasses from the huge precast concrete lion or quietly digging in the savanna sands. Then the jungle calls. Here the tree climbers are full of children being watched by the giant gorilla. Then it's on to the mountains where the climbing wall becomes the mountain of choice. An open grassland provides an area for traditional games of chase or where balls can be kicked around. Back in the school neighborhood, the children find one more piece of equipment with numerous skill development challenges (Figures 4a-12, 4a-13, 4a-14, and 4a-15).

In anticipation of a new school being built, the PTA had conducted fundraisers over several years. The PTA monies funded this play area, which was completely installed by parent volunteers. The safety surfacing chosen for this play area and the kindergarten area is engineered wood fiber. It is much less expensive than rubber products, lasts a long time, meets the Americans with Disabilities Act (ADA) accessibility requirements, and can be put in place by volunteers.

Storybook Courtyards

Early in the planning process for CEO, the children indicated they wanted story gardens. When this wish surfaced in their early drawings of what they wanted to see outdoors at their new school, the design team decided to talk with the children

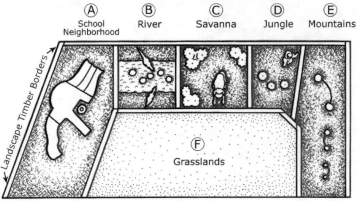

Playgroung Design for Clemson Elementary
1st & 2nd Grade Play Space - Conceptual Design

(A) School Neighborhood (B) River (C) Savanna (D) Jungle (E) Mountains

Landscape Timber Borders

(F) Grasslands

Sidewalk

(A) Area where playground equipment is located

(B) Blue shredded rubber makes river: Two alligators along "river"

(C) Lion lies in savanna

(D) Gorilla watches as children climb "trees"

(E) "Mountains" include climbing wall

(F) Grasslands provide an open area for activities

Note:
Safety surface is engineered wood fiber except in river

FIG 4a-12: Planning for this play area began by fitting children's ideas into a geographical theme. (COURTESY OF BARBARA SIEGEL RYAN.)

FIG 4a-13: "Don't fall in the river or the alligators might get you" is a familiar call of children crossing the "river" on "stepping stones." (COURTESY OF GINA K. MCLELLAN.)

FIG 4a-14: The lion watches over all the play that takes place in the savanna. (COURTESY OF GINA K. MCLELLAN.)

SCHOOLYARDS, PLAYGROUNDS, AND BACKYARDS ✳ 213

FIG 4a-15: The gorilla eyes children climbing trees in the jungle. (COURTESY OF GINA K. MCLELLAN.)

FIG 4a-16: These fourth graders are maintaining the cauldron of flowers in the Harry Potter courtyard. (COURTESY OF GINA K. MCLELLAN.)

to get a better idea of what they were suggesting. Through that interview process, it became obvious that they wanted gardens that reflected certain stories. The design team then decided that the four courtyards between the six wings of the new school would be ideal for story gardens.

To get input from as many children as possible in selecting which stories should be reflected in these gardens, the media specialist had children identify their favorite books with gardens as integral parts of the stories. As the books were identified over a period of about two weeks, each book was put on display in the school library. Finally, the children voted. The stories selected for the four courtyard gardens were *Alice in Wonderland*, *Peter Rabbit*, *The Secret Garden*, and *Harry Potter* (Figure 4a-16).

Details of the design process used with these gardens can be found in the case study in Chapter 2.

Interior Courtyard for Native Plants

A small courtyard opened to the sky but surrounded by administrative offices and a conference room was the perfect setting for a small garden for reading and receptions. A focus on native plants for the area made sense in terms of sustainability, and a landscape design class at Clemson University again took the lead in the design and implementation. This courtyard radiates a peaceful feeling with a fountain accenting the native plants, and provides a friendly home for the school's pet rabbit.

It was important in designing an interior space such as this to keep in mind its inaccessibility in terms of getting maintenance equipment into it. The native plant approach was an excellent choice requiring little maintenance. One indigenous plant that proved to be too aggressive was removed after two years. Cast aluminum benches and a walk-through arbor are key elements of this garden's atmosphere. Funding for the interior courtyard garden came from the Clemson Elementary School Homework Center and the Clemson Garden Club.

The Barn

Children are known for their love of animals, so it should not have surprised the CEO planners when dozens of students requested a barn for their new school. The question then became "how can it be done"? The design team first looked around to see if another elementary school anywhere had a barn. When they didn't find one, they began to research the potential pedagogical connection between barn based programs and the K–5 curriculum standards. Not only did standards directly link to animals and farms, but the interdisciplinary education possibilities using a barn seemed endless (Figures 4a-17, 4a-18, and 4a-19).

The design team then began to research barn types with the help of agri-

FIG 4a-17: Benefits to children resulting from interactions with animals are endless. (COURTESY OF GINA K. MCLELLAN.)

FIG 4a-18: Animals provide an extensive interdisciplinary stage for teaching and elicit contagious enthusiasm among the students. (COURTESY OF GINA K. MCLELLAN.)

FIG 4a-19: Programs in the barn at Clemson Elementary School mix lessons in math, science and language arts with activities with animals. (COURTESY OF GINA K. MCLELLAN.)

FIG 4a-20: *Great Clemson Cow Drop* T-shirt designs help set the atmosphere for this event. (COURTESY OF GINA K. MCLELLAN.)

FIG 4a-21: Waiting to see which grid the cow picks is fun for everyone, especially if the observer "owns" a grid on the field. (COURTESY OF GINA K. MCLELLAN.)

culture and animal science students at Clemson University. The approximate location for a barn was determined and entered in the master plan. Wanting a barn for the CEO program and getting one would, of course, mean securing the money to build one. A parks, recreation, and tourism management class at the University began to work with the elementary school students to devise a fundraiser for the barn, and the Great Clemson Cow Drop was born. A cow drop operates on the premise that a T-shirt purchase gets the purchaser a grid on the cow drop field. Grids are randomly assigned after shirt sales end and a cow is brought onto the gridded field at the appointed time. For Clemson Elementary, it was another activity at the annual fall carnival. The cow then wanders around the field grazing and when her "product" is dropped in a grid, the owner of that grid wins the prize money. The cow drop was held three consecutive years to raise enough money for a barn. The fourth year raised money to build the paddock fences and outfit the barn with stall mats, feed buckets, and cleaning supplies (Figure 4a-20, 4a-21, and 4a-22).

FIG 4a-22: The Clemson Elementary barn allows multiple venues for handling animals and children. (COURTESY OF GINA K. MCLELLAN.)

FIG 4a-23: This 24' by 24' barn and its paddock is a versatile learning environment for Clemson Elementary School. (COURTESY OF GINA K. MCLELLAN.)

The barn was delivered to Clemson on a flatbed truck in large pieces. A parent volunteer who was a contractor pulled a crew off a job, brought them to the school, and assembled the barn on the prepared footings in less than two days (Figure 4a-23).

Experimental Gardens and Greenhouse

While the school was still under construction, there was no access to the actual construction site for work related to the CEO program. Access was, however, allowed to the area behind the school, so the design team completed the plans for an experimental garden area and began implementation. The slope was relatively steep so the plan called for 6 × 6-foot (1.8 × 1.8 meters) raised beds to be built into the hillside. Clemson Elementary School had been assigned an AmeriCorps team for 6 weeks, and one of the team's projects was to build the 17 raised garden beds (Figures 4a-24 and 4a-25).

FIG 4a-24: Volunteers of all ages helped plant daffodils on "Super Bulb Saturday." (COURTESY OF GINA K. MCLELLAN.)

FIG 4a-25: The product of "Super Bulb Saturday" once spring arrives is a lively display of hundreds of bright yellow daffodils. (COURTESY OF GINA K. MCLELLAN.)

These beds were designed to be adopted by classes who wanted to experiment with growing things—vegetables, lettuce, fruits. Less than two months after completing the beds and eight months before the school would be occupied, the CEO program received 2,000 daffodil bulbs through the America the Beautiful Fund. It was January when the bulbs arrived, so parent volunteers lined up a donation of enough potting soil to fill all 17 beds. Then they sent a note home with students announcing "Super Bulb Saturday," hoping to get about 20 volunteers to move soil into the beds and plant the bulbs. On the designated Saturday morning, 140 volunteers showed up to work; and in less than two hours, soil and bulbs were in place. The first spring the school was open, there were 17 beautiful beds of daffodils. The greenhouse planned for the CEO has not yet been built. Grants are being sought to fund that facility.

Nature Trail

With over ten acres of deciduous hardwood forest with a beautiful stream and a natural spring, a nature trail was one element that had to be part of CEO. Resource management students in parks, recreation, and tourism accepted the responsibility of inventorying the area and determining the best route for the nature trail. Once the location was marked, a local Boy Scout troop under the guidance of a troop leader and forestry professor, began construction of the nature trail. The scouts and leader identified significant forest elements as they worked and did research for interpretive signs along the trail. They printed and laminated interpretive signs and built and mounted posts to hold the signs (Figure 4a-26).

The natural spring and an old-growth area of timber were located across the stream necessitating a bridge. A civil engineering professor had his students design, build, and mount two bridges across the stream. The bridges are steel construction with wood decking, are bolted onto concrete footings on both sides of the stream, and will last a very long time.

FIG 4a-26: Clemson Elementary students love trips along their nature trail. These Clemson University students have captivated their audience with tales of carnivorous plants. (COURTESY OF GINA K. MCLELLAN.)

A graduate class in conservation biology from Clemson University inventoried the entire forest acreage and the stream and provided benchmark counts of mammals, tree species, freshwater species, and aquatic insects. They also built and mounted bat houses and nesting boxes for owls and other birds (Figure 4a-27).

Outdoor Classroom

One Boy Scout who worked on the nature trail needed an Eagle Scout project and offered to build an outdoor classroom along the nature trail. It was constructed on a gently sloping hillside leading down to the stream and can accommodate up to two classes of students at a time. The setting is one that piques the interest of any child. The high quality of craftsmanship that went into the benches and teacher's table will assure their durability for years to come.

FIG 4a-27: A rocky stream on school property is a welcomed place for discovering the secrets of nature. (COURTESY OF GINA K. MCLELLAN.)

Adventure Play Area

The playground at the base of the hill and behind the school is geared for the older grade levels. The original idea was to make this area as much like a true adventure play area as possible. Due to the nature of an adventure playground, there was little support for it by the teachers, so it was altered to fit a model of creative play rather than adventure play. Although there is one piece of play equipment and a climbing wall, the rest of the area is being devoted to creative play. Fifteen poles of varying heights are fixed in the ground and have no rules for use. They can be whatever the children decide to make them. New components will be added to the area as money is available, and the next item on that list is a fort built into the hillside (Figure 4a-28).

FIG 4a-28: This winged climbing wall offers children numerous options for maneuvering the walls by going up, around, over and from one to the other. (COURTESY OF GINA K. MCLELLAN.)

Edwards Amphitheater

A U-shaped area at the back of the school that centers directly on a 100-year-old hickory tree was the perfect setting for an amphitheater. It was designed by the architect during the planning of the school; but by the end of that design process, it became obvious that there would be no money to construct it within the budget allocated for the new school.

The amphitheater was a desirable facility for many reasons, so the design team looked to other sources of funding. It was redesigned by a parent on the team who was an architect himself. With a new drawing in hand, the search for funding began in earnest.

A former long-time president of Clemson University had once owned the land the school was built on, and he also served on the Building Task Force. To honor this well-respected member of the Clemson community, donors with ties to the University provided funds to help build the amphitheater. With additional funding from the after-school program, the amphitheater became a reality.

The dedication ceremony was rightfully a celebration of Dr. R.C. Edward's contributions but was also a celebration of the Clemson Elementary Outdoors project and the roles of the "three Clemsons" in building it.

CONCLUSION

Clemson Elementary Outdoors is a work in progress. Dr. Paul Prichard has retired as principal, and Dr. Ken Weichel, the new principal, is continuing the development efforts. CEO should always be changing, and change will keep it vibrant. It is a testimony to what Clemson Elementary School, Clemson University, and the City of Clemson have accomplished by joining forces as partners with a united goal of providing quality outdoor play and learning environments for the children of Clemson.

By spring of the first year the school was open, more than 20,000 hours of volunteer labor had been logged. More than 800 Clemson University students had worked on planning, design, and implementation of the CEO. More than $70,000 in equipment and supplies were on the ground, and the CEO project was still moving at full speed. Three years later, the number of volunteer hours had doubled, as had the number of Clemson University students who had helped. Expenditures were over $170,000.

The *Giving Tree* hangs on a wall looking out into the amphitheater, and bears the names of major contributors to the CEO project. These donors never asked for recognition; they only wanted to help with the cause. There are hundreds of volunteers whose contributions are great, and they, too, never asked for recognition. What they are all content with is the knowledge that they have helped to provide places at this elementary school where environment-based education can thrive and help students "realize that school isn't supposed to be a polite form of incarceration, but a portal to the wider world" (Louv, 2005) (Figure 4a-29).

FIG 4a-29: *"The Giving Tree,"* a small but important way of saying "Thanks" to all who made Clemson Elementary Outdoors a reality. (PHOTO CREDIT: GINA K. MCLELLAN.)

CREDITS

Clemson Elementary Outdoors Design Team:

Dr. Paul N. Prichard, Principal

Dr. Gina K. McLellan, Clemson Elementary Outdoors Master Plan

David Allison, Building Task Force Representative

Donza Mattison, Project Architect, McMillan, Smith, and Partners, Architects, PLLC

Clemson Elementary Faculty and Staff

Clemson Elementary Students

Professor Mary Haque, Clemson University Horticulture Department

Dr. Lolly Tai, Landscape Architecture Department at Clemson University

Clemson University students in the Departments of Parks, Recreation and Tourism Management, Horticulture and Landscape Architecture

Clemson Elementary Outdoors Construction Team:

Chris Nigro, Lead Parent Volunteer

Clemson Elementary PTA

Clemson Elementary After School Care Program

Clemson Elementary Administrators, Faculty and Students

Parent and Community Volunteers

AmeriCorps

Dr. Serji Amirkanian, Storybook Courtyard Gardens thematic elements

Dr. Scott Schiff, Nature Trail bridges

Jim Cobb, School District of Pickens County

Renee Roux, Vic Shelburne, Barbara Weaver and Carolyn Taylor for Music
   Garden, Nature Trail, Reading Garden and fundraising
Robert Haselton, Barn construction
Greenworld, Inc. for storybook courtyards hardscapes
Clemson University students in the Departments of Parks, Recreation and
   Tourism Management, Horticulture, Landscape Architecture, and Civil
   Engineering

Whitehall Elementary School, Anderson, SC

Opening date: May 2004 Carolina Fence Garden and Renovated Memorial
Outdoor Learning Lab
Acres: .5 (.2 hectare)
Cost: $100,000 not including community volunteer help
Funding: Grants, volunteers, service learning, in-kind donations, school fund
raising

MISSION AND PURPOSE

The Whitehall Elementary School collaboration had multiple objectives such as
honoring the memory of Dennis Hepler, a former principal of the school, while
celebrating the concept of outdoor education by providing spaces for learning in
the landscape. Pedagogical objectives included providing an opportunity for students
to learn and develop useful skill sets through participation in a project with
community impact.

THE DESIGN TEAM

Using a service learning model in which students apply what they are learning in
class to projects for "real-world" clients outside of the classroom setting, Clemson
University design students and faculty worked with elementary school administrators,
teachers, students, and community leaders to design learning landscapes
for Whitehall Elementary School (Figure 4b-1).

THE DESIGN

The design for Whitehall Elementary School includes a memorial park, a Carolina
Fence Garden, a woodland nature area, a vegetable learning garden, and a

landscape design for the front entrance of the school. The Carolina Fence Garden includes plant material and structures unique to South Carolina. This garden can be used to teach students about history and state symbols, such as yellow jessamine, the state flower; the Carolina Wren, represented by a birdhouse to provide shelter for the state bird; and clusters of blue granite, the state rock (Figure 4b-2).

FIG 4b-1. An urban forester instructs college design students in how to assess tree health on the Whitehall Elementary School memorial garden site. (COURTESY OF MARY TAYLOR HAQUE.)

EDUCATIONAL ASPECTS

Objectives of the Sustainable Schools project included goals of involving both university and K–12 school students in identifying environmental problems, using critical thinking skills to propose solutions, and the taking of action to effect change. Environmental issues addressed in the projects included energy efficiency, recycling, soil and water conservation, low maintenance, biodiversity, and wildlife habitat creation and preservation. The sustainable schools project is creating outdoor learning environments while contributing to the personal, intellectual, and social growth of participants. In the movement from observation to action coupled with reflection, writing, and celebration, students in the service learning paradigm have integrated research, design, and sustainability; oral, written, and graphic communication; collaboration; and community connection. Interdisciplinary cooperation within the institution, continuity between the institution and the community, and dialogue with the greater service learning community encourage both students and faculty to become

FIG 4b-2. This newly planted "Carolina Fence Garden" is used to teach students about state history and culture at Whitehall Elementary School. (COURTESY OF MARY TAYLOR HAQUE.)

citizens of the world, modeling a process that others can emulate and build upon in an ongoing cycle of individual and community growth and interaction.

PARTICIPATORY ASPECTS

Service learning is providing institutions of higher education and K–12 schools with opportunities to meet, collaborate, and work toward common goals. Students are learning about research, design, and sustainability; oral, written, and graphic communication; collaboration; and connection. During the transition from observation to action, students and faculty are becoming citizens of a greater community where they affect change while modeling a process for others to emulate. This collaborative process, which included research and analysis; planning and design; implementation and action; sharing and celebration; reflection and evaluation; and recognition, allows all members of the learning community to participate in the planning and design of the garden as well as in the construction, use, and maintenance of the garden (Figure 4b-3).

FIG 4b-3. College students become active citizens of a greater community when they affect change through service learning projects for K–12 schools. (COURTESY OF MARY TAYLOR HAQUE.)

UNIQUE CHARACTERISTICS OF THE GARDEN

The garden reflects both the unique past and the future of Whitehall Elementary School as it honors a former principal while creating learning stations featuring plants and other elements native to South Carolina. The collaborative design process provided unique opportunities for students to compile a portfolio of their work, which included both design drawings and reflective writing, a type of writing in which students analyze and process what they are learning. Student work was also celebrated and displayed at the official project groundbreaking ceremony and again at the formal dedication attended by school, city, and county officials and community members (Figure 4b-4). Every student in the university design class earned South Carolina Wildlife Federation certification as a "Habitat Steward" for successfully completing the Habitat Steward program and providing outstanding environmental and community stewardship and leadership.

FUNDING

Volunteers and members of the school landscape committee conducted successful fund-raising efforts simultaneously with the design process. Contributions included in-kind donations of plants, labor, and supplies from local businesses and citizens. Four Anderson County Council members designated improvement funds for the project, and the Master Gardeners Association of Anderson County approved a local grant. Additional grant fund-

FIG 4b-4. Whitehall Elementary School pupils practice communication skills at the groundbreaking ceremony. (COURTESY OF ANGIE BRUHJELL.)

ing from the Cooperative State Research, Education, and Extension Service, U.S. Department of Agriculture, supported the project. The National Wildlife Federation (NWF) and the South Carolina Wildlife Federation (SCWF) also provided resources through workshops and through their schoolyard habitat program.

THE DESIGN TEAM

Strong reciprocal community relationships were formed as both university and elementary school students worked with teachers, parents, volunteers, and administrators to design educational landscapes for Whitehall Elementary School. Clemson University students were welcomed as vital partners along with the outdoor learning lab committee. The committee included the current building administration, five retired Whitehall principals, the Anderson County Director of Transportation, the Director of Operations for a large construction firm, as well as the PTO president, vice-president, and volunteer chair. Other vital members included selected teachers, representatives from Keep America Beautiful of Anderson County, an urban forester, the president of the student body, members of the Master Gardeners, Association of Anderson County, and School District Five buildings and grounds personnel. Members of the design team also partnered to help construct the project.

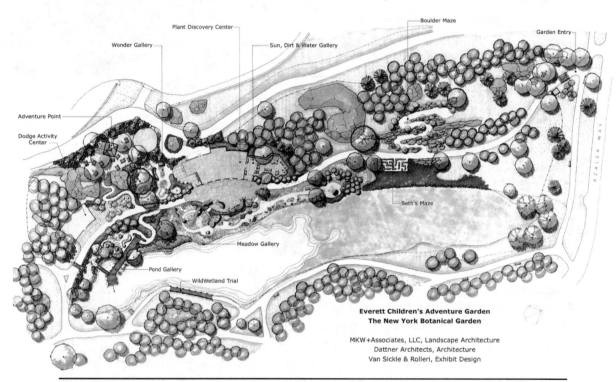

Plant Discovery Center

Boulder Maze

Wonder Gallery

Garden Entry

Sun, Dirt & Water Gallery

Adventure Point

Dodge Activity
Center

Beth's Maze

Meadow Gallery

Pond Gallery

WildWetland Trial

AZALEA WAY

**Everett Children's Adventure Garden
The New York Botanical Garden**

MKW+Associates, LLC, Landscape Architecture
Dattner Architects, Architecture
Van Sickle & Rolleri, Exhibit Design

Everett Children's Adventure Garden, The New York Botanical Garden, New York, NY. (COURTESY OF
NEW YORK BOTANICAL GARDEN.)

CHAPTER 5

Sustainable Landscape Concepts

With the beginning of the new century, many are finding that the increased ecological awareness brought about by Rachel Carson and others in the 1960s is just as important, or perhaps even more so today. As a result, many educational institutions are looking for effective ways to integrate environmental sustainability into their curriculum, and parents are looking for ways to help their children become environmentally sensitive stewards. Landscapes can provide stimulating settings for producing and shaping beliefs, and can provide opportunities for students to envision and affect change in a positive way. Developing healthy habits such as recycling waste and reducing consumption are powerful ways to take action. Children can also learn to design sustainable landscapes that provide economic benefits through energy efficiency and financial savings through reduced maintenance while enhancing the quality of life for future generations. Their education may be strengthened by a conscious effort to teach children to feel environmental responsibility. Major categories to plan for when designing environmentally friendly landscapes include:

1. Water conservation

2. Energy conservation

3. Low maintenance

4. Waste reduction (reduce, reuse, and recycle)

5. Wildlife habitat

Look for information on how to establish a National Wildlife Federation certified habitat in Chapter Two, but read further here to find information about enhancement of microclimate and biodiversity, reduction of resource inputs and waste, and ways to save money while creating an environmentally friendly and healthy landscape for and with children. Children have the potential to literally make the world a better place. Teachers, parents, and other caregivers should take advantage of the idealism of youth to spark enthusiasm for the environment and teach children how to be stewards of the land. Youth are empowered when they discover that they can take action and make a difference in the world around them.

Water Conservation

Water is the most desired play element for children, and is a valuable natural resource that needs to be protected and conserved. Droughts in recent years have spotlighted our dependence on previously plentiful water supplies even in areas like the Southeast, where water seems abundant compared to many areas in the Southwest. Water rationing and outright bans on watering landscapes have imposed severe limitations on the landscape industry as well as on gardeners. Teaching children to prepare for drought now is a sensible alternative to suffering the consequences later. When basic horticultural principles are employed with an emphasis on water efficiency, landscapes use much less water and are drought tolerant. Combining water conservation techniques with landscaping is a concept known as Xeriscape or "dry landscape." Xeriscaping combines sound horticultural practices to conserve water while maintaining a beautiful landscape. The seven basic Xeriscape principles are:

1. Careful planning and design

2. Appropriate lawn areas

3. Thorough soil preparation

4. Appropriate use of plant materials

5. Effective and efficient watering methods (Figure 5-1)

6. Use of mulch on trees, shrubs, and flower beds

7. Proper landscape maintenance.

FIG 5-1. Xeriscape principles are critical to the success of the Carolina Children's Garden, which is in the sandhills of South Carolina. Water drains quickly through the sandy soils, so appropriate use of shade, mulch, lawn, and plant selection is important. (COURTESY OF RANDY L. WILSON.)

Each of these principles should be used when designing and managing a landscape. The greatest water efficiency is realized when all seven principles are used in combination. Studies have shown water-use reductions of 30 to 60% or more in landscapes that employ the seven basic principles of Xeriscape. Combining lower maintenance costs with greater survivability of landscape plants in times of water shortage, a Xeriscape is economically attractive. Xeriscaping is a good way to teach children to become socially responsible stewards of our environment.

PLANNING AND DESIGN

When designing a new landscape or renovating an existing one, planning the landscape on paper is the best place to begin. Follow the design process outlined in Chapter Two, and be sure to note the site's microclimates (Figure 5-2). To achieve the greatest water efficiency, the landscape plan can incorporate "hydrozones"—areas within a design that receive either low, moderate, or high amounts of water. All plants within a zone have the same water requirements and can be watered as a group.

Appropriate Lawn Areas

Children love to play on grass. It's cool, soft, natural surface makes a great place to run, do cartwheels, and play tag and other games. Lawn areas usually receive

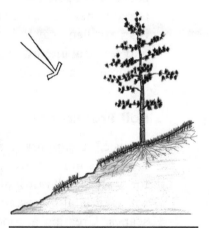

FIG 5-2. The microclimate for steep south or west facing slopes is often hot and dry. If plants are not properly established, erosion occurs and valuable water is lost as runoff. (COURTESY OF GAGE COUCH.)

FIG 5-3. A small grassy area surrounded by drought tolerant plants provides water-conserving space for free play in the Carolina Children's Garden. (COURTESY OF RANDY L. WILSON.)

more water and require more maintenance than any other area in the landscape, so they should be used appropriately. Grasses should be carefully selected depending on location, use and desired maintenance programs. In-depth information on establishing lawns is available from most extension offices.

Mowing the lawn at the proper height will help improve the drought-tolerance of turfgrass. If grass is mowed frequently enough, the lawn clippings should be left on the lawn to mulch the turf and reduce fertility requirements. The beauty and quality of a lawn cannot be replaced, but the traditional size, design, and maintenance programs must be changed to meet water restrictions and drought conditions. Native grasses provide a low-maintenance alternative, and meadows of native grasses can provide beautiful, water-conserving habitat for wildlife. Transitioning from a traditional mowed lawn to a taller meadow look is an excellent way to incorporate variety, rhythm, and seasonal interest in a way that is interesting to children (Figure 5-3).

Soil Preparation

A basic life-support system of the landscape, soil is the medium for root growth and a reservoir for water and nutrients. Properly conditioned soil is of vital importance to the health of landscapes. Creating a good soil environment from the start will bring great dividends in the future, and children take great pleasure in the process (see sections on composting and vermicomposting) (Figure 5-4). A good soil is porous and will

FIG 5-4. Properly conditioned soil makes it easier for children to grow healthy plants. (COURTESY OF BILL JORDAN.)

drain freely, yet retains water and nutrients in a form available to plants. When unsure about the soils in a landscape, call your county extension agent or bring in a soil sample for a complete analysis and recommendations for improvement. Addition of organic matter to the soil is the single most important method of improving soil structure. Organic matter increases water and nutrient-holding capacity, aeration, and drainage. Plants establish more rapidly when planted in well-prepared soils. They are healthier and more vigorous, and they have greater disease and drought resistance.

Some sections of the country receive sporadic rainfall, and excessive moisture may be a problem in poorly drained areas during winter and spring. Drainage may be improved by changing the slope of the site, adding subsurface drainage, or planting at a higher grade.

Plant Selection

Lush, green landscapes and seasonal color provided by a variety of plants are a hallmark of many parts of the country. Xeriscapes can achieve this beauty while reducing water consumption. Xeriscaping does not require that landscapes become cactus gardens in all regions. However, careful planning and plant selection are important to ensure the investment and longevity of landscape plants in a Xeriscape (Figure 5-5). Any plant is a candidate for use in a Xeriscape; the key to success is how the plant is used. In general, the greatest success is achieved when plants are placed in an environment most similar to the plant's native habitat. However, many plants are adaptable and will perform equally well in different situations. Determining a plant's adaptability often requires research into its cultural requirements, which must be compatible with the plant's placement in the landscape plan.

When selecting plants for a landscape, a designer must consider a number of site conditions such as sun exposure, wind, soil conditions, and drainage patterns (Figures 5-6

FIG 5-5. Many plants are available at nurseries. Be sure to select ones that are well adapted to your site conditions. (COURTESY OF MARY TAYLOR HAQUE.)

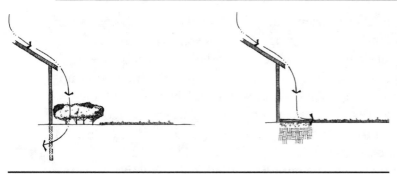

Figures 5-6 and 5-7. Drainage patterns should be considered when designing around buildings. To avoid moisture problems in basements, water should drain away from the building and then be dispersed over a surface that can absorb water. (COURTESY OF GAGE COUCH.)

and 5-7). It is important to know the sun/shade patterns of the landscape, for some plants are tolerant of morning sun but not of the intensely hot afternoon sun, while other plants require both to flower prolifically. Soil type, structure, and pH are factors that will determine the success of a particular plant. Although soil factors can be modified for a given planting, the dominant soil conditions will ultimately be the most important when choosing plants.

Plants requiring areas that are wetter than the site being designed should be used in an area that will naturally receive more water, such as a low spot, near a spigot, or where runoff from the roof or paved areas will provide extra water. Likewise, plants that are adapted to areas that are drier than your site should be located in the design where they will benefit from good drainage, such as slopes, tops of berms, or nonirrigated areas (Figure 5-8).

It is important to bear in mind, however, that a plant tolerant of dry conditions may be stronger and faster growing when it receives extra moisture. Just because a plant is drought tolerant does not mean it has to be used in a dry spot in the landscape. Drainage is often important, and careful attention should be given to placement of species requiring good drainage.

FIG 5-8. Low areas near the distant lake have been planted with moisture-loving plants, while higher areas on sandy soils in the foreground were planted with drought-tolerant selections, creating hydrozones in the Carolina Children's Garden landscape. (COURTESY OF RANDY L. WILSON.)

It is very important to note that most plants are drought tolerant only after they become established in the landscape. It is critical, therefore, that irrigation be provided when necessary for the first and second growing season so that children will have successful experiences with growing plants.

Effective and Efficient Watering Methods

The use of efficient irrigation systems is a technique inherent to Xeriscape planning. Irrigation systems should provide appropriate amounts of water at critical times. The irrigation system must be designed to correlate directly to the planting zones, known as "hydrozones." The planting zones are created by grouping together plants of similar water requirements. Turf areas need to be irrigated by a separate system or by using timers to control the amount of water the turf receives versus the requirements for ornamental shrubs, perennials, and annual beds. Irrigation systems are available in various forms: the traditional pop-up sprinklers and overhead sprinklers and the more water-efficient subsurface, drip and soaker-hose systems.

Drip and microsprinkler irrigation systems have many advantages.

1. They are precise.

2. They keep the foliage dry.

3. They are simple to install.

4. They can be used almost anywhere.

5. They reduce the number of replacement plants necessary by ensuring better plant survival.

6. They reduce erosion and water loss due to evaporation.

7. They reduce splash-transmitted, soil-borne diseases associated with traditional sprinkler irrigation.

8. They reduce or prevent mildew and decay because water does not hit house siding.

9. They reduce weed populations.

10. The landscape can be enjoyed at any time because there is no water spray to inhibit activities.

11. They efficiently supply water slowly so that puddling is not a problem.

12. Because water is placed directly at the root zone, the plant's water requirements are met by using much less water than conventional methods.

A soaker hose is also an economical choice for an irrigation system. The hose is small and easy for children to handle. Installation is relatively simple and the hose works well in small gardens.

Drip systems, soaker hoses, and subsurface systems have a low profile in the landscape, so vandalism is almost eliminated. However, they can be easily damaged accidentally by children digging in a garden. These systems use much less water than conventional irrigation systems and create attractive Xeriscape landscapes and gardens.

Sprinklers for appropriate turf areas can be used efficiently. If children will be playing on the lawn, be sure to choose a system that minimizes the possibility of accidentally running into irrigation heads. Watering deeply and infrequently encourages deep rooting of plants, which promotes greater drought tolerance (Figure 5-9).

FIG 5-9. Irrigation was not available at this school site, so children used buckets to water this newly planted tree. (COURTESY OF BILL JORDAN.)

Mulching Trees, Shrubs, and Flower Beds

As much as 75% of the rainfall landing on bare ground is lost due to evaporation and runoff. This loss can be enormously reduced when the proper mulch is utilized. Mulch helps to ensure plant survival and is an important component of Xeriscapes. The two basic types of mulches are organic and inorganic. Some examples of organic mulches are pine straw, pine bark mininuggets, pine bark mulch, shredded hardwood bark, wood chip mulch, composted leaves, and grass clippings. Inorganic mulches include pebbles, gravel, black plastic, and landscape fabrics. Although many materials can be used for mulches, price, availability, and aesthetic appeal often dictate choice.

The best mulches are usually fine-textured and nonmatting organic materials. An organic mulch should decompose slowly, be free of weed seed, and should not be easily washed away by rainfall. Mulches that decompose quickly, such as grass clippings, are less desirable. Gravel mulches reflect heat to the plant's canopy, thereby increasing water loss from the leaves. Children are tempted to throw gravel at each other, so avoid pebbles and gravel in children's landscapes. Organic mulches have many benefits in the landscape. They:

1. Increase water-holding capacity of the soil.

2. Reduce the amount of water lost by runoff.

3. Moderate extreme soil temperature fluctuations.

4. Reduce weed competition.

5. Reduce the incidence of soil-related diseases.

6. Prevent soil erosion.

7. Reduce soil compaction, improve soil structure, and add nutrients and humus to the soil.

8. Create an aesthetically pleasing design feature.

9. Prevent mechanical damage to trees and shrubs caused by mowers and weed-eaters.

10. Prevent splash-back and staining of house foundation and siding.

FIG 5-10. Organic mulches should be spread out to the drip line of trees to promote plant health. (COURTESY OF BILL JORDAN.)

Woody landscape plants need an application of approximately three inches of a good mulch. This should be applied under the plant and at least out to the drip line, because the root system can extend two to three times the spread of the plant (Figure 5-10). Mulches are critical in a successful Xeriscape and cannot be overemphasized.

Proper Landscape Maintenance

Xeriscape designs that implement all seven principles have been shown to reduce maintenance by as much as 50%. There are nine main reasons for reduced maintenance. Xeriscape designs:

1. Reduce water loss and soil erosion through careful planning, design, and implementation.

2. Reduce mowing by limiting lawn areas and utilizing proper fertilization techniques.

3. Reduce fertilization through soil preparation.

4. Reduce pruning of trees and shrubs through proper plant selection and through restricted applications of water and fertilizer.

5. Reduce replacement plants through proper watering methods and soil preparation.

6. Reduce weeds through proper mulching.

7. Reduce disease and pest problems by creating less stress on plants through the methods listed above.

8. Reduce irrigation through proper maintenance and selection of plants with healthier root systems.

9. Reduce costly damage to house/structures and foundations through proper selection, placement, and minimum watering near the house.

Xeriscape maintenance practices make disease and pest problems less prevalent because they reduce stress on plants. The plants have been hardened-off by using good irrigation techniques. Correct amounts and timing of fertilizers, especially nitrogen, keep the plants healthier. Soil temperature extremes and weed competition are partially eliminated due to mulching. All of these maintenance practices keep plants from being stressed, reducing pest and disease problems.

Water requirements can be lowered because root systems of plants are healthier (more fibrous and deeper) when proper care and a good maintenance schedule are followed. By being aware of plant signs that indicate the need of water, a gardener can irrigate more efficiently, conserve water, and produce healthier plants.

Teamwork among administrators, teachers, children, parents, landscape designers, landscape contractors, and maintenance crews is crucial to maximize efficiency of the seven Xeriscape principles. A successful Xeriscape allows gardeners more leisure time to enjoy the environment that they have created as part of the team. In addition, all involved can experience the satisfaction of having contributed to the quality of life for others by conserving a limited, precious, and threatened natural resource: water (Figure 5-11).

FIG 5-11. Teamwork between elementary, high school, and college students resulted in the design and installation of a water conserving landscape at Townville Elementary School. (COURTESY OF BILL JORDAN.)

Energy Conservation

Landscapes can be designed to make schools, playgrounds, and gardens comfortable and energy efficient as well as fun and educational. Proper landscape design with climate in mind can help children on playgrounds and in gardens avoid problems such as heat exhaustion or skin cancers later in life. Comfortable, safe, and energy conserving landscapes can also help protect the environment because fewer natural resources are used.

HUMAN COMFORT AND CLIMATE

Human comfort is affected by several aspects of climate including sun (solar radiation), wind, temperature, and precipitation (rain, fog, dew, sleet, snow). These factors can be modified to some degree to help make schools and landscapes more comfortable to live and work in. Natural elements like vegetation, water, and landforms as well as man-made materials can be used to modify local climate and create more comfortable and livable "microclimates."

MICROCLIMATE

The microclimate is the climate on your site (Figure 5-12). You can modify the microclimate through design choices. For example, if your children's garden is to be in a cool, mountainous region, you may locate it on a sunny southern slope to take advantage of a warmer microclimate. If you live in a hot, humid region, you

FIG 5-12. Microclimates can be created by planting trees to slow winter winds or to block the sun's rays. (COURTESY OF GAGE COUCH AND BARBARA SIEGEL RYAN.)

can surround your playground with abundant shade to create a cooler microclimate. Nearby bodies of water may increase your site's humidity or decrease its air temperature, creating a microclimate within the larger context of the region. Oceans, lakes, pools, and fountains also provide physical and psychological cooling effects (Figure 5-13).

Different from the average local conditions, the microclimate may be more sunny, shady, windy, calm, rainy, moist, snowy, or dry. These factors influence the type of plants that may or may not grow in your microclimate.

FIG 5-13. Even a scarecrow seems cooler when sitting next to water on a hot day! (COURTESY OF MARY TAYLOR HAQUE.)

LAND FORMS AND TOPOGRAPHY FOR CLIMATE CONTROL

Landform plays an important role in controlling and directing wind. When siting a school or garden, keep in mind the principle that cold air sinks and warm air rises. Do not locate the building on top of a hill where wind speeds are often 30% higher, or in the bottom of a valley where cold air pockets exist. These high and low points should be left as natural areas, creating wildlife corridors and beautiful natural areas for scenic views and shared recreation.

Locating schools on gentle slopes in between high and low points preserves the views throughout the region. With proper planning, bike and

FIG 5-14. Bike trails like the Silver Comet Trail in Atlanta, GA, provide alternate transportation routes and recreation opportunities. (COURTESY OF MARY TAYLOR HAQUE.)

walking trails can network through these green corridors. This provides an energy-efficient alternative to automobiles and provides children and adults recreation opportunities in their community (Figure 5-14).

USING PLANTS FOR CLIMATE CONTROL

Plants play a significant role in climate control and in helping to achieve energy efficiency. They are the best of all solar radiation control devices (Figure 5-15). Trees, shrubs, groundcovers, and turf, or even a combination of these, are effective in reducing direct as well as reflected solar radiation. An understory of mulch, shrubs, and groundcovers should be planted under trees, especially if they are surrounded with paving. Trees planted in clusters will keep each other cool.

FIG 5-15. Deciduous trees provide excellent solar radiation control. (COURTESY OF GAGE COUCH AND BARBARA SIEGEL RYAN.)

USING TREES FOR SOLAR RADIATION CONTROL AND EVAPOTRANSPIRATION

The specific placement of plants has direct effects on temperature control. Trees cool buildings and outdoor areas not only by shading, but also by cooling the air around them through a process called evapotranspiration (Figure 5-16).

Shading and evapotranspiration, the process by which a plant actively moves and releases water vapor from trees can reduce surrounding air temperatures as much as 9°F (−13°C). Since cool air sinks to the ground, air temperatures under trees can be as much as 25°F (−4°C) cooler than air temperatures above asphalt paving nearby. Further, studies by the Lawrence

Berkeley Laboratory found summer daytime air temperatures to be 3° to 6°F cooler in tree-shaded neighborhoods vs. treeless areas. A consciously well-planned landscape can reduce an unshaded home's summer air-conditioning costs by 15% to 50%. In the case of a small mobile home in Pennsylvania, a study reported air-conditioning savings of as much as 75%. (http://www.eere.energy.gov, accessed 2005).

On playgrounds in temperate areas, use deciduous trees that drop their leaves during the winter and allow the sun's rays to filter through the branches. Consider safety and avoid brittle trees that may break in a storm and cause safety or litter problems.

USING PLANTS FOR WIND CONTROL

Wind speed can influence perceived air temperature in both summer and winter. For example, a 10 mph (16 kph) northwesterly wind can make an air temperature of 44°F (7°C) feels like 32°F (0°C). Evergreen or coniferous trees and shrubs can reduce the influence of cold winter winds. A windbreak, planted along the edge of a playground, perpendicular to prevailing winds, can provide protection from cold winter winds, helping to make playgrounds more comfortable in winter (Figure 5-17).

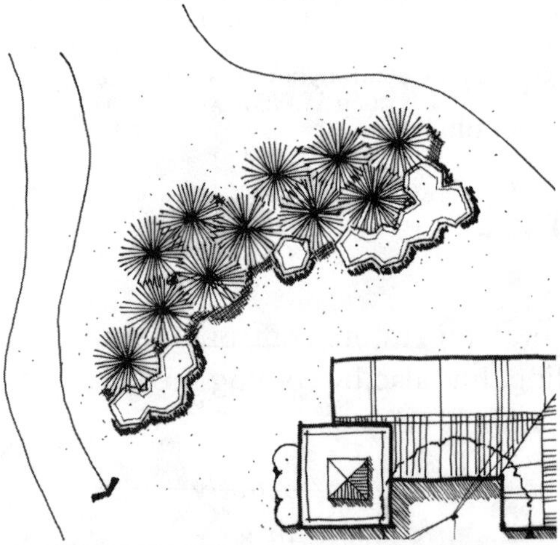

Breezes can be directed in the summertime to cool outdoor play areas. Planting trees to funnel prevailing winds into the area can keep children cooler.

FIG 5-16. Both trees and man-made structures provide shade at the Children's Garden of Brookgreen Gardens in South Carolina. Trees also cool surrounding areas through evapotranspiration. (COURTESY OF MARY TAYLOR HAQUE.)

FIG 5-17. Plants can be placed to divert winter winds around outdoor play areas and buildings, creating a more comfortable and energy efficient setting. (COURTESY OF GAGE COUCH.)

MAN-MADE SHADING DEVICES AND MATERIALS FOR CLIMATE CONTROL

Arbors

In exposed areas where immediate shade is needed, an arbor or trellis planted with vines is a quick solution. Because deciduous plants follow climatic variations, a vine will be covered with shady leaves in summer and bare in winter, providing a self-adjusting device that changes with the seasons.

Dark- and Light-Colored Surfaces

The built environment includes many types of surfaces such as roofs, walls, and pavement. Elements that are dark absorb heat; conversely, light surfaces reflect heat and stay cooler. Thus, asphalt absorbs heat while concrete reflects heat. Dark-colored surfaces such as roofs, asphalt basketball courts, and parking lots contribute to the heat island effect and should be cooled when possible. The sun may be captured indirectly from heated retaining walls, pavements, and isolated objects such as stone, and can help to make use of outdoor play areas during cold seasons.

The measure of a surface's reflectivity is known as albedo. Although a light-colored surface reflects heat, some find it uncomfortable to the eye due to glare. Glare can be reduced when designing with concrete, for example, by texturing the surface, which disperses light rays in several directions. Use a balance of trees and selected surface colors to obtain the most energy-efficient play environment.

RECYCLED, RENEWABLE, AND LOW ENERGY-CONSUMING MATERIALS

When choosing construction materials for your landscape, use biodegradable, recycled, and low energy-consuming materials, which are locally produced (Figures 5-18 and 5-19). Recycled concrete sidewalks make attractive retaining walls. Local municipalities can save money and space in local landfills by letting you have the large blocks of concrete associated with demolition or redevelopment of an urban area (Figure 5-20). Soil, cement, brick, and stone are also good materials for thermal mass; they will absorb heat during the day and radiate heat out at night. Outdoor play areas of such materials can often be used comfortably day and night in both winter and summer if shaded by deciduous trees.

Figures 5-18 and 5-19. Instead of sending a dead tree to the landfill, have it cut to make seats or stepping surfaces. (COURTESY OF MARY TAYLOR HAQUE.)

Steel, aluminum, and plastics are considered energy-intensive materials and should be used in moderation or when they have been recycled. Using alternative renewable materials will extend our ability to adequately maintain our resources for future generations. By purchasing locally produced building materials, you will save transportation costs involving both money and energy, and will support your neighbors in the local labor market (Figure 5-21).

FIG 5-20. This retaining wall at Wonderland Gardens, GA is made from a combination of recycled concrete sidewalks and stone. (COURTESY OF MARY TAYLOR HAQUE.)

Porous Paving Materials

Paved play surfaces, roads, and parking areas can get very hot. Asphalt parking areas can reach 195°F (90.5°C) in the summer. Rain falling on such hot surfaces can warm to 90°F (32°C) before running off into creeks or lakes where it harms temperature-sensitive species of plants and animals. Such runoff also carries

FIG 5-21. Using renewable, local materials to build this bench saved transportation costs and energy. (COURTESY OF MARY TAYLOR HAQUE.)

toxic pollutants. Parked cars on hot pavement are not only uncomfortable to get into; they emit gas fumes that contribute to air pollution.

Porous paving materials allow 15 to 25 percent of rainwater to seep through tiny holes in the pavement. They act as a filter, catching oils and chemical pollutants while also allowing cooler earth temperatures from below to cool the pavement. Light colors can be used to make porous paving more reflective, further reducing temperatures.

An exciting example of a more sustainable landscape paving material, porous paving is strong, durable, and is less susceptible than traditional concrete to freeze–thaw cracking because of the open spaces. These materials can be used to teach children how to cool temperatures while improving water quality in their neighborhood.

CHECKLIST FOR LANDSCAPE DESIGN WITH CLIMATE CONTROL AND ENERGY EFFICIENCY (Figure 5-22)

☐ Plants are placed to block hot sun.

☐ Evergreen plants are placed to buffer cold winter winds.

☐ Plants are used to direct summer breezes.

☐ Light-colored paving material is used on paved play surfaces, roads, and parking areas.

☐ Textured paving surfaces are used to reduce glare.

FIG 5-22. Checklists and sketches are powerful tools for analyzing your site when designing for climate control and energy efficiency. (COURTESY OF BARBARA SIEGEL RYAN.)

☐ Porous paving materials are used to reduce storm-water runoff and cool temperatures.

☐ Low energy-consuming, locally produced, and recycled materials have been selected.

Low Maintenance

Landscape maintenance usually includes pruning, mowing, watering, weeding, and controlling insects and diseases. Following are ideas to make maintenance of children's gardens more efficient.

To Reduce Pruning

A well-designed landscape should not require much pruning. Select plants with an ultimate height and spread to fit the space that it is intended for. Far too many people plant small shrubs from one-gallon pots without realizing that they may grow a foot or more a year and soon cover the sidewalk or play equipment. Such plants will either have to be pruned every year or replaced with an appropriate-sized specimen.

Specify plants with a natural form (i.e., columnar, rounded, vase shaped, weeping, etc.) appropriate for its spot. For example, a graceful forsythia will not have be pruned into an ugly round "meatball" if it is given plenty of room to spread out. The natural look is popular and easy, too. Design with informal balance rather than formal balance so that plants do not have to "mirror" each other in the design, and much less pruning will be necessary.

To Reduce Watering

Specify plants that can adapt to the available soil moisture and that are drought tolerant if necessary. Plants native to the area are often appropriate. Be especially careful in selecting plants for south- or west-facing slopes where water runs off and sun is intense.

Avoid containers and planter boxes that collect little natural rainwater. Containers are exposed to drying wind, sun, and heat. If planters are used, leave the bottom open to the ground so that plant roots can access water tables and water can be pulled by capillary action.

If plants are to be surrounded by paving materials, specify porous paving or a material such as brick layed on sand so water can seep through the cracks and provide plants with more moisture.

Locate plants outside of roof overhangs. Materials such as attractive river stones or mulch can add texture and interest in such areas to reduce the amount of soil moisture lost through evaporation.

To Reduce Weeding

Specify two- to three-inch thick mulches of a coarse texture to shade out weeds and to provide a dry surface that does not promote germination of weed seeds that may blow into a bed. Select plants that are aggressive enough to compete with weeds and that will shade them out as much as possible. Spunbond fabrics that allow water percolation and air exchange may be used under mulches to discourage weeds in particularly difficult areas.

To Eliminate Spraying for Insects and Diseases

Design with plants that have as few pest problems as possible. Locate plants with particular attention to cultural details such as sun, drainage, moisture, and climatic requirements so that they will not be exposed to stress conditions. Stress increases susceptibility to disease and insect infestation.

Invite trained personnel who can "scout" for pest problems in the community. A good scout reduces the necessity of preventative spray programs that often call for spraying when it is not necessary. If problems are discovered, ask for natural pest controls, such as natural predators.

Both children and adults enjoy putting up birdhouses for insect eating birds like Purple Martins. Their flight is delightful to watch and they consume many unwanted insects.

To Reduce Mowing

Turfgrass makes a great play surface for children, but it's sometimes overdone. Where appropriate, reduce turf areas and replace them with ground covers, mulch, natural wooded areas, or meadows that do not require constant mowing. Where turf is necessary, specify slow growing species or cultivars. Use ground covers or mulches instead of grass around trees to reduce hand edging and trimming and to protect trees from mechanical damage and the future disease or insect infestation that often results. When laying out borders between lawn areas and shrub beds, woods, or meadows, design with lines that allow mowers to negotiate smoothly without having to back up.

MISCELLANEOUS TIPS FOR LOW-MAINTENANCE DESIGN

In high-use areas where turf is difficult to maintain, use an inexpensive alternative like mulch.

If the budget allows, porous paving may be used on pedestrian areas in heavy shade where grass is difficult to grow and where a gathering space is needed.

Some trees produce fruit that might be beautiful on the tree, but when placed improperly in the landscape can cause "litter" problems as they drop their fruit or shed twigs onto a manicured lawn, sidewalk, or playground. Sweet gum and crabapples trees are examples of plants that should not be placed over grassy or paved areas where litter would be considered a maintenance problem. When designing around existing plants with such litter problems, incorporate a deep ground cover that will absorb fallen fruit, twigs, etc.

Some plants like southern magnolia and American holly have low-growing limbs that reach the ground and cover up any fruit or leaf drop. Specify that such plants be placed so they can keep their limbs to the ground, hiding fallen fruit, leaves, and twigs. Children love to climb Southern magnolias, and they make great forts with fragrant flowers and interesting fruit.

When designing and implementing a new landscape, specify proper planting and installation techniques; a high-quality implementation job reduces stress on plants and encourages a vigorous, healthy landscape that requires less maintenance.

Native Plants

If your children like nature and want to select low-maintenance plants that are well adapted to your climate, soils, and available water, choose native plants. Natives provide an ecosystem friendly habitat for birds and butterflies, which add color, movement, and song to your landscape. Native plants are indigenous and can restore a sense of place, providing relief from the homogenous landscapes seen wherever you go. They offer a wide array of color, texture, form, and fragrance to stimulate your senses and add beauty to your landscape.

Using a diverse selection of plants will give you year round seasonal interest. Spring, summer, fall, and winter will each hold a special charm, and you can marvel at the changing seasons. Diversity also brings stability, and you are less likely to lose a large section of your plants to insects or disease.

Do not destroy wild stands of native plants by digging them from the woods or meadows. Many native plants are available commercially. They should be bought from reputable nurseries where they have been propagated or grown without damage to wild habitats. Ask a local landscape architect, urban forester, grower, extension agent, or member of the Native Plant Society for help with native plants that perform well in your area.

Composting

As landfills are filling up and garbage incineration is becoming an unacceptable practice, it is clear that change is in order to ensure successful disposal of waste. Reducing consumption and waste, as well as recycling waste, are two exercises that provide partial solutions. Composting takes care of waste by converting it into soil for use in the garden. The process is educational, interesting, and easy for children. They can help build compost bins, and can place organic waste in a pile and wait for it to decompose while studying the biological, chemical, and physical processes involved. Most of the work of decomposition is completed by microorganisms, including fungi, bacteria, and actinomycete. The work of these microorganisms can be explored by daily temperature readings and even competitions between children to get separate compost piles to the highest possible temperatures or to hold the high temperatures the longest. Compost piles under optimum conditions reach temperatures of 120°F to 150°F (49°C to 66°C). By understanding the principles of physics, chemistry, and biology that act physically on the compost process, children begin to understand the workings of the scientific and natural world.

One safety concern with composting is combustion when temperatures rise too high. Teachers and administrators should be aware of this danger and regulate the size of the piles, so excessive heat will not build in the centers. Turning piles frequently will also help alleviate this potential problem, which can become a learning experience for children.

Instead of bagging and sending fallen leaves and grass clippings to the landfill, compost them in a designated area on site. As children tune in to the living world around them, they will realize the importance of protecting and enriching the soil. Supporting the earthworms and microorganisms in their own soil helps children form an ancient system that supports native plants in a beautiful and functional way.

CHECKLIST: IDEAS TO HELP YOU DESIGN FOR LOW MAINTENANCE

☐ Specify plants whose ultimate height and spread will fit the space available.

☐ Use an informal design.

☐ Use plants whose natural form (i.e., columnar, rounded, vase shaped, weeping, etc.) is appropriate for the space.

☐ Use plants that are drought tolerant, particularly on south- or west-facing slopes.

☐ Do not use containers and planter boxes that collect little natural rainwater unless they are open from the bottom so that plant roots can access ground water.

☐ When paving around plants, use porous paving materials such as brick laid on sand so water can seep through the cracks.

☐ Use organic mulches two to three inches deep.

☐ Use plants that are aggressive enough to compete with weeds.

☐ Use landscape fabrics under mulch to deter weeds.

☐ Use plants with minimal pest problems.

☐ Use plants that are adapted to local climatic conditions.

☐ Use trained personnel to "scout" for pest problems.

☐ Use ground covers, woods, meadows, or mulches to replace unnecessary turf.

☐ Use slow growing species of turf when possible.

☐ Use ground covers or mulches near trees.

☐ Use smooth bed lines to allow mowers to negotiate easily.

☐ Use low-maintenance alternatives such as mulch or porous paving for high-use or shady areas.

☐ Avoid using plants with litter problems.

☐ Around existing plants with litter problems, incorporate mulch or a deep groundcover to absorb fallen fruit and twigs.

☐ Use proper planting and installation techniques.

☐ Use native plants.

☐ Compost organic waste.

CASE STUDIES

Awbury Arboretum: Nature Trails and Wildlife Habitats, Philadelphia, PA

Arboretum established: 1916
Educational programs established: 1980s
Acres: 55 (22.3 hectares)
Cost Estimate: N/A
Funding: Foundations, individuals, corporations, and government funding

MISSION AND PURPOSE

Awbury Arboretum is a public garden for education and "the quiet enjoyment of nature." Its mission is " . . . to preserve and interpret Awbury's historic house and landscape, thereby connecting an urban community with nature and history" (Awbury Arboretum Field Trips, 2004a." Awbury's unique location in the heart of an urban Philadelphia neighborhood strongly influences the nature of the programs and services it provides, including: a School Field Trip Program, Summer Nature Program, a new Landscape Apprentice Program for at-risk young adults, a community garden, volunteer and service learning opportunities, public outreach events, and rental of the Francis Cope House for weddings, conferences, and other community events (Kaufman, personal communication, 2005). Its Children's Educational Program ties all its lessons to the current Pennsylvania curriculum standards.

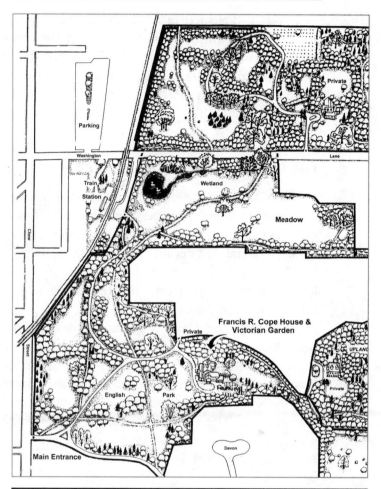

The 55-acre (22.3 hectares) Awbury Arboretum provides children with the opportunity to learn from the historic house and landscape. (COURTESY OF AWBURY.)

It was established in 1852 by Henry Cope, a Philadelphia civic leader and shipping merchant who built his home at Awbury. Later, 30 additional homes were built for Henry's extended family. In 1916, the current 55-acre (22.3 hectares) landscape and the historic Francis Cope house were given in trust by Cope Family members to City Parks Association, to be used as a public garden (Awbury Arboretum, 2004b).

THE PLANNING AND DESIGN TEAM

Gerald Kaufman, the executive director of Awbury, together with eight staff members and 22 board members, are committed to preserving and interpreting the values and interests of the founding Cope family, including environmental stewardship, social justice, and strong connections to the surrounding community. Kaufman said, "We are preserving the aesthetic values evident in the historic landscape and Cope House designs, while adapting to current imperatives (Awbury Arboretum, 2005)."

Currently, the team is updating their strategic plan for the 55-acre (22.3 hectares) property "that will educate, inform and engage visitors and the surrounding community." They plan to conduct extensive audience research through focus groups and surveys to determine the community's interests, the questions they have about the historic site, and the way they would like to spend their leisure time. The team plans to use the research results to brainstorm themes and activities that would best interpret Awbury's house and landscape (Awbury Arboretum, 2004b).

THE DESIGN

Today, Awbury offers a rich Children's Educational Field Trip Program during the school year that supports the Pennsylvania curriculum standards as well as an active Summer Nature Program (Awbury Arboretum Field Trips, 2004a).

Elsie Viehman, Director of Education, said "For some of the children in the inner city, there are few trees in their neighborhood and Awbury provides them the opportunity to fully immerse themselves in nature. We provide opportunities for active learning" (Viehman, personal communication 2005) (Figure 5a-1). According to Jenny Carey, a Board Member, "Awbury is not what you might consider to be a traditional 'Children's Garden,' but it is a garden that is wonder-

FIG 5a-1. Gathered in front of the 1862 Cope House, children use binoculars as part of the *Adaptations* lesson. (COURTESY OF ELSIE VIEHMAN.)

fully used by large groups of mainly minority, inner city children. It is within walking distance of at least eight schools. Approximately 5,000 kids participate in Awbury's education program during the year!" (Carey, personal communication, 2005).

Unique Characteristics of the Garden

Awbury Arboretum provides a rich natural setting for children to experience and learn from the historic house and landscape. Each of the environments provides opportunities for learning and participation "in a fully non-threatening, natural environment where all lessons are hands-on and minds-on" (Viehman, personal communication 2005).

Educational and Participatory Aspects

FIG 5a-2. Awbury Arboretum's environmentally oriented programs expose children to a diversity of plants and wildlife. Students built a giant bird's nest out of twigs. (COURTESY OF ELSIE VIEHMAN.)

The Children's Educational Field Trips are 90 minutes in duration and accommodate 10–60 children from schools, home schools, clubs, scouts, day care, and recreation centers. Classes are divided into smaller groups of 8–10 for more effective and hands-on learning. The environmentally oriented programs expose children to plants that are common as well as unusual (Figure 5a-2); insects and animals such as cicadas and birds; recycling and water issues such as composting and wetlands (Figure 5a-3); and history

FIG 5a-3. Many of Awbury Arboretum's education programs fulfill the Pennsylvania State Curriculum Standards regarding "Environment & Ecology." Children observe frog behavior at the pond's edge. (COURTESY OF ELSIE VIEHMAN.)

FIG 5a-4. Through the "Discovery" education program, children explore the meadows, woods and wetlands. Kids get a close up look at a slug. (COURTESY OF ELSIE VIEHMAN.)

such as the Victorian times and the Native Americans. The educational program is grouped into preschool–grade 1 and grades 2–5, 2–8, and 5–8. The program is designed to educate children about a variety of themes and is described below. Teachers receive pre- and post-visit materials to help integrate their experience at Awbury into the curriculum (Awbury Arboretum Field Trips 2004a; Awbury Arboretum, 2005).

THE CHILDREN'S EDUCATIONAL FIELD TRIP PROGRAM

GRADES	FULFILLS PENNSYLVANIA STANDARDS	PROGRAM
Preschool–1 (during any season)		*Discovery:* Children explore Awbury's meadows, woods and wetlands (Figure 5a-4). Guides encourage 3–6-year olds to become "young scientists" and use their senses as they look for treasures like leaves, seeds, and bugs. Fairy Tale Forest: Using children's literature as a basis, children

		explore Awbury's fields and forest, gardens, and ponds to find real examples of nature depicted in familiar stories.
2–5	-Environment & Ecology 4.7	*Birds at Awbury:* In Awbury's bird sanctuary, children discover the life and language of our feathered friends through careful observation and thought-provoking activities based on the Pennsylvania Songbirds Curriculum.
2–8 (April–June)	-Environment & Ecology 4.1	*Wetlands:* Awbury's pond and stream habitats are ideally scaled for young observers to hike as they search for bullfrogs, dragonflies, red-winged blackbirds and migratory birds. Students also discover new native species planted streamside to enhance the wetlands' ability to retain and purify storm water runoff. Scooping and identifying pond critters included.
2–8	-History 8.2 -Environment & Ecology 4.8	*Native American:* Examines the first human inhabitants of the Delaware Valley and the natural resources they used to survive. Students will explore the arboretum grounds searching for plants, animals, water, soil, and rocks that the Lenape used in their daily lives before and during Colonial times. They also are invited to handle artifacts and play games as they imagine what everyday life was like for Lenape children (Figure 5a-5).
2–8	-History 8.1 & 8.2	*Victorian Days:* Students are exposed to what life was like for Quaker children living in Awbury's Cope House in the 1860s. They experience the differences between past and present as they participate in authentic parlor and lawn games, compare antique kitchen

FIG 5a-5. The guide engages children in the Native American concentration game, "Steal the Firewood." (COURTESY OF ELSIE VIEHMAN.)

implements with contemporary ones, and design a quilt square. Special attention is given to the architectural features of the Victorian House on the site.

2–8 (December– March)	-Environment & Ecology 4.7	*Winter Woodlands:* The challenge of survival emerges vividly during the winter months. Students look at plant adaptations such as buds, bark, and sap; compare animal adaptations such as hibernation and migration; and try to understand animal behavior by deciphering tracks in the snow.
5–8	-Environment & Ecology 4.1	*Nature's Recycling I:* Cleaner watersheds mean cleaner water! This lesson highlights the difference between natural and built watersheds and shows how responsible choices by students can contribute to a cleaner water supply. Familiarity with the water cycle is required; an EnviroScape® model is used to demonstrate the consequences of stormwater runoff.

5–8	-Environment & Ecology 4.2 and 4.6	*Nature's Recycling II:* Look for real-life examples of photosynthesis, decomposition and biodegradability throughout the arboretum. Can you find evidence of the nutrient cycle in our forest? Students compare landfills with composting and apply their knowledge in a relay race.
5–8	-Reading, Writing, Speaking, and Listening 1.4	*Words at Work:* Students "interview" a tree, name a plant, "collect" verbs and adjectives, write descriptive paragraphs, and/or compose a poem. They take their memories home in a keepsake journal.

The Summer Nature Program is very active from July through August. Children have the opportunity to choose from a number of hands-on nature activities organized around a variety of themes as described below (Awbury Arboretum Summer Nature Program, 2005):

WEEK	DATE	PROGRAM
1	July 5–7	*The Secret Garden:* Children discover secrets of nature by getting to know animals in this enchanted bird sanctuary.
2	July 11–14	*Wetland Wonders:* Children learn how water works to keep us cool, how plants work to keep water clean, and how people work to keep plants growing.
3	July 18–21	*Predator or Prey?:* Children get up close and personal with arboretum wildlife as they observe from behind the lens of a hidden camera.
4	July 25–28	*PlantStation:* Children use the arboretum as a giant game board trying to find both common and exotic plants.
5	August 1–4	*Hurricanes, Earthquakes, Tsunamis, Oh My!:* Children have fun learning about some of nature's scariest phenomenon
6	August 8–11	*Nature's Music:* Children are invited to attend the Awbury Symphony of cicadas, birds, and crickets while learning to make musical instruments of their own.

Awbury's Outdoor Learning Environments include the following Theme Gardens (Welcome to Awbury 2004):

- ♣ *Historic Francis Cope House:* An 1860–1862 house is listed on the National Register of Historic Places. Its Gothic-Italianate features designed by Yarnell and Cooper is characterized by arches, balconies, and triangular gables (Figure 5a-6).

FIG 5a-6. Through "Victorian Days" program, students are exposed to what life was like for Quaker children living in Awbury's Cope House in the 1860s. Cope House on a fall day. (COURTESY OF ELSIE VIEHMAN.)

- ♣ *Victorian House and Garden:* A Victorian-era garden behind the Cope house is planted with old-fashioned roses, peonies, hollyhocks, and snapdragons (Figure 5a-8).

- ♣ *English Naturalistic Landscape Style:* An English landscape, designed by William Saunders, is modeled after the 18th Century English landscape movement. It is characterized by rolling terrain, winding roads, woodland surrounding, and broad vistas (Figure 5a-7).

- ♣ *Stream, Ponds and Wetland:* A precious resource of open-water "riparian corridor" that supports a diversity of wildlife.

- ♣ *Meadow and Former site of Paramore Farm:* A natural meadow that captures rainfall and stormwater runoff and channels it toward the wetland area.

FIG 5a-7. Through the "Discovery" program, children explore the meadows, woods and wetlands. (COURTESY OF ELSIE VIEHMAN.)

- ♣ *McNabbtown:* A picnic site that was once the historic site of McNabbtown with 1870s rowhouses for immigrant workers.

- ❧ *The Secret Garden:* A walled meditative garden and bird sanctuary.

- ❧ *Haines Field:* A field that showcases many outstanding specimen trees.

- ❧ *Awbury Community Garden:* A garden with more than 50 garden plots where residents grow vegetables and flowers. Included are raised beds for those with physical disabilities.

FUNDING AND MAINTENANCE

Awbury Arboretum is a nonprofit organization. Awbury receives funding from foundations, both private and corporate; government grants and contracts; private individuals; and endowments to support operations (Kaufman, personal communication, 2005).

> *"The cycles of life, watching a seed sprout, grow, flower, produce seed, and return to the soil to nourish the next crop of flowers is a metaphor kids can grasp, and relate to their own lives."*
>
> —Barbara Richardson (Rupp, 2005)

CREDITS

The Awbury Arboretum Design Team

Gerald Kaufman, Executive Director
Elsie Viehman, Education Director
Jennifer Karsten, Education Manager

Everett Children's Adventure Garden at the New York Botanical Garden, Bronx, NY

Garden and Educational programs established: May, 1998 (NYBG established in 1891)
Acres: 12 (4.9 hectares)
Budget for initial project: $15 million ($8.5 capital, $2 endowment, $4.5 operating)
Funding: Individual, corporate, and government grants

Visitors are greeted at the Everett Children's Adventure Garden entrance with an artful arbor and colorful blossoms. (COURTESY OF LOLLY TAI.)

MISSION AND PURPOSE

The New York Botanical Garden's (NYBG) Everett Children's Adventure Garden is a unique public garden where children learn about plant science in a hands-on and engaging way. Interactive exhibits convey different plant science concepts and processes through signage, exhibits, programs, and explainers.

The project goals as described in the 1993–1998 plan are (Eberbach, 2001):

- To enhance the quality and vitality of basic science education for elementary school-age children, their teachers, and their families.

- To restore immediate experiences with plants and nature to children in a safe discovery-oriented environment.

- To enhance the Garden's appeal to families and expand weekend and afternoon visitation by children and caregivers.

THE PLANNING AND DESIGN TEAM

During the initial project, the key New York Botanical Garden staff involved were Catherine Eberbach, Manager of the Children's Adventure Program, Glenn Phillips, Manager of School Programs, Donald Lisowy, Manager of Teacher Enhancement, Barbara Thiers, PhD, Administrative Curator, Cryptogamic Herbarium, and Charles Peter, PhD, Associate Curator (Eberbach, 2001).

The team, known as the Discovery Group, engaged the opinions of children and adults through front-end, formative, and summative survey and evaluations.

According to Eberbach, "In 1993, The Discovery Group conducted front-end evaluations of 12 focus groups of elementary school children, teachers, and parents to assemble information about attitudes toward science and the outdoors and specifically, about participants' knowledge of plant biology as well as their reactions to possible Garden activities." Results of the findings were used to make decisions about the garden design "that would strengthen the connection between the design of the exhibits and programs and visitor understanding, experience, and interest." Formative evaluations for 10 exhibits were conducted during the design development stage. The exhibits selected used real plants, posed operational challenges, informed the design of other exhibit components, or were cognitively challenging. In 1998, Randi Korn & Associates, Inc. implemented a summative evaluation of the Garden. The study not only surveyed visitors during their visit, but also included post-visit telephone interviews. The entire design was developed from 1992–1998. Everett Children's Adventure Garden opened to the public in 1998 (Eberbach, 2001).

THE DESIGN

The Everett Children's Adventure Garden was designed for children of ages 5–12, in family and school programs to learn about plant science. The programmatic goal is to teach and help children understand that (Eberbach, 2001):

- Plants have the life process
- Plants have life requirements and
- Plants and their environments are always changing

> *"The process goal is to engage urban children and their families to actively do science as they explore plants and their environments. To cultivate a positive attitude towards science, the Project would like all children to see themselves as capable of participating in scientific activities. In effect, all children should be willing and able to say, 'I can do science.'"* From *"The Children's Adventure Project"*
> —Eberbach, 2001

The Everett Children's Adventure Garden is a 12-acre outdoor and indoor facility designed especially for children (Figure 5b-2). Changing landscapes, themed galleries, and interactive exhibits provide a living and dynamic stage

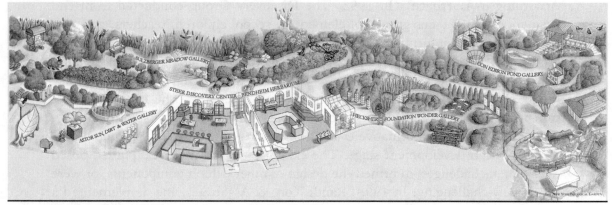

FIG 5b-2. Everett Children's Adventure Garden Site Plan. (COURTESY OF NYBG.)

for hands-on learning about plant science (Andersen, personal communication, 2005).

The Garden was designed for visitors to explore the garden through a self- or staff-guided tour. They have the opportunity to experience more than 40 hands-on nature discovery exhibits/activities through the interaction with mazes, topiary caterpillars (Figure 5b-3), a giant flower model, plazas, a waterfall (Figure 5b-4), a natural wetland, gardens, an herbarium and much more. The path through the garden leads to

FIG 5b-3. Topiary caterpillars covered with colorful seasonal plantings bring whimsy into the garden. (COURTESY OF LOLLY TAI.)

FIG 5b-4. This waterfall is one of several water features in the garden. It overlooks the Con Edison Pond Gallery. (COURTESY OF LOLLY TAI.)

FIG 5b-5. Children climb to the top of Boulder Maze to use the telescope for views of the wetland. (COURTESY OF NYBG.)

such sites as the Boulder Maze for climbing (Figure 5b-5), a Touch Tank for plants that live in water (Figure 5b-6), an indoor laboratory for doing experiments and looking through microscopes and to prompt the use of all the senses at every activity. All the exhibits are designed to be fun, inviting hands on, and to encourage child-centered explanation (Guide to the Everett Children's Adventure Garden, n.d.).

EDUCATIONAL AND PARTICIPATORY ASPECTS

The Everett Children's Adventure Garden is organized into four outdoor and two indoor learning galleries. Each gallery or area of the garden correlates with a different theme about plants. Interactive signs and exhibits within each gallery convey aspects of the theme. The signs and exhibits work hand in hand with the living, growing plants and animals in the garden featuring themes about plant diversity, the life cycles of flowering plants, animal/plant relationships, and pho-

FIG 5b-6. Children love to pick up the plants to see their roots at the Touch Tank. (COURTESY OF NYBG.)

tosynthesis. The Steere Discovery Center provides children the opportunity to learn about the scientific process (Andersen, personal communication, 2005).

All programs are created in accordance with New York City Standards, New York State Science Standards. The programs also respond to National Science Education Standards for developing (1) an understanding of the characteristics and life cycles of organisms; (2) an understanding of diversity and adaptation of organisms; (3) an understanding of science and technology; and (4) the ability to do scientific inquiry (New York Botanical Garden, 2002).

SIX LEARNING GALLERIES—FOUR OUTDOOR AND TWO INDOOR

Four Outdoor Galleries

FULFILLS NY STATE STANDARDS	GALLERIES AND THEMES
	Outdoor Galleries (Fall/Spring/Summer):
1, 2, 4, 5, 6, 7	The Heckscher Foundation for Children's Wonder Gallery: Roots, stems, leaves, and flowers are in the spotlight as students compare and contrast these different plant parts; invent their very own plant; and make observations about the diversity of plant fragrances, colors, shapes and sizes (Figure 5b-7).
1, 2, 4, 5, 6, 7	The Arthur Hays and Iphigene Ochs Sulzberger Meadow Gallery: Students learn about the life cycle of flowering plants; interact with garden features such as a giant

FIG 5b-7. Students read and learn about plant parts through the interactive signs. (COURTESY OF NYBG.)

butterfly, larger-than-life flower model and puppet pollinators; and pretend to pollinate the flowers as if they were insects. The flowers attract pollinators and children observe first-hand pollination in action (Figure 5b-8 and Figure 5b-9).

1, 2, 4, 5, 6, 7   The Vincent Astor Foundation Sun, Dirt, & Water Gallery: Students investigate how the sun helps plants live and grow and why plants are so important—photosynthesis.

1, 2, 4, 5, 6, 7   The Con Edison Pond Gallery: Students explore an ecosystem and discover plant/animal interactions; investigate what lives near and around a wetland habitat as they build their own bird's nest; collect pond samples; and hunt for cattails, duckweed, frogs, turtles; play the Food Web Game, and more (Figure 5b-10).

(ANDERSEN, PERSONAL COMMUNICATION, 2005; GUIDE TO THE EVERETT CHILDREN'S ADVENTURE GARDEN, N.D.).

Note: The activities and interpretive text in all galleries of the Everett Children's Adventure Garden also support a level of science inquiry as mandated by the New York City learning standards and the National Science Education Standards.

FIGS 5b-8 and 5b-9. (Left) Students interact in the flower exhibit and learn about what's in a flower. (COURTESY OF NYBG.) (Right) A child has fun in the flower exhibit as he pretends to be a butterfly and pollinates the flower. (COURTESY OF NYBG.)

FIG 5b-10. Students interact with the natural area. (COURTESY OF NYBG.)

Age Levels

The signage in each gallery is flexible enough to accommodate children between 6 and 11 years old, or grades 1–6, but the reading level is aimed at grades 3–4. There is a significant prereading (pre-K and K) audience, and (where content is appropriate) it is intended that the signage be read to them by parent, teacher, or explainer (Andersen, personal communication, 2005).

Two Indoor Galleries

Learning takes place at the Steere Discovery Center during all seasons. In the Texaco Kids Lab, kids use hand lenses, microscopes, mortar and pestles, and other tools. They participate in plant experiments, making careful observations and discovering that all science starts by asking questions. In the Bendheim Kids Herbarium, kids are exposed to a library of preserved plants. They examine plant parts by using microscopes and hand lenses, explore discovery boxes, create leaf rubbings, and learn how to prepare a plant specimen for preservation (Guide to the Everett Children's Adventure Garden, n.d.).

ACTIVITIES CHILDREN ARE DRAWN TO MOST FREQUENTLY

According to Natalie Andersen, the current Vice President for Education, "Children love to put together the large flower model, to jump on the lily pads which shoot water, to dip in the pond to scoop out a variety of creatures that live there along with the ducks, frogs, turtles, and plants and, of course, to find their way through mazes (Andersen, personal communication, 2005).

FUNDING AND MAINTENANCE

Funding and leadership for the Everett Children's Adventure Garden was provided by Edith and Henry Everett. Major support was provided by William and Linda Steere, The National Science Foundation Grant, The Kresge Foundation, Marian S. Heiskell, Cleveland H. Dodge Foundation, William Randolph Hearst

Foundation, Altman Foundation, Texaco Foundation, Leon Lowenstein Foundation, Inc., Charles Hayden Foundation, The Lewis Calder Foundation, Howard Hughes Medical Institute, LuEsther T. Mertz Charitable Trust, The Vincent Astor Foundation, The Horace W. Goldsmith Foundation, The Heckscher Foundation for Children, Consolidated Edison Company of New York, Inc., The Greenwall Foundation, Mitsubishi International Corporation Foundation, and The New York Times Company Foundation, Inc. (Andersen, personal communication, 2005; Guide to the Everett Children's Adventure Garden, n.d.).

PROJECT EVALUATION AND CONCLUSION

The success of a project relies on evaluation and making changes with the lessons learned. With the addition of the Everett Children's Adventure Garden, family attendance increased from 30,000 in 1992 to 180,000 in 1999. School visitors also increased from 32,000 in 1992 to 90,000 in 1998. As a result, these visitors increased the demands for services and facilities such as stroller and bus parking, ticketing, toilets, and tables. It is important to prepare the garden staff to handle crowds and to be informed educators, to facilitate, and answer questions. For busy family or caregivers, it's important to communicate the educational messages succinctly and in an easy to read manner. The success of a garden is based on the adjustments and changes made through on-going evaluation (Eberbach, 2001).

SINCE 1998

The Adventure Garden is constantly evolving. After 3 years of successful operation, an evaluation of the Everett Children's Adventure Garden was conducted as planned in the original design. Ongoing evaluation of such an innovative facility is necessary to update and refine existing exhibits. Randi Korn & Associates, Inc. conducted this evaluation in 2001. In the summer of 2005, the enhancements were completed (Andersen, personal communication, 2005). They include:

New signage for all exhibits using a bold, vibrant palette and inquiry-based questions encouraging active observing, questioning and hypethesising. With the help of graphics, exhibits can be used either by children, by their teacher, by a parent or by an Explainer. Even children with poor or no reading skills can use the graphics visually and find and match the plant, or observe the phenomenon depicted.

❧ An orientation sign and a new Adventure Trail to introduce the visitor to the Garden and explain that this is a place to use their senses.

❧ The outdoor gallery names were changed to reflect what they teach.
> **Old Name**: The Arthur Hays and Iphigene Ochs Sulzberger Meadow Gallery.
> **New Name:** The Arthur Hays and Iphigene Ochs Sulzberger Meadow Gallery: Life Cycle Lane.
> **Old Name**: The Heckscher Foundation for Children's Wonder Gallery.
> **New Name:** The Heckscher Foundation for Children Gallery: Plant Part Paradise.
> **Old Name:** The Con Edison Pond Gallery.
> **New Name:** The Con Edision Gallery: Habitat Hub.
> **Old Name:** The Vincent Astor Foundation Sun, Dirt & Water Gallery.
> **New Name:** Vincent Astor Foundation Gallery: Sun Central.

❧ Each gallery has an introductory sign to tell visitors what they will be seeing and learning about.

CREDITS

The Original Design Team of the Everett Children's Adventure Garden at the New York Botanical Garden (at the Time of the Project) between 1992 and Opening in 1998

Catherine Eberbach, Manager of the Children's Adventure Program
Glenn Phillips, Manager of School Programs
Donald Lisowy, Manager of Teacher Enhancement
Barbara Thiers, PhD, Administrative Curator, Cryptogamic Herbarium
Charles Peter, PhD, Associate Curator

CONSTRUCTION TEAM

MKW & Associates, Landscape Architects
Dattner Architects, Architecture
Van Sickle and Rolleri, Exhibit Design

To maximize the educational value of the visit, A Teacher's Guide to Everett Children's Adventure Garden was created and is sent to teachers prior to their visit. It offers background information and suggestions for activities to do before, during and after the visit. An education staff leads the 1-hour guided tour.

The Dodge Activity Center was opened for Professional Development classes for teachers as well as being an additional program site and a lunch facility in winter.

Another new addition to the educational process is Adventure Garden SEEDS (Science Exploration and Education Discovery Series). Each unit is designed to help teachers improve their students' science literacy and utilize the Adventure Garden as an extension of the classroom (Andersen, personal communication, 2005).

Unit 1: Plants Parts—K–1

Unit 2: Plant Adaptations—Grades 2–3

Unit 3: People and Plant Interactions—Grades 4–5

CREDITS

The Enhancement Project Team

Natalie Andersen, Vice President for Education
Debra Epstein, Director of Children's Education-Programming
Carbone Smolan Agency Design Team

FUNDING AND LEADERSHIP

Bristol-Myers Squibb Company and Bristol-Myers Squibb Foundation, Inc., Mr. and Mrs. Jonathan C. Clay; Con Edison, Cleveland H. Dodge Foundation, Inc., Edith and Henry Everett, William Randolph Hearst Foundation, Mr. and Mrs. Andrew Heiskell, and Verizon Foundation.

Camden Children's Garden, Camden, NJ. (COURTESY OF VENTURI, SCOTT BROWN AND ASSOCIATES.)

CHAPTER 6

Curriculum, Fundraising, Community Partnerships, and Service Learning

Educating Teachers on How to Use Gardens

The increased use of children's outdoor environments for teaching and learning reflects an increasing number of benefits to the children fortunate enough to be involved in this type of learning. A growing base of research is indicating a wide range of benefits from two primary tangents. One is the improvement of the child's ability to learn based on *how* a child is affected by an outdoor environment. The second is the direct connection of *what* is learned relative to the outdoor environment in which it is learned. For example, when a child spends time outdoors, that child enjoys a natural buffer from life's stresses. When stress is reduced, the child is able to focus better on learning. This is *how* a child is affected, followed then by *what* the child actually learns in the outdoor environment (Figure 6-1).

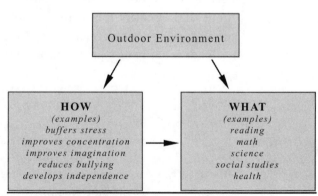

FIG 6-1. Dichotomy of environment-based education effectiveness. (COURTESY OF GINA K. MCLELLAN.)

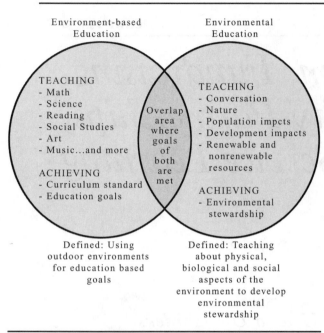

Environment-based
Education

Environmental
Education

TEACHING
- Math
- Science
- Reading
- Social Studies
- Art
- Music...and more

ACHIEVING
- Curriculum standard
- Education goals

Overlap
area
where
goals
of
both
are
met

TEACHING
- Conversation
- Nature
- Population impcts
- Development impacts
- Renewable and
  nonrenewable
  resources

ACHIEVING
- Environmental
  stewardship

Defined: Using
outdoor environments
for education based
goals

Defined: Teaching
about physical,
biological and social
aspects of the
environment to develop
environmental
stewardship

FIG 6-2. Environment-based education in contrast to environmental education. (COURTESY OF GINA K. MCLELLAN.)

The use of outdoor environments for education-based goals is called *environment-based education*. This differs from the more common *environmental education*, which focuses on the understanding of physical, biological, and social aspects of environments with the goal of developing environmental stewardship and responsibility (Figure 6-2). Although environment-based education can include environmental education, it expands the realm of what can be taught in an environmental setting to include many subjects such as math, reading, music, art, and social studies.

In many school settings, little attention is paid to identifying what kind of learner a child is and how to best reach that child. Most children can be identified as auditory, visual, or kinesthetic learners. Although some children are dominant in one style of learning, some may cross heavily into a second category. Classrooms are well suited to auditory and even visual learners, but those who are dominantly kinesthetic learners need a more experiential environment that is easily found in the outdoors.

The concept of environment-based education is not a new one. Luther Burbank, a leading educator in the early 1900s, strongly supported the concept.

> *"Every child should have mud pies, grasshoppers, water bugs, tadpoles, frogs and mud-turtles, elderberries, wild strawberries, acorns, chestnuts, trees to climb, brooks to wade, water lilies, woodchucks, bats, bees, butterflies, various animals to pet, hay fields, pine-cones, rocks to roll, sand, snakes, huckleberries and hornets and any child who has been deprived of these has been deprived of the best part of . . . education."*
> —Luther Burbank's Environment-Based Education Philosophy

John Dewey, another well-known educator, called for this form of education with his claim that all studies arise from one earth and the life lived upon it. In more recent history, Howard Gardner added naturalist intelligence to his theory of multiple intelligences, thus providing even more support for education in nature.

> *"Tell me, I forget.*
> *Show me, I remember,*
> *Involve me, I understand."*
>
> —Native America Proverb

Increasing documentation of the benefits of environment-based education is rising from the field of educational research. The State Education and Environmental Roundtable is focused on studying environment-based education, but its report, "Closing the Achievement Gap," in 2002, is generally unrecognized by the education community (Louv, 2005). This document, written by Gerald Lieberman and Linda Hoody, reports on results of 150 schools in 16 states over 10 years, that modeled environment-based education. These schools report student gains in major subject areas, improvement in standardized test scores, a rise in grade point averages, and skill development in problem solving, critical thinking, and decision making.

Numerous benefits are being reported from a variety of sources as research increasingly focuses on environment-based education. Some of the benefits include:

- Children with attention-deficit/hyperactivity disorder (ADHD) symptoms are able to concentrate better after contact with nature (Taylor et al., 2001).

- Children with views of and contact with nature score higher on tests of concentration and self-discipline (Wells, 2000).

- When children play in natural environments, their play is more diverse, with imaginative and creative play that fosters language and collaborative skills (Moore and Wong, 1997).

- Exposure to natural environments improves children's cognitive development (Pyle, 2002).

- Nature buffers the impact of life's stresses on children and helps them deal with adversity (Wells and Evans, 2003).

- Play in a diverse natural environment reduces bullying (Moore and Wong, 1997).

- When it comes to reading skills, place-based education is a knight in shining armor with students in these programs typically outperforming their peers in traditional classrooms (Sobel, 2004).

OBSTACLES TO ENVIRONMENT-BASED EDUCATION AND SUGGESTED SOLUTIONS

With new research supporting the benefits of environment-based education and successful examples of environment-based education arising with increased frequency, the question as to why more teachers do not avail themselves of this style of teaching must be explored. The dominant reasons as to why environment-based education is not embraced, as described by teachers themselves, fall into eight categories. These are listed below, accompanied by suggestions for moving beyond the obstacles.

1. *Lack of understanding:* There is often a lack of understanding of what environment-based education is. This translates into a misunderstanding that if one does not know a lot about the environment, one cannot teach in the outdoors. Teachers should become more familiar with what environment-based education means, a task easily accomplished with a visit to the Web site of The National Environmental Education and Training Foundation and its link to Education and the Environment for K–12 (http://www.neetf. org, accessed 2005). When teachers understand that environment-based education is a shift in the environment *used* for teaching and not teaching *about* the environment, involving their students in environment-based education will be easy to implement (Figure 6-3).

FIG 6-3. Collecting aquatic specimens from a pond gives students an experiential environment-based lesson in science. (COURTESY OF GINA K. MCLELLAN.)

2. *Lack of environmental experiences:* It is well documented that adults who are comfortable in the outdoors got that way from childhood experiences, and those experiences help to strengthen positive environmental attitudes (Chawla, 1988). Teachers may well be hesitant to move education processes into the outdoors simply because their own early experiences did not include many outdoor experiences. When a teacher is not comfortable in the outdoors but realizes that positive impacts accrue to students using the outdoors, that teacher should select one short activity that he or she feels comfortable doing in the outdoors. During that trial activity, the teacher can tune in to how the students react and how they perform. Simple evaluation of the activity by the teacher will provide good feedback, and teachers should not hesitate to ask for help with these activities from parents or others in their community.

3. *Outdoor fears:* This deterrent comes in two primary forms. One is a general fear of the outdoors on the part of the teacher or a fear of specific things in the outdoors such as insects (Bixler and Floyd, 1997). The second form is the fear of a child getting hurt, but there are basic precautions that can be taken to avoid this. Thousands of children play on school playgrounds daily, but the numerous advantages to this play time are not undermined because of fear that a child *could* get hurt. Occasionally, a teacher must deal with a child's fear of the outdoors, with those fears usually based on lack of experience. One teacher reported that a first grader on a nature trail walk was in tears and afraid. The child was from Saudi Arabia, and had never experienced a wooded environment before that day. With reassurance from the teacher and the child's growing confidence with each step along the trail, he soon was as comfortable as the other children. Environment-based education should not be undermined based on fear. Minimize the risks through precautions and move confidently into the outdoors. Otherwise, fear of the outdoors becomes an excuse for not pursuing environment-based education rather than a justifiable reason.

4. *Time:* Time, or a lack of it, is a frequently mentioned reason. Everyone recognizes the demands on a teacher's time—time to plan, time to grade, time to write reports, and time to develop individual education plans. What a teacher needs to realize relative to environment-based education is that the interdisciplinary opportunities that present themselves in the outdoors can actually save large amounts of time. The natural incentives offered to chil-

dren in the outdoors can provide the motivation, encouragement, and creativity to accomplish the tasks set forth by the teacher in a more efficient and timely manner than the traditional classroom setting can. This efficiency can more than make up for any time used to move students to and from the environment (Figure 6-4).

5. *Inflexibility of schedules:* This objection to using the outdoors for teaching is usually associated with schedule rotations and class changes. Advance planning can assure that even a short period of time can be an effective period of time in the outdoors. Another option used in schools with students changing classes on a set schedule

FIG 6-4. The booklet published by a first-grade class after a walk on the nature trail includes an essay and drawing by every student in the class. (COURTESY OF GINA K. MCLELLAN.)

is to provide periodic flex schedules so that a double or triple period can be accommodated in an outdoor setting. Plus, this approach provides an interdisciplinary opportunity that can be shared by teachers in different subject areas. It just takes a little cooperation among teachers and a little advanced planning to achieve significant payoffs for the students.

> *"Our 5th grade teachers had assumed that a change in the normal day-to-day schedule would be something the students couldn't handle well. The truth is they were intently focused on the outside learning activities and totally unconcerned about the change in their schedule."*
> —Andy Darring, a teacher.

6. *Training:* Teachers with no experience in environment-based education usually fall into one of two categories: those who want to try environment-based education, and those who don't. For those who want to try this approach, training can be an invaluable tool in jump starting them into environment-based education. A few techniques and a few activities taught

to the teacher can open a whole new world of learning for students. This training can come from people who teach outside the formal school structure such as an educational specialist in a nearby botanical garden or a local author. The training can come informally in a Web-based format tackled by an individual teacher. It can also be found through numerous professional groups and con-

FIG 6-5. Rudy Mancke, host of ETV's *NatureScene*, leads a training session for teachers on the Clemson Elementary School nature trail. (COURTESY OF GINA K. MCLELLAN.)

ferences that focus on environment-based education, and it can be garnered from a huge variety of educational resources in books, journals, and on the Web. For teachers who don't want to try environment-based education, the hope is that through the successes of colleagues and their students and a little guidance from administrators and other teachers, they will try this approach and see some immediate successes (Figure 6-5).

7. *Prissy factor:* This term is often used lightly, but focuses on a real obstacle and that is there are teachers who simply don't want to get dirty and don't want their students to get dirty. Their assumption is that the outdoors is dirty. Environment-based education is not synonymous with getting dirty, but if children do get dirty in the process, they can clean up. And if they do get dirty, they probably learn something in the process. Solutions to this problem exist. It's always best when it is addressed in a simple, sensible way by the teachers. Some teachers have every child keep an old pair of shoes at school to wear when they go to the nature trails, ponds and creeks. Some have each child keep an oversized shirt to wear over their school clothing. Some simply send a note home the day before an outdoor learning excursion asking the parents to send their child to school the next day in play clothes that won't be damaged if they get soiled.

8. *Breaking the routine:* Perhaps one of the most unfortunate obstacles to environment-based education is that some teachers are so ingrained in their current methods that they see no reason to change their routine. They are

comfortable with the way things are currently done; they are afraid to try anything new; they are close to retirement; and the list goes on. Routine is a difficult cycle to break. Although it is always preferred that a teacher try environment-based education because he or she wants to, some schools have taken a strong stand to encourage inclusion of this approach.

JUSTIFYING ENVIRONMENT-BASED EDUCATION

As the above list of obstacles is examined, it is noticeable that two items usually on a list of obstacles to achieving educational goals are not on this list—lack of money, and lack of student interest or motivation. Environment-based education has few if any costs beyond the normal cost of education. The outdoors is already "built." It does not necessarily need any alterations to be used as a learning environment.

A lack of student interest or motivation is simply not a problem. Children have an innate curiosity towards the outdoors and typically relish being in it. One of the reasons discipline becomes almost nonexistent in the outdoors is because the children are so focused on what they are doing outside that they are just not interested in being disruptive. They also want to be able to return to the outdoor environment another time, and are quite content to behave to make that return trip possible. Teachers using environment-based education have also noticed spectacular improvement in the academic and behavioral performance of children with attention-deficit disorder and ADHD symptoms because these children thrive in an environment that accommodates their varying tendencies.

The benefits of environment-based education are still being assessed. More research is needed to further support the gains being made in education through this approach. With the indications to date being so positive for children in terms of both *how* they learn and *what* they learn, teachers have a golden opportunity to try environment-based education, evaluate it with their own students, and be part of the information gathering and research processes currently underway.

Fundraising and Building the Project

Implementing outdoor environments for children is often a "good news–bad news" story. The "good news" consists of creative ideas and designs for the garden or schoolyard; the "bad news" is that budgets don't exist to implement those creative ideas and designs. This chapter will focus on the three aspects of fundraising that provide the basis for how to seek and find the money necessary to bring a project to fruition. These aspects are the philosophical bases of fundraising, the practical approaches to fundraising, and the potential sources of funding.

PHILOSOPHICAL BASES OF FUNDRAISING

The thought of raising funds for any project strikes fear in the heart of most. We don't feel qualified. We don't like to ask for money. We are not comfortable enough with our own personal monies to feel comfortable asking others to part with their monies. Understanding a few of the philosophical bases of fundraising can help the potential fundraiser understand how to begin the fundraising process. The philosophical bases of fundraising shared here were derived through first-hand experience with numerous projects. They are the thoughts that provide focus and, perhaps most importantly, the nerve to proceed with the necessary steps of raising money.

1. **If you want money for a project, you have to ask for it:** A popular bumper sticker says, "It will be a great day when our schools get all the money they need and the Air Force has to hold a bake sale to buy a bomber." Sitting back and waiting for money to come to your project without asking for it would be like waiting for the Air Force to hold bake sales. It just isn't going to happen. Once you philosophically accept the fact that if you want money, you have to ask for it, and then you can move forward in your quest.

2. **The largest number of donated dollars comes from private individuals:** It may come as a surprise, but the most donated dollars come from individuals, not corporations and foundations. According to Giving USA (2004), the annual publication of the American Association of Fundraising Counsel, nearly 80% of $241 billion in charitable donations in 2003 was given by private individuals. The philosophical focus of fundraising for children's outdoor environments should include individual donors as a major emphasis.

3. **Fundraising is not begging:** Fundraising should rather be considered an exchange of a donation for work that a donor cannot do. In raising money for children's outdoor environments, this tenet becomes increasingly evident. The busy parent who cannot fit time into a schedule to help organize volunteers or to be part of the planting crew may assuage any guilt feel-

ings by providing a monetary donation. There are numerous parents and community members who do not feel qualified to do certain types of tasks but willingly donate money in place of their hands on obligations. To secure such donor commitments, the fundraising team or individual fundraiser must determine the best way to articulate what the project is all about and its indubitable value so that this potential donor will want to exchange money for your work.

4. **When you ask for money, people can and do say no:** You may be soliciting money for the greatest children's environment ever, but no one is obligated to donate money for it. They are not obligated as a parent, as a community member, as a business person, or even as a personal friend. The person or persons seeking funding must be comfortable with this fact and not take a negative answer personally. The fundraiser should, however, try to determine if the potential donor is saying no because of a lack of information or understanding of the project, because they really want more time to think about the project, or because they just don't like the project. If the fundraiser sees one of these as a possibility, the door should be considered still open and a different approach applied at a later date.

5. **Believe in your cause:** The old adage that enthusiasm is contagious is never truer than in fundraising activities. The most successful fundraiser must believe in the value of the cause and be able to communicate it to others who have little or no conception of the cause. The fundraiser must be able to defend the cause and answer a variety of questions voiced by potential donors. This can literally be practiced ahead of time with other fundraising team members playing the devil's advocate role. Verbalizing your defense in advance helps you sound out a solid defense of the project should it be needed.

6. **Operate with your hopes high and your expectations low:** Somewhere in between high hopes and low expectations is a reality goal. It's quite like a child telling a parent he needs $100 for a new pair of tennis shoes. His high hope is for the coolest shoes on the market, but based on previous experience, his low expectation is for a pair of normal shoes on sale. The end result is actually a pair of pretty neat shoes that cost $50, a reality goal somewhere between high hope and low expectation. This same mental state applied to fundraising prevents the burst balloon syndrome when the neg-

ative reply is received or when the amount given is less than wanted. The words in an old Rolling Stones song reflect this approach with, "You can't always get what you want, but if you try, sometimes you might just get what you need." When a high expectation is met, there is plenty of room then for celebration rather than rote expectation.

7. **I'm a person; you're a person. Just ask!** The fundraiser must realize that the person being asked likely has the same kinds of anxieties about money that the fundraiser does. We learn many things about money as we grow and mature, and one of these precepts is that being anxious about money is a normal behavior. Consider the fundraiser and donor on level ground, and acknowledge that the donor may be as anxious about parting with the donation as the fundraiser is about asking for it. The fundraiser's positive attitude about the cause and enthusiasm for the cause can help to quell the anxiety. Recognize that the asker and the giver have much in common!

PRACTICAL APPROACHES TO FUNDRAISING

With the fundraiser fully aware of the philosophical principles outlined above, the practical approaches to fundraising can begin. The approaches discussed in this section have been gleaned from dozens of fundraisers focused on raising money to design and build children's outdoor environments. These efforts have included children's gardens within large botanical gardens, in the middle of cities, and in schoolyards. They have also included a variety of other children's outdoor environments ranging from nature trails to barns to playgrounds. What all of these fundraising endeavors have in common is that the same practical approaches to fundraising apply.

1. **Communicate your vision:** Virtually every project begins with a vision. The vision may be clear and complete in your mind, but the potential donors can't see that vision without help from you. It is an absolute necessity to translate your vision into visual graphics of some kind to share with potential donors. The visuals can take the form of a Web site, brochures, models, or gift catalogs.

2. **High-quality visuals are the only acceptable visuals:** Whatever your choice in visuals, they must be high quality. You want them to look so good that a donor will pass them on to other potential donors. In this day of

desktop publishing, it is within any fundraiser's realm to produce excellent visuals within any given budget.

3. **Decide in advance how you will recognize your donors, and communicate this to them during the fundraising campaign:** Although donors don't necessarily expect anything in return for a donation, most of them will appreciate some kind of recognition. This can be handled through recognition in newsletters and status reports. Updates on projects are a good communication tool and a good place to recognize donors frequently. A more formal approach to donor recognition is with permanently mounted plaques naming donors, or donor giving trees, which easily allow for multi-level contribution recognition in a permanent and visually aesthetic form (Figure 6-6).

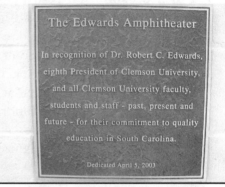

FIG 6-6. When an outside entity coordinates fundraising for an environment, it may be desirable to post a special recognition plaque desired by that entity. (COURTESY OF MARY TAYLOR HAQUE.)

4. **Plan, plan, plan, and activate your plan:** Planning is a basis for many successful ventures, and fundraising is no exception. A fundraising plan will provide focus and save time. The perception among fundraisers working on children's environments is that one hour of good planning will save four hours of work because you know where you are headed. We don't typically get in a car to drive from Maine to Minnesota without first checking a map. A few minutes of map time can save hours of driving time. Planning to fundraise works like map time and abates unnecessary effort.

Within the planning phase, the organizer's blueprint should include:
   a. A concise statement of your vision of the project
   b. A summary of what is needed to carry out the plan
   c. A chart of anticipated gifts
   d. An organizational chart identifying all leadership roles and responsibilities
   e. Projected costs to carry out the fundraising efforts
   f. A timetable with deadlines for each component of the fundraising effort
   g. Evaluation checkpoints

This blueprint will look different for every project and may be expanded or shortened depending on the complexity of the project. A one-shot individual fundraising activity for a specific purchase of playground equipment will look much simpler than a project to design and develop 20 different outdoor environments at a new school.

5. **Know what makes potential donors tick:** Know the background on your potential donors. Do they lean toward programs that enhance education? Do they focus their giving on community service? Do they have a penchant to enhance the aesthetics of a community? Do they allow for a broad spectrum of programs and activities? Do they prefer to fund construction as opposed to programs or vice versa? Do they have children? When you know the donor's preferences and past giving history, you can direct your contact with that donor toward these preferences.

6. **Know who stands to benefit from the planned project:** If you can identify who will potentially benefit from a given project, you can focus your donor solicitations on those who stand to benefit whether it be economically or socially. If a planned children's garden is in an area of the city where a particular realtor dominates, that realtor has a vested interest in a garden that enhances that area of the city and gives the realtor an additional marketing element. A business owner with three young children approaching school age could be a viable donor for a new playground and nature trail at the school his children will attend. There are numerous ties to be made between beneficiaries and donors with just a little preliminary research.

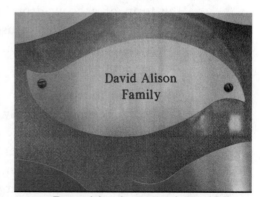

David Alison
Family

7. **Thank before you bank:** This is such a basic premise of fundraising that it is found in virtually every piece of literature that addresses fundraising. Decide during the preliminary planning stages how you want to thank your donors. Stick with the "thank you" plan, and make sure the thank you letters, notes, and/or gifts are sent immediately, hence "before you bank" (Figure 6-7).

FIG 6-7. Recognizing donors can be tastefully done with a permanent recognition place such as a leaf on a giving tree mounted near the environment. (COURTESY OF MARY TAYLOR HAQUE.)

8. **Keep your donors updated:** Donors have contributed because they believed in what you are trying to do. It is mandatory that you provide follow up information on the project. This can be in the form of a newsletter or other high-quality printed material about the project, and can be used as another source for recognizing your contributors. This correspondence should provide detail about what is currently being done on the project, photographs that give some idea of the status, and projected timelines for upcoming stages.

9. **Invite your donors to your dedication:** When it's time to dedicate your new garden, trail, play area, or other children's environment, invite the donors to the dedication. Remember, they have done much to make the environment possible. This is simply a goodwill gesture and one the donor will appreciate and remember.

In addition to the approaches discussed above, there are principles to apply to specific individual fundraising events that grow out of the planning steps above:

1. **For individual fundraising events, match the fundraiser to the cause:** More fun and interest can be added to an individual fundraising event when the cause and the event can be thematically connected. For example, students at an elementary school wanted to build a barn at their school. The only way to do this was through fundraising. As they searched fundraising ideas with the help of parents and teachers, a themed event took shape in the form of a "cow drop." The opportunity to raise money for a barn through an event that focused on a cow doing what comes naturally was the perfect connection to garner interest and a tremendous amount of community support.

2. **Match the fundraising event to the number of volunteers:** Successful fundraising events require well-organized volunteers in plentiful numbers. It is important to recognize during the planning stage that the fundraising event must be able to operate with the number of volunteers potentially able to assist with it. If a municipal government is raising funds for a children's garden in a city, that government unit may be capable of presenting a quality fundraiser with only city employees involved. If, however, a school plans a fundraiser that relies on numbers of items sold, a much larger base

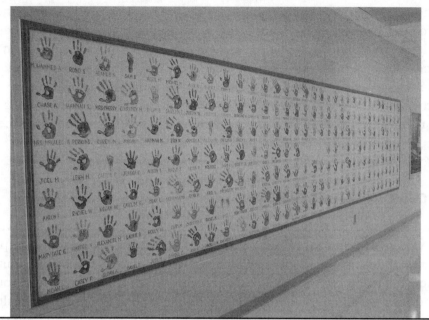

FIG 6-8. Children's handprints mounted on tiles raised nearly $10,000 for one school's outdoor environments. (COURTESY OF MARY TAYLOR HAQUE.)

of volunteers or sellers is needed. Setting goals and garnering volunteers committed to meeting the goals is the basis for success (Figure 6-8).

3. **Match the fundraiser to the market:** An often overlooked premise of fundraising, particularly for individual events, is the decision to sell something for which there is no market. Schools have failed on numerous occasions when trying to sell candles when they were not in vogue, selling expensive candies and decorative products when economies were in recession, and duplicating fundraisers being conducted in the same geographic area. With obesity as an increasingly familiar health issue, candy and cookie fundraisers should be approached with caution, especially in school settings. Great successes have been reported when fundraisers provided a marketable item that was high quality and usable.

4. **Match the organization with the fundraiser:** This tenant is sometimes related to the legality of a fundraiser rather than the ability or desire of the organization to conduct the fundraiser. If, for example, a state PTO does

not allow its individual member PTOs to conduct lotteries, then the raffle for the big screen TV cannot be done through the PTO. It may still be done with that school as the beneficiary of the money raised, but it will need to be conducted through a different organization that does allow lotteries. Lotteries, while highly popular as a fundraiser, may even be against the law in a given state. There are small print disclaimers in these cases such as the wording "no purchase required," which might allow the event to proceed, but it is always advisable to seek a legal interpretation for allowable lotteries before planning even gets underway.

SOURCES OF FUNDRAISING

Novice fundraisers as well as experienced ones can become quickly overwhelmed by the variety of potential funding sources. This section focuses on four primary categories of funding, and analyzes each relative to various types of organizations and their funding needs for children's environments. It is important throughout the fundraising planning stages to keep the donor's perspective in mind. Although the fundraiser may be overwhelmed by the variety of potential funding sources, the donor may also be overwhelmed by the variety and number of requests to donate. Aristotle sums this up:

> *To give away money . . . is an easy matter and in any man's power. But to decide to whom to give it and how much and when, and for what purpose and how, is neither in every man's power nor an easy matter.*
>
> —Aristotle

Traditional or Grass Roots Fundraising

School-related organizations often focus their fundraising activities on traditional or grass roots fundraising, which simply means asking for money for your organization. This is because most of their fundraising is done by ordinary people focused on specific acquisitions that can be garnered under the hat of one or several fundraising activities. The second reason for the traditional or grass roots approach in school settings is that the fundraisers are usually teams of parents comfortable with their ability to pull off a traditional fundraiser but with little or no knowledge of how to reach beyond that level. It is important for the fundraising organization to realize that without some extraordinary effort, traditional or grass roots projects will garner minimal financial support, thus requiring repetitions over several seasons or years to meet its fundraising goal. One elementary school PTO had three years to raise funds for playground equipment while a new school was designed and built. The money raised in that period was just enough to fund some desired playground equipment for the new school, but it took three years to reach the goal.

Assuming a traditional or grass roots fundraising effort is the best activity for the job at hand; the organization can begin by using the talents of its own members. The thought to keep in mind is that by doing their own fundraising, the organization will gain self-sufficiency and some independence. Numerous benefits will accrue to the fundraising organization including:

1. Confirmation of the project goals with each donation.

2. Pride that the project is something the community wants and sees a need for.

3. The acknowledgment of the community that this project is important enough to warrant the numerous hours of work the organization members are contributing.

4. An increase in membership reflecting the magnetic draw of the project.

5. Good publicity because the efforts will ultimately benefit children in the community.

To be sure the benefits accrue, the fundraising organization must be sure to:

1. **Maximize the profit:** In the school setting, grass roots fundraising is usually focused on how to make the most money in the least time. After all, parents are usually the fundraisers, and are motivated to add something to the school setting that will benefit their children while at that school, so time is of the essence. To maximize profits, consider which fundraising events will be most economical and efficient in terms of volunteers. Although it is easy to fall back on the bake sales and carwashes, it is important to not underrate your ability to undertake the big event. A school with 600 students might clear a profit of $200 on food at the fall carnival but can clear $20,000 with a well-organized gift wrap sale because the products from the latter are something nearly everyone can use, and the marketing and sales materials for it are provided through the company that provides an umbrella of fundraising opportunities for organizations.

2. **Make long-range plans:** Assume the organization will be in the fundraising business for a long time; a safe assumption when the organization is related to a school. When the perfect fundraising activity is found, keep it. Make it an annual event saving time and money because you don't have to reinvent the wheel every year. Profits can more than double within only one to two years, and each year more experienced leaders and ideas accumulate.

3. **Find a good secretary and treasurer to keep records:** Previous records are constantly sought as benchmarks and save innumerable hours of guesswork. They must be precise and complete. These records can pave the way for a smoother fundraiser in subsequent years, can provide insight into costs to aim for on bid items, and provide fundraising dates to include in newsletters and other donor reports.

Grants

Grants are like people—they come in many sizes and shapes. Some school organizations avoid them because they are either too busy with traditional fundraising or the members of the organizations feel unqualified to seek them. The first step in dealing with grants is to realize there are many types of them, and that you must match the grant source to the cause for which you are seeking the money. This section provides a short overview on grants and encourages the fundraising organization to seek out a qualified grantwriter if grants appear to be in that organization's future.

There are seed grants, matching grants, challenge grants, operating grants, program grants, construction grants, general support grants, continuing support grants, multiyear grants, and more. Some foundations giving grants require preproposals; some require full proposals following a specified format; some require application submissions. Some have once-a-year grant cycles; some have open calendar grant cycles. Some will fund programs only; some will fund construction. Some give funding in specific geographic regions; some give funding nationwide. Some focus on particular segments of society: underprivileged, elderly, disabled. Some focus on particular activities or interests: music, environment, art, sports. With all the potential variations, it is easy to see why seeking grants requires significant upfront research to even establish the viability of seeking grants by most fundraising organizations.

Early in the grant application process, the organization seeking funds must decide to whom it plans to submit grant proposals. It is therefore important for that organization to get some key information synthesized and written down. A focused statement of the problem or concern must be delineated, and once it is, the organization can begin to tie its concern to those of the potential donors. For example, if a garden is going to be developed in an economically deprived area, the concern for providing gardening opportunities to underprivileged children can be linked to funding organizations with concerns for underprivileged children. This precept applies whether the builder approaches foundations with unsolicited proposals or applies for specific grants offered by a foundation, agency, or other organization.

Next, the seeker must direct its concerns into outcome oriented objectives. Think in terms of "what do we need to do to get to where we want to go." Ultimately, it is these objectives that link directly to the budget requested in the grant. The seeker will also develop a list of actual steps to be followed in achieving results, and these steps must include specifics of who will do what and when it will be done. This sets a timeline for the entire project.

Many granting organizations want to know how the project will be evaluated. The evaluation plan should include a description of how the seeker will know what is achieved, how well it is working, and how to maintain it through the future. Finally, a budget must be developed that links back to the objectives. Although different funding organizations will require different degrees of specificity, the budget should generally be tailored to the complexity of the project. A budget accompanying a request for $2,000 for planting materials will be quite different from a construction grant that includes hardscapes and irrigation.

The persuasive flow of logic should be obvious in all proposals, regardless of length or complexity. Above all, it is mandatory that the instructions and guidelines of the granting organization are followed exactly. They maintain the right, and frequently exercise it, to throw out grant applications and proposals that do not meet the requirements. There are numerous books and resources on the internet and in libraries that can provide more detailed guidance pertaining to grantwriting. It is also advisable whenever possible to seek the assistance of an experienced grantwriter who is willing to help your organization in the grant submission process.

Gift Catalogs

Gift catalogs are shopping guides of available funding opportunities for particular projects. A gift catalog includes drawings, photos, descriptions, and prices of specific elements of the overall project. In one community where a new elementary school was being constructed, the lead volunteer for the outdoor project printed color copies of a gift catalog that featured a page for each of the 22 areas planned for the school's outdoor project. These ranged from courtyard gardens to playgrounds to a greenhouse. Each page visually depicted the finished product, and included a cost breakout of what was needed for that area. By sharing the catalog with potential funders during personal visits, five of the areas were funded by local businesses and organizations. These donations alone totaled nearly $60,000.

The success of gift catalogs lies in the fact that they visually depict what is to be. The planners of any children's environments may well have perfectly defined visions in their heads, but to convince someone else to provide funding requires that the vision be transferred to the potential funder. A well-illustrated depiction of an environment in a gift catalog makes this transfer possible. Gift catalogs also have the advantage of being passed on from one funder to another potential funder.

Business Partners

Business partners, like donors, come in all shapes and sizes. Although a business partner may be an initial donor for a project, they can become a long-time supporter for the school or organization behind the children's environment. A foundation based in New York, for example, may fund the initial construction of a music garden in Georgia; but it is not likely that this foundation would remain an ongoing business partner. On the other hand, a local restaurant that garners much of its income from families in the local area would have much to gain by being an ongoing business partner for a local children's garden or schoolyard.

Consider business partners in categories of what they might offer relative to what your organization needs. This means that if your needs are primarily focused on money, the business partnership will then be monetary. If you need construction assistance such as grading and retaining walls, your business partnership will be one of in-kind services. These overall types of partnerships might also include time and volunteers, education and training, or perhaps marketing and advertising. This list continues to expand as the needs are identified.

No matter what purpose the business partners will serve, the approach to building those partnerships is basically the same for all of them, and it starts with the garden or schoolyard organization matching their goals with the interests and community connections of the potential business partner. Many of the same actions identified in the grants section of this chapter apply to identifying business partners.

Business partners have many benefits they can pass on to children's environmental projects. They may have expertise in areas that will be helpful during design and construction phases. They may have employee volunteer programs in which employees donate time to community projects. They may provide monetary support in terms of donated materials and equipment or donated services such as printing. They may provide instructional services to children using the developed environments or judges and awards for competitions based in a particular environment. No matter how the environment and the business partner ultimately work together, there are several basic steps that can lead to a successful partnership.

Steps to a successful business partnership begin with some of the same basics used in grantwriting. First, develop a comprehensive list of what the environment needs. This can come from the PTA, the planning committee, or the organization supervising the project development. Second, based on the list of needs you developed, decide on appropriate businesses to contact. Approach businesses that can potentially help your cause, but don't approach them on a basis of what you can do to help them. Geographic proximity should be a major consideration in this identification. If the business is located nearby, that business may feel the partnership will be more productive. Do not, however, exclude from consideration a business located in the next town or an adjoining county. That business's services may easily extend beyond neighborhood borders.

Next, decide how the businesses will be approached, and remember that personal contact is the best approach. This is the only way the business can truly see the benefit of the partnership you are asking them to be a part of. Know the business before you meet with its representative, and know what you want to suggest in terms of a partnership. Also, know exactly what the next step will be so you can discuss it on the spot while you have the attention of the potential partner. Always thank the business for considering your proposal of the partnership. Thank them in person and follow up with a letter.

Successful partnerships will ultimately depend on several factors. These include:

- Keep the lines of communication open between the business and the organization and then communicate frequently.

- Recognize the business partner in as many ways as possible including newspaper articles, speeches and other presentations, newsletters, and so on.

- Thank the business frequently, especially at each point where another major goal is reached such as completion of grading, planting a garden, or turning the fountain on for the first time.

- Publicly acknowledge the input the business has had in the planning, design and implementation of the environment.

- Invite the business to garden and school activities and recognize its contributions.

Although remembering the above suggestions for a successful business partnership, it is also necessary to avoid certain actions. One important thing to remember is to avoid overusing the business. To prevent this, decide on the way to best work with that business; and when the business agrees with that tact, stick with the program and don't try to add more. Second, do not over commit the business. Remember that business people are busy people and should not be expected to attend numerous meetings or appointments. Third, never underestimate the amount of time it will take your organization to build and maintain a business partner. It is often assumed that once the partner is on board, that's the end of the recipient organization's work. In reality, the care and nurturing of a successful business partnership never ends, and the ways your organization gives back to that business partner will continually evolve (Figure 6-9).

FIG 6-9. Name imprints on bricks that then provide the paths through a children's garden is a popular means of raising funds for a specific site. (COURTESY OF MARY TAYLOR HAQUE.)

Experiential Service Learning Partnerships

Service learning is a teaching methodology that combines community service with academic learning in a meaningful way through action and reflection. Over 30 children's gardens have been designed for schools and public gardens in South

Carolina by graduate and undergraduate students and faculty at Clemson University using this pedagogy (Figure 6-10). Communities across the world can benefit from this approach to learning, which has many academic as well as community benefits.

ACADEMIC BENEFITS OF SERVICE LEARNING

Research regarding service learning provides evidence that participants gain from this experience in a variety of ways (Billig, 2000; Eyler et al., 2001; Gray et al., 2000). A small sample of positive outcomes includes the following:

FIG 6-10. College classes can assist K–12 schools with design of outdoor environments. (COURTESY OF MARY TAYLOR HAQUE.)

1. Service learning enhances interpersonal development and the ability to work well with others while developing leadership and communication skills (Figure 6-11).

2. Service learning increases commitment to serve, and volunteering in college is related to involvement in community service later.

3. Service learning enhances students' ability to apply what they have learned in the classroom to "real-world" situations, connecting theory to practice.

4. Participation in service learning contributes to career development (Eyler et al., 2001).

FIG 6-11. Service learning students learn to work well with others while improving their community. (COURTESY OF MARY TAYLOR HAQUE.)

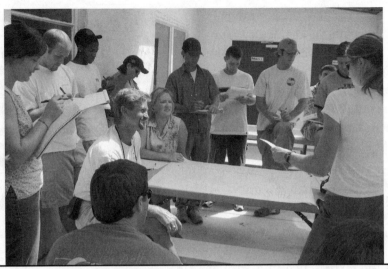

FIG 6-12. College students engage in "real-word" problem solving as they interact with their client, the manager of the South Carolina Botanical Garden, to help design a children's garden. (COURTESY OF MARY TAYLOR HAQUE.)

Community-oriented service learning teaches students early on that the involvement of the community is an essential part of the process of design. Students' interaction with the client group is key to getting students excited about a project (Bixby, 2000). Students strengthen analysis and critical thinking skills as they identify problems and devise solutions (Figure 6-12).

HOW TO FIND A SERVICE LEARNING PARTNER

Institutions or individuals seeking design assistance may approach nearby colleges and universities to invite faculty, graduate, and undergraduate students to partner on the design and/or installation of children's gardens. If you are searching for an academic partner in higher education, begin by checking to see if the university has a service learning center. Such centers often help link academic and community partners, and they will provide you with names and contact information of potential faculty partners. If the institution does not have a service learning center, contact the department chair in the department most closely aligned with your needs. Departments of landscape architecture, horticulture, parks, and recreation often participate in design-related community service learning projects, and the chair can give you the names of appropriate faculty to contact. Allow plenty of lead time, because faculty often commit their classes to proj-

FIG 6-13. Young people can reflect, celebrate and build community by sharing information about plans such as this one for Wonderland Garden in Atlanta, Ga. (COURTESY OF MARY TAYLOR HAQUE.)

ects a year or more in advance. An early start also allows time to apply for grants if funding is limited.

Service Learning Methodology

Service learning methodology on landscape design projects includes research and analysis; planning and design; implementation and action; and sharing, reflection, celebration, evaluation, and recognition (Figure 6-13). Begin by establishing a partnership between an educational institution and a community partner desiring assistance with design. Students can conduct research about the site and case studies about other children's gardens, as well as interview clients in a user needs analysis. When working with K–12 school landscapes, college classes engage the school children and teachers in the process, so service learning is integrated at all levels from K–18. Students can work individually or in teams to create preliminary drawings to be critiqued by the client committee, the professor, and by each other (Figure 6-14).

Reflection, evaluation, and celebration are the final steps in the service learning methodology. Students can write poems and reflection papers about their projects. As writing students become immersed in the complexities of the issues

FIG 6-14. Peer review is an important part of critiques on service learning projects. (COURTESY OF MARY TAYLOR HAQUE.)

FIG 6-15. Students can "write to learn" as part of the reflection process. (COURTESY OF MARY TAYLOR HAQUE.)

facing the clients, they learn both traditional course material and "real-world" lessons. They can "learn to write" and "write to learn" simultaneously (Santrock, 1999). The process of becoming a skilled writer can make students better thinkers, speakers, readers, and listeners (Ellis, 1998) (Figure 6-15).

FIG 6-16. Journals and portfolios are often used as both reflection and assessment tools. (COURTESY OF MARY TAYLOR HAQUE.)

Students often compile a portfolio of their work including reflective writing, a type of writing in which students analyze, process, and begin to make sense of what they are learning during the semester (Figure 6-16). They can also consider how they might build upon and improve their performance in future interactions with clients. Student work can be celebrated in the classroom with formal presentations followed by refreshments and student–client discussions. Their work can also be celebrated and displayed

FIG 6-17. Creative projects such as this metal butterfly ornament can be unveiled and celebrated at groundbreaking ceremonies. (COURTESY OF MARY TAYLOR HAQUE.)

at groundbreaking ceremonies and dedications, which are also attended by school, city and county officials, and community members for school and/or municipal children's gardens (Figure 6-17). Presentation of certificates is a nice way to reward students during a celebration event and is an excellent way to combine evaluation and celebration. Organizations like The National Wildlife Federation and its affiliates provide resources through workshops and through their schoolyard habitat program. They will also evaluate projects and certify ones that meet their criteria. They also certify students and volunteers as "Habitat Stewards" if they successfully complete the Habitat Steward program and provide outstanding environmental and community stewardship and leadership.

Such events also provide opportunities for students to practice oral communication skills as they present their work to various groups and individuals including parents, students, teachers, planning committees, and colleagues (Figure 6-18). Celebratory receptions are effective at completion points during a project process, and can be held during project presentations, on the last day of class, at project dedications, or ground breaking ceremonies, for example.

Reflection, Celebration, and Recognition

Factors that motivate faculty involvement in service learning include a clear mission, infrastructure support, and the "development of a common campus language for public service activity" (Holland, 1999). Other motivational strategies include support for peer development activities among faculty, and incentives and rewards including publicity, awards, support for dissemination activities, and fundraising and grant support. Consistency across all elements of the public service vision may be the most essential aspect of an institution's commitment to

FIG 6-18. Community partners meet with students for critiques, presentations, and celebration events. (COURTESY OF MARY TAYLOR HAQUE.)

public service. "Such consistency is essential to encouraging many faculty to view service as a legitimate and valued component of their scholarly life and work" (Holland, 1999).

Faculty and students can practice sustained and broad reflection while inviting additional evaluation, feedback, discussion, and sharing through presentations at regional, national, and international meetings (Figure 6-19). A network of experienced service learning faculty associates can act as mentors and resources to support both new and veteran service learning faculty across an institution (McGuiness, 1996) and internationally through conferences and electronic communication. "Our institutions of higher learning might certainly take heed, not only by encouraging students to do such service, but by helping them stop and mull over, through books and discussions, what they have heard and seen. This is the purpose, after

FIG 6-19. Renee Keydoszius presented her service learning project at the American Society for Horticultural Science Southern Region Meeting, inviting feedback and evaluation. (COURTESY OF MARY TAYLOR HAQUE.)

FIG 6-20. This landscape implementation class contributed over a thousand hours to community service while learning skills to build a children's garden. (COURTESY OF MARY TAYLOR HAQUE.)

all, of colleges and universities—to help one generation after another grow intellectually and morally through study and the self-scrutiny such study can sometimes prompt" (Coles, 1993).

HOW COMMUNITY PARTNERS CAN REWARD SERVICE LEARNING CLASSES

College students working on designing children's gardens as a service learning project often devote hundreds of hours to researching, analyzing, and designing the project, with class projects totaling in the thousands of hours over a semester (Figure 6-20). Community partners can reward this effort in several ways:

1. Designate a leader and/or committee to represent your garden. Make sure they provide all of the materials such as base maps requested by students in a timely manner. Most college students are working on a semester or quarter system, and they must move fast.

2. Come to every occasion you are invited to and give constructive information and feedback to students. For example, students will be seeking your

input as they prepare the site and user needs analysis, and they will need to get your opinion on the preliminary plans to allow time for revisions and corrections before the final plan is drawn up (Figure 6-21).

FIG 6-21. Students learn from positive feedback as well as from constructive criticism. (COURTESY OF MARY TAYLOR HAQUE.)

3. Voice your appreciation and gratitude for the work students are doing at the beginning, throughout the duration, and at the conclusion of the project.

4. When critiquing plans, be sure to point out the positive elements as well as those that need to be improved (Figure 6-22).

5. Providing refreshments during a site visit or after a presentation is a good way to reward students for their hard work.

6. A certificate of accomplishment personalized for each student lets them know their work was appreciated, and is also useful to include in their port-folio. If personalizing multiple certificates is too difficult, make one out for the class. Copies can be made for each student.

7. A letter of commendation at the end of the semester expresses gratitude and can also be included in a student's portfolio as recognition for their accomplishment. These can be personalized for each student or addressed to the class as a whole.

FIG 6-22. Project partners must plan to attend meetings to give input and feedback throughout the project process. (COURTESY OF MARY TAYLOR HAQUE.)

CASE STUDIES

The Ethnobotany Garden in the South Carolina Botanical Garden

Opening date: May 2004

Acres: 8,233 square feet (764.8 square meters)

Cost: $20,000 not including volunteer work hours

Funding: Clemson University
United States Department of Agriculture
South Carolina Department of Health and Environmental Control
Sustainable Universities Initiative
South Carolina Botanical Gardens
Howard Hughes Medical Institute

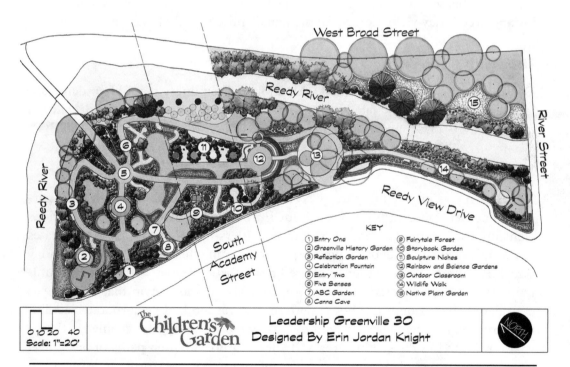

KEY

1. Entry One
2. Greenville History Garden
3. Reflection Garden
4. Celebration Fountain
5. Entry Two
6. Five Senses
7. ABC Garden
8. Canna Cave
9. Fairytale Forest
10. Storybook Garden
11. Sculpture Niches
12. Rainbow and Science Gardens
13. Outdoor Classroom
14. Wildlife Walk
15. Native Plant Garden

0 10 20 40
Scale: 1"=20'

The Children's Garden
Leadership Greenville 30
Designed By Erin Jordan Knight

NORTH

An ethnobotany garden seeks to educate the public on an array of plant uses that have persisted in different cultures throughout history. (COURTESY OF RENEE KEYDOSZIUS.)

MISSION AND PURPOSE

The ethnobotany garden seeks to educate the public on an array of plant uses that have persisted in different cultures throughout history. As fuel for fire, fodder for livestock, furniture, or flooring, plants are part of our everyday life. The term "Ethnobotany" describes the study of people's relationships to plants. "Because ethnobotany focuses not just on plants, but on how people use plants, it can offer even very young children the opportunity to reflect on what they eat, what they wear, where they live, and how the things they use were made" (Pevec, 2003). The plants that are cultivated in this area are those that have been important to human cultures for hundreds of years because of their usefulness. Through interaction with this garden, children, as well as the public in general, will come to have a greater appreciation of the dependency of humans on the plant kingdom to provide us with foods, fibers, building materials, cosmetics, and medicines. Our goal is to expose visitors to the history that pervades so many of the plants around us and to create opportunities for discovering new uses for plants that before had been designated merely as "ornamentals" or "weeds." That humble weed may yield a powerful medicine and unsightly foliage a brilliant dye.

THE DESIGN TEAM

Designer Stephanie Zabel worked with an interdisciplinary team of garden staff, landscape professionals, faculty, students, community volunteers, and children from an after-school program at the South Carolina Botanical Garden (SCBG).

THE DESIGN

The design was inspired in part by layouts of traditional herb and medicinal gardens that were once utilized throughout Europe. The plan incorporates various elements used in the gardens of Moravian settlers who fled to the United States in the 18th century to avoid religious persecution in what is now the present-day Czech Republic. Their gardens reflected a simplistic lifestyle and a need for utilitarian plants and a practical layout, yet they also made certain that beauty was considered. Based on a geometric pattern, the garden beds incorporate rectilinear, circular, and semicircular patterns. To establish unity, the geometric theme is also reflected in the seating area and curved arbor. Garden paths of pea gravel allow water to percolate into the garden without creating storm water management problems. The paths allow for easy pedestrian circulation and also allow access for children to harvest, weed, and replant the beds. A central axis runs through the middle of the garden, enclosing a circular bed with an obelisk in the middle. The axis terminates at a sitting area under a semicircular alcove in a stone retaining wall. Over 50 useful plants are housed in the Ethnobotany Garden, each with a unique set of past and present uses. Many are quite familiar to the modern-day palate: rosemary, basil, oregano, thyme, and the lesser-known edible flowers of borage and calendula. Others present their stately functions with inviting aromas such as the anise-scented leaves of winter tarragon and the healing silver dollar eucalyptus. Common, overlooked "weeds," including Queen Anne's lace, yarrow (Figure 6a-1), and mullein, are celebrated in the garden, as each has been used for centuries as folk medicine. For example, Passionflower, also known as maypop, is a native vine of North America. Passionflower calms and soothes tension and nervous anxiety. Native Americans soothed various inflammations by applying a root poultice to the affected area. They also brewed a tea of the plant to treat anxiety (Buchanan, 1995). Today, passionflower is still used in European countries to treat similar conditions (Figure 6a-2).

FIG 6a-1. Yarrow was widely utilized throughout the continent by many Native American tribes and continues to enjoy modern usage. Yarrow has been used by Alaskan Natives for everything from colds to open wounds and reducing high fevers (Garibaldi, 1999). (COURTESY OF RENEE KEYDOSZIUS.)

EDUCATIONAL ASPECTS

People have used plants as foods, fibers, medicines, dyes, and tools throughout the ages. Therefore, one cannot underestimate the relationship that occurs between humans and plants, or fail to notice the extensive role of plants in everyday life. Ethnobotany is the study of the significant interactions that constantly occur between cultures and the botanical world. "People/plant relations are so central to human livelihoods that courses or programs in Ethnobotany could potentially cover a vast range of topics" (Hamilton, 2002). The scope of ethnobotany incor-

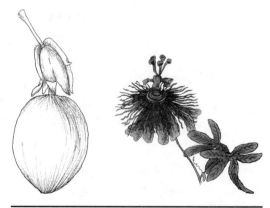

FIG 6a-2. Passionflower, also known as maypop, is a native vine of North America sometimes used to calm and soothe tension and nervous anxiety. (COURTESY OF RENEE KEYDOSZIUS.)

FIG 6a-3. Graduate student Meghan Baker developed outdoor lessons in the Ethnobotany garden using South Carolina state curriculum guidelines. (COURTESY OF MARY TAYLOR HAQUE.)

porates aspects of botany, chemistry, anthropology, history, and economics to explain and interpret human–plant interactions. A multidisciplinary field, ethnobotany addresses the interactions between human cultures and plants in both historical and contemporary contexts. Ethnobotanical study, with its interdisciplinary nature and focus on the placement of information within its full cultural context, is a model of liberal arts education (Anderson, 1997). As such, it is particularly well suited to the young, who are still moving within the interconnectedness and possibilities of the world of knowledge, rather than within its narrow specializations. Children are often curious about how clothes, crafts, food, and buildings are made, and they may one day become scholars studying how people use plants (Figure 6a-3). An ethnobotany garden or portable "trunk" carrying samples from the garden to schoolrooms can be used to teach many lessons that meet general education goals and curriculum guidelines. Following is a checklist of such goals and guidelines developed for the South Carolina Botanical Garden Ethnobotany Garden.

Ethnobotany Garden Lesson Plan
Educational Goals and Curriculum Guidelines

I. Educational Goals of the Ethnobotany Trunk

1. Teach the importance of plant–human interactions through lessons on enthnobotany, plant origins, environmental conservation, and modern-day botanical medicines.

2. Develop an understanding of human dependence on plants and natural habitats for ultimate survival.

3. Reinforce "hands-on" learning through relevant activities such as dyeing with plants, creating homemade teas, using edible flowers, and observing the culturally important plants in our local environments.

II. Applicable South Carolina Curriculum Guidelines (Grades 3–5)

- *Science*

Grade 3:
  Inquiry:
  Use the senses and simple tools to gather information about objects or events such as size, shape, color, texture, sound, position, and change (qualitative observations). (A2, A3, A4, A5)
  Life Science:
  Investigate and predict ways living things will interact with each other and the environment. (L1, L2, L3, L4, L6)
  Earth Science:
  Identify that soil provides support and nutrients for plant growth. (L1, L2)

Grade 4:
  Inquiry:
  Use the senses and simple tools to gather information about objects or events such as size, shape, color, texture, sound, position, and change (qualitative observations). (A2, A3, A4, A5)

Grade 5:
  Inquiry:
  Use the senses and simple tools to gather information about objects or events such as size, shape, color, texture, sound, position, and change (qualitative observations). (A2, A3, A4, A5)
  Life Science:
  Evaluate the impact of the environment on populations of organisms. (L1, L2, L4, L6)

- *Visual Arts*

Grades 3–5:
  Understanding and Applying Media, Techniques, and Processes:
  Use a variety of media, techniques, and processes to communicate ideas, experiences, and stories through their artwork. (A2, A3, A4, A5, Additional Activities)
  Understanding the Visual Arts in Relation to History and Culture: Describe how history, culture, and the visual arts can influence one another. (L5, A5)

- *Language Arts*

  Writing Purposes:

  3-W2.2: Continue using writing to learn, entertain, and describe. (Additional Activities)

  4-W2.2: Demonstrate the ability to use writing to learn, entertain, and describe. (Additional Activities)

  5-W2.2: Demonstrate the ability to use writing to learn, entertain, and describe. (Additional Activities)

- *Communication: Listening*

  3-C2.1: Demonstrate the ability to follow multistep oral directions. (L3, A1, A2, A3, A4, A5, Additional Activities)

  3-C2.2: Demonstrate the ability to listen for meaning in conversations and discussions. (All lessons applicable)

  4-C2.1: Demonstrate the ability to follow multistep oral directions. (L3, A1, A2, A3, A4, A5, Additional Activities)

  4-C2.2: Demonstrate the ability to listen for meaning in conversations and discussions. (All lessons applicable)

  5-C2.1: Demonstrate the ability to listen for meaning in conversations and discussions. (L3, A1, A2, A3, A4, A5, Additional Activities)

- *Social Studies*

III. People, Places, and Environments: Geography

3.9: The learner will demonstrate an understanding of the world in spatial terms. (L3)

3.12: The learner will demonstrate an understanding of interactions between the environment and society. (L1, L3, L4, L5, L6, A1, A4, A5)

4.7: The learner will demonstrate an understanding of places and regions. (L3, L5, L6)

5.10: The learner will demonstrate an understanding of places and regions. (L3, L5, L6)

Key:

L1 = Lesson 1

L2 = Lesson 2, etc.

A1 = Activity 1

A2 = Activity 2, etc.

PARTICIPATORY ASPECTS

The ethnobotany garden has become a learning tool that stimulates interest in the wondrous array of plant species and their many uses. Children in the Sprouting Wings program and visitors to the SCBG have a wide range of plant species to harvest for use in crafts and other projects such as dyeing wool (Figure 6a-4). Sprouting Wings is an after-school gardening and nature exploration program for underserved elementary school students across the upstate of South Carolina.

To promote creative thinking and add interest in the landscape, a class of university students participated in the garden creation by crafting an object outside of class to install in the garden. Artwork included decorative stepping stones of concrete and stained glass (one with a dragonfly and one with a butterfly focal point), a spectacular metal butterfly to adorn the garden, a bat condominium, stain glass birdhouse, and a broken tile birdhouse to enhance wildlife habitat (Figure 6a-5). Two weeks after the installation of the tile birdhouse, a pair of house wrens began building a nest. The South Carolina Department of Health and Environmental Control recognized the team of students and staff who implemented the garden as "Champions of the Environment" after an assessment visit at the end of the semester. The garden, which includes food, water, nesting sites, and cover for wildlife, has also been certified as a wildlife habitat by the South Carolina Wildlife Federation (SCWF), and children help with the ongoing maintenance and upkeep.

FIG 6a-4. Children in the Sprouting Wings program harvest horseradish for culinary and craft uses. (COURTESY OF MEGHAN BAKER.)

UNIQUE CHARACTERISTICS OF THE GARDEN

The Ethnobotany garden is an innovative and educational resource that has a broad span of practical applications. Because children are the primary audience, their specific needs were of greatest importance during the design process. Safety, five-sense stimulation, spaces for solitude and decompression, and details that give rise to creative play are crucial principals in designing garden spaces for children (Knight, 2001). Beds in the Ethnobotany garden are small and easily accessible so that children are able to harvest plant material and replant annuals and biennials. Details such as colorful birdhouses of tile, dragonfly stepping-stones, and a giant metal butterfly add interest and magic to the garden space. Sitting areas are child sized and low to the ground. A wide set of entrance steps pro-

FIG 6a-5. To promote creative thinking, add interest, and enhance wildlife habitat, a class of university students crafted artistic objects to install in the garden. (COURTESY OF MARY TAYLOR HAQUE.)

vides an ideal place for a class to sit. Because children might be tempted to "graze" on plants, highly toxic plants were excluded. Each selected species offers a plethora of exciting and surprising uses that often go unnoticed. Most importantly, each serves as a tangible link between human and botanical worlds.

ACTIVITIES MOST POPULAR WITH CHILDREN

Children enjoy planting the seeds of annual plants and harvesting plants like the silver dollar eucalyptus to make dyes for a skein of wool. They love the mystery associated with creating a bright orange dye (Clemson University's color) from the blue green leaves, especially when working with Clemson students who volunteer in the garden (Figure 6a-6).

FUNDING

Grant funds were used to design and build the garden. Utilizing service learning, university students joined faculty, garden staff, and a retired master carpenter to build the garden, including a wooden obelisk, a key focal point of the garden. The class built 12 other obelisks for use in other gardens and to sell as fundraisers at the SCBG spring plant sale. The sprouting wings children who helped build and maintain the garden create and sell wreaths, potted plants, and crafts at the plant sale to help raise money for their program.

MAINTENANCE

The garden is maintained by sprouting wings children, garden volunteers, and paid garden staff.

CONSTRUCTION TEAM

An interdisciplinary team of garden staff, landscape professionals, faculty, students, community volunteers, and children from an after-school program created the Ethnobotany Garden at the SCBG (Figure 6a-7). Participants combined academic service learning and experiential education in a cooperative, community project to design, install, maintain, and interpret the garden. As part of a larger plan for a series of themed children's gardens within the SCBG, the Ethnobotany garden is a model environment for both active and passive learning for children. The

FIG 6a-6. Children enjoy harvesting plants like the silver dollar eucalyptus to make dyes with the help of university students. (COURTESY OF AMY DABBS.)

FIG 6a-7. College students combined academic service learning and experiential education in a cooperative, community project to design, install, maintain, interpret, and raise funds for the ethnobotany garden. (COURTESY OF MARY TAYLOR HAQUE.)

semester following the design development, students enrolled in a Landscape Implementation class partnered with the SCBG staff, volunteers, and Sprouting Wings to install the garden. One important agenda for an educational landscape is as an instructional resource, reinforcing and enhancing learning activities along integrated, multicurricular lines (Takahashi, 1999). Sprouting Wings participants were especially excited about helping build the garden created for children, because this would be a prime educational resource for teaching about the natural world. They assisted in the propagation and planting of the Ethnobotany Garden, and are assisting in its maintenance and regeneration while continuing to learn about both plants and their cultural and contextual uses. While Sprouting Wings children were propagating plants under the direction of a graduate student and SCBG staff, undergraduate students were constructing a stone retaining wall designed to respond to the site topography and to create a sense of space. These landscape implementation students worked under the direction of a professional stonemason and SCBG staff members, who conducted a workshop to teach university students masonry skills. College students and faculty working on this service-learning project contributed over 1,000 hours to their community while learning more about both the art and the science of landscape design and implementation. The students at Clemson University benefited from the instruction of a professional stonemason, an experienced carpenter, and a team of professional educators and horticulturalists from the South Carolina Botanical Garden in addition to the knowledge absorbed from their textbook and from the professor and graduate students in charge of the class. Evaluation and assessment by organizations like the South Carolina Department of Health and Environmental Control DHEC and SCWF provide yet another avenue of information and feedback for participating students.

> *"Children are intrigued by the miniscule details that give an object beauty or interest; often adults take the simple and small elements for granted"*
> —Knight, 2001

CREDITS

The Ethnobotany Garden in the South Carolina Botanical Garden Designer

Stephanie Zabel: Landscape designer (Figure 6a-8)

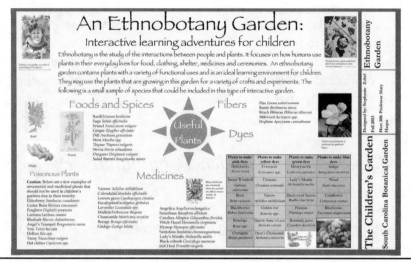

FIG 6a-8. Designer Stephanie Zabel developed this research poster to illustrate Ethnobotany concepts. The individuals cited below contributed to the article about the Ethnobotany Garden. (COURTESY OF STEPHANIE ZABEL.)

The Ethnobotany Garden in the South Carolina Botanical Garden Planning and Construction Team

James Arnold: Manager, South Carolina Botanical Garden

Meghan Baker: Clemson University graduate student grant writer and project director

Gary Burgess: Lead stonemason

Rodger Carpenter: Lead carpenter and SCBG volunteer

Amy Dabbs: Sprouting Wings Program Coordinator

Mary Haque: Clemson University professor in charge of service learning component

Brad Jordan: Construction manager, South Carolina Botanical Garden

Renee Keydoszius: Clemson University graduate student assisting with service learning component

Lisa Petty: Assistant Sprouting Wings Program Coordinator

FIG 6a-9. Calendula, a well-known edible flower that has the distinction of being not merely a culinary herb, but also a medicinal and dye plant. (COURTESY OF MARY TAYLOR HAQUE.)

Carri Carver Wallace: Clemson University graduate student grant writer and project organizer

Lisa Wagner: Director of Education, South Carolina Botanical Garden

Michael Whitmire: Clemson University graduate student assisting with service learning component

Greenville Children's Garden (Community Partnership)

Opened: September 10, 2005
Acres: 1 acre (+.4 hectare)
Cost: Nearly $50,000 raised ($40,000 spent to date) with $20,000 in in-kind donations, not including volunteer work hours.
Funding: Funding sources are individual, company donations, and brick sales.

MISSION AND PURPOSE

The Children's Garden at Linky Stone Park in Greenville, SC, celebrates Greenville's children and teaches them through plants and play what makes their community special and unique. History, arts, education, nature, reflection, and other themes are featured in the Children's Garden. Educating and entertaining children through discovery opportunities is a guiding principle. Children enjoy this garden because they sense that it belongs to them. It was through their guidance that the garden took shape, and it is through their play that it truly comes to life.

This garden is the result of the foresight, teamwork, and creativity of Leadership Greenville Class 30 (LG XXX), a dynamic and engaged group sponsored by the Chamber of Commerce, designed to cultivate civic involvement and educate outstanding individuals destined to lead their community. Through a partnership with the City of Green-

Many people worked together to create the Children's Garden at Linky Stone Park, and because it was a community effort, it is a reflection of the community it serves. (COURTESY OF DAVID KNIGHT.)

ville Parks and Recreation Department and a dedicated team of volunteers, LG XXX made a generous and lasting gift to Greenville's children.

> *Children's gardens are an asset to all metropolitan areas, but they are needed in cities like Greenville in particular. Greenville is a beautiful city, and much of the region surrounding it remains very natural and picturesque. However, the Upstate is experiencing unprecedented growth, and the rural childhood many children of this region knew is often being replaced by a suburban one, far more isolated from nature. A study conducted by Smart Growth America (Ewing, 2002) on sprawl in the United States, ranks Greenville/Spartanburg as #5 on the list of Most Sprawling Metropolitan Areas. What is more, four of the top five ranked communities are located along the I-85 corridor. The highway that runs through the heart of Greenville County unites it with cities such as Atlanta, GA (#4) and Greensboro (#2) and Raleigh-Durham (#3), NC, in more ways than one. It ties them in bonds of unprecedented development that far outpaces the population growth. It is when youth are isolated from nature that the creation of special spaces for them within the urban fabric becomes most critical. The members of Leadership Greenville XXX identified this need and met its challenge.*

THE PLANNING AND DESIGN TEAM

The Design Team was organized through the leadership, vision, and long-term commitment of Brice Hipp, member of LG XXX, who initiated the children's garden concept and served as project Chair. Without her dedication, the garden would not be in bloom today. Hipp enlisted Erin Jordan Knight to serve as landscape designer and consultant, and after providing the contracted deliverables, Knight remained intimately involved in the project's development and implementation stages as a volunteer.

Before the project began, Hipp met with Paul Ellis, Director of Parks and Recreation of the City of Greenville, to discuss the concept's feasibility as well as possible site locations. Ellis proposed locating the new garden at Linky Stone Park, a site already landscaped as a project of Leadership Greenville XIV, and equipped with the existing infrastructure as well as an expert maintenance staff necessary to support the garden. The site was ideally located on the Reedy River

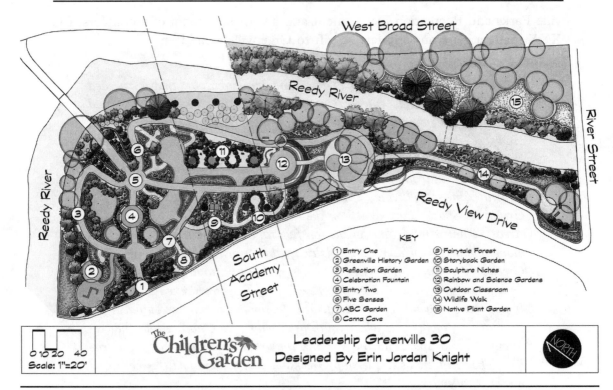

West Broad Street

Reedy River

River Street

Reedy River

Reedy View Drive

South Academy Street

KEY

① Entry One		⑨ Fairytale Forest	
② Greenville History Garden		⑩ Storybook Garden	
③ Reflection Garden		⑪ Sculpture Niches	
④ Celebration Fountain		⑫ Rainbow and Science Gardens	
⑤ Entry Two		⑬ Outdoor Classroom	
⑥ Five Senses		⑭ Wildlife Walk	
⑦ ABC Garden		⑮ Native Plant Garden	
⑧ Canna Cave			

0 10 20 40
Scale: 1"=20'

The Children's Garden

Leadership Greenville 30
Designed By Erin Jordan Knight

NORTH

FIG 6b-1. The Master Plan for the garden, designed by Knight, reflects collaboration between LG XXX members, children, City Parks and Recreation staff, and the community. The design is a plant-based combination of play and educational opportunities. (COURTESY OF ERIN JORDAN KNIGHT.)

within a planned corridor for a significant greenway development of parks, bike paths and open spaces.

Once the site was selected, the Design Team began the process of clarifying the project vision through surveying children and community members for design ideas, researching children's gardens, and determining subcommittees and roles for each participant.

THE DESIGN

Knight taught the team about children's gardens and their potential characteristics and features. She and Paul Ellis led a brainstorming session with the team about all the ideas appropriate for the Greenville Children's Garden (Figure 6b-1).

The group discussed each idea in an open forum. They were asked to rank their favorite three elements to incorporate. Of the group's 20 favorite ideas, 18 became part of the final design. Eighty-one percent of all proposed ideas were ultimately incorporated.

A similar group discussion was conducted at local schools, under the guidance of teachers in the community. Teachers briefly introduced children to the idea of a garden created just for them, and then asked them to draw or write about what they would like to see there. The most popular responses involved requests about animals (i.e., animal sculptures, wildlife habitat, and ponds with fish and turtles), a theme recurring 111 times in the overall 655 suggestions (Figure 6b-2).

FIG 6b-2. Children throughout Greenville County answered survey questions through the guidance of teachers and produced drawings or descriptions of their hopes for the garden. Here is one child's proposal.

The second most popular request was for fountains, ponds, or other water features, which were mentioned a total of 87 times. Some of the children's ideas for water include a chocolate shooting fountain, a flower bending over fountain, a fountain children can walk through, and a dancing fountain.

Of course, many types of active play common on the typical playground were suggested, perhaps because this is what children are familiar with in landscapes designed for their use. Trees and flowers also received much recognition, getting 43 and 57 requests, respectively. Other themes that were mentioned related to music, nature, the arts, and literature. A recurring theme was the request from children for validation. They wanted to feel important and special. Suggestions included a sign stating, "We Love Children!"; "a trained parrot that says nice things to children"; "a wall where kids can sign their names"; and "red carpet sidewalks."

Another group of children met on-site to brainstorm garden ideas. They drew their garden plans on the columns of the Academy Street Bridge, which runs overhead, bisecting the park. These columns were later painted in a rainbow of colors and covered with themed murals (Figure 6b-3).

FIG 6b-3. After surveys were compiled, a group of children met on-site to refine the results and brainstorm specific garden components. Here, a child uses chalk to draw ideas on bridge columns that illustrate their proposals.
(COURTESY OF ERIN JORDAN KNIGHT.)

HISTORY GARDEN
Historic River Cane

River cane (Arundinaria gigantean) is the only native American bamboo, and it is the "reed" that gave the Reedy River its name. Found in flood plains throughout the southeastern United States, it is a member of the Grass family (Poaceae), and grows to over 25 feet in height. A smaller subspecies called switch or mountain cane (Arundinaria gigantea tecta) grows to about 4 feet high. Like all grasses, river cane blooms and produces seed, but only does so infrequently (sometimes as long as 50 years between blooms). Cane reproduces by spreading underground with rhizomes and putting up new shoots every 12 to 18 inches.

Archeological records indicate that Native American people began to use river cane nearly 9000 years ago. Because it is found in such a wide range of sizes and because it can be manipulated in a variety of ways, river cane was one of their most important plant species. It was used for arrows, spears, blowguns, baskets, sleeping and work mats, and even woven into the walls of lodges. Native Americans may have even planned the relocation of their villages around the abundance of river cane. When they began to deplete the canebrakes (thickets of river cane) near a particular village, they would begin nearly a year ahead to prepare their move near to a lush and healthy canebrake. When they rebuilt their homes in the new location, they cut the black locust saplings in the canebrake for lodge poles and then cane to weave between the poles to pack with mud and form the walls.

Early explorers of the southeast recounted seeing thick canebrakes many miles across. These canebrakes were likely maintained by fires set by the Indians who learned that fire killed off most competing plant species and made a healthier canebrake. Many species of animals thrived in the canebrakes, such as bear and bison and even the Carolina Parakeet. Early white settlers grazed cattle and horses in canebrakes which was comparable to the finest pastures. While the great canebrakes are gone today, you can still find small canebrakes along rivers and streams throughout its range, and many people are again learning the value of river cane in preventing erosion of stream banks and providing wildlife habitat. Almost everywhere you see river cane today, there is evidence of Native American habitation nearby.

Here, we have replanted historic river cane so that it will stabilize the river banks, be a home for animals, and be discovered and studied by the children who visit the garden.

FIG 6b-4. Signage plays a critical role in the garden, as it expands on the educational opportunities found there. Children and local artists illustrated each sign while experts researched and wrote text on a variety of topics. Here, you see Adam Kerechanin's drawings and Wes Cooler's text for the River Cane signage in the History Garden. (COURTESY OF ERIN JORDAN KNIGHT.)

The final garden design consists of over 20 major theme areas, each encompassing the requests of children and class members, or the spirit of their ideas, and also reflecting Greenville itself.

The Greenville History Garden celebrates the city and its rich past. Children learn about important agricultural plants of Greenville's past, such as wheat, corn, oats, cotton, tea, and river cane in *The Historical Plants Garden* (Figure 6b-4). They learn about textiles, an industry important to

Greenville and significant to the very site, in *The Textile Garden*. There, plants used for dyes, fabrics, or other elements of the cloth-making process grow and children can weave grasses through a loom. *The Water Table Celebrating Greenville History* involves troughs of water at varying heights and is proposed for a later phase of garden implementation. It will circulate water that falls from one level to another, spinning a mill wheel as the Reedy River once did.

The Reflection Garden will provide children overwhelmed by the social and interactive play of other areas a chance to be quiet and observe nature. Plantings will provide color and textural interest and offer interesting discoveries in all seasons.

The Celebration Fountain is an interactive fountain of play opportunities for children of Greenville. It, too, is proposed for a later phase of implementation.

The **Five Senses Gardens** delight all the senses and provide opportunities for wonder and discovery. The *SMELL* garden will enhance experience with herbs and aromatic plants. The *SEE* garden includes many plant performers that exhibit distinct behaviors and those that create significant visual interest. The *TASTE* area showcases berries and fruits and edible flowers. In the *TOUCH* garden, children will interact with plants that have textures of interest. The *HEAR* garden features outdoor musical instruments.

The ABC Garden takes young children on an alphabet lesson (or older ones on a botanical one) of flowers and herbs from A (Anise Hyssop) to Z (Zinnia) (Figure 6b-5).

In the **Canna Cave**, children can escape into a world of overgrown flowers and seclusion. These cannas were originally grown in the garden of Linky Stone and now form a magical enclosure in which children can hide and play.

FIG 6b-5. A child examines an obedient plant in the ABC Garden. (COURTESY OF MARY TAYLOR HAQUE.)

The **Fairy Tale Forest** celebrates the themes of children's favorite fairy tales. As children near the Hansel and Gretel Candy Cottage, they discover candy-themed plants—from lollipop-like allium flower balls on stick-like stalks to chocolate cosmos and peppermint.

In the **Storybook Garden**, children find Peter Rabbit sitting within a small picket fence overlooking a "vegetable garden" of hostas. Then, children must search for *The Secret Garden*. Other friends from literature are found there, too (Figure 6b-6).

FIG 06b-6. In *The Secret Garden Enclosure*, children will find much "magic" hidden, just as in the story. In the hand-carved stone engraving, stating that "Every joy on earth was found in the secret garden" crafted and donated by David Gillespie, children can find hidden keys within the beautiful lettering. Murals painted by Rick Forest span the seasons and include many subtle details from the story. (COURTESY OF MARY TAYLOR HAQUE.)

Sculpture Niches, created of evergreen shrubs, are opportunities for future art displays and/or seating areas in the garden.

The **Rainbow Garden** displays annual flowers within the painted bricks that line the boundaries of its beds (Figure 6b-7).

The **Science Gardens** include *The Geology Garden*, which is constructed of the major rock types found in the Upstate, SC, region (Figure 6b-8). *The Ecology Garden* introduces children to the Reedy River and to concepts concerning water quality. Interpretive signs teach children about watersheds, pollution, and what kids can do to protect water resources. A riparian buffer

FIG 06b-7. Fletcher Group, Inc., a local environmental engineering firm, designed the geology wall and installed both that feature and the rainbow garden as their annual staff retreat; a tremendous gift to the garden. (COURTESY OF FLETCHER GROUP, INC.)

FIG 06b-8. Caption to come.

teaches children about biofiltration. *The Botany Garden* is planted with flowers and vines that attract a garden's major pollinators: birds, butterflies, bees, and moths. This garden also teaches children about seeds, parts of a flower, and pollination. *The Biology Garden* will grow vegetables that contain the vitamins that fuel and nourish the human body.

The Outdoor Classroom, a ring of mature trees in the garden, ideal for outdoor lessons.

The **Wildlife Walk** and **Native Plant Gardens**, future phases of the garden, will exhibit a wildlife habitat area and plants native to Upstate, SC.

FUNDING

The LG XXX team began work on the marketing and public relations and fundraising very early in the design process. This project was made possible through a combination of generous contributions from local businesses and individuals, in-kind donations, and volunteer labor.

IMPLEMENTATION

Garden implementation was primarily a volunteer effort, expertly organized by Heather Bergerud, Volunteer Coordinator (Figure 6b-9). Horticulture students

FIG 06b-9. Heather Bergerud, Volunteer Coordinator, and Lilah Campbell plant annuals in the bands of the Rainbow Garden. Children love the bright, bold color of this feature that unifies the Science Gardens. (COURTESY OF DAVID KNIGHT.)

FIG 06b-10. Clemson Horticulture Students under the direction of Dr. Jim Faust and Bill Jordan completed the majority of bed preparation as well as much plant layout and installation, an effort that transformed the garden. (COURTESY OF ERIN JORDAN KNIGHT.)

from Clemson University under the direction of Dr. Jim Faust completed most bed preparation and much of the plant installation. Bill Jordan of Clemson University grew all specialty plants for the garden from seed and found that the tiny seedlings brought out child-like interest in his horticulture students. They bickered over who got to touch the tiny sensitive plants that would close at the brush of a fingertip, and marveled at the brilliant red of the Hopi red dye amaranth seedlings, destined for the textile garden.

Workdays brought LG XXX members, children from local schools, master gardeners, high school students, local business people, other volunteers, and City Parks and Recreation crews together to invest in a garden that seems to be not only for children, but for the child in all of us (Figure 6b-10).

MAINTENANCE AND EVALUATION

The City of Greenville's Parks and Recreation Department's Falls Park Staff are responsible for the garden maintenance and care, under the direction of Jordan Franklin, Public Garden Manager.

Initiating a garden through community partnership takes a great deal of planning, effort, and organization from a diverse and dedicated team of partners. When creating a garden, the critical questions to ask are: *Where is the garden going to be located? Who will be involved in the garden's development? How will we fund the project? How do we implement the design? Who will take care of long-term maintenance?*

The most wonderful aspect of such a project is that it is a true reflection of the people it serves, and thus is more likely to be utilized, maintained, and celebrated (Figure 6b-11).

FIG 06b-11. Children were an important part of every workday, and it was through their contribution that other volunteers grew truly excited about the project. (COURTESY OF ERIN JORDAN KNIGHT.)

FIG 06b-12. Visitors celebrate the Children's Garden grand opening and explore its many features. Here people of all ages enjoy the ABC Garden which teaches plant identification as well as the alphabet. (COURTESY OF MARY TAYLOR HAQUE.)

CREDITS

The Children's Garden at Linky Stone Park, Design Team

Leadership Greenville XXX

Brice Hipp, Chairperson of Leadership Greenville XXX Children's Garden Team

Erin Jordan Knight, Landscape Designer

Heather Bergerud, Volunteer Coordinator

Paul Ellis, Director of Parks and Recreation and Don Shuman, Assistant Administrator of Parks and Grounds for the City of Greenville

Construction Team

Assistance with workdays, writing or editing text of signs, signage illustrations, and design and implementation of garden features: Children, artists, carpenters, gardeners, and other volunteers.

Major Volunteer Contributions:

Eric Bergerud: Design and implantation of the outdoor musical instrument

Fletcher Group, Inc.: Design and implementation of the Geology Garden and Rainbow Garden

David Gillespie: Hand-carving of *The Secret Garden* stone

Dr. Jim Faust and his Clemson University horticulture students enrolled in the 2005 annuals and perennials course, planting and bed preparation

Bill Jordan: Growing of specialty garden plants, many other horticultural contributions, carpentry, implementation

Stephen Nix: Carpentry and implementation

Contracted Construction/Installation Team Members:

Rick Forest, Garden Muralist

The Garden Arch, Rob Hunt, Designer/Builder, Plant and sod implementation

American Wood Fences and Decks, Construction and carpentry contractor

Conclusion

hildren benefit in many ways from well-designed outdoor environments including schoolyards, gardens, and playgrounds. Providing children with spaces that meet all of their critical needs not only gives the child a special place for play, but can also benefit them throughout life. Studies indicate that children's intelligence increases when stimulated by constantly changing environments where play is not predetermined, and the freedom of nature provides emotional release from the stresses of childhood. Today, when children are increasingly isolated by the impacts of sprawl, it is particularly important to provide gardens to meet their specific needs and interests. City planners, developers, park officials, and others should be contacted to encourage them to minimize isolation and urban sprawl by using regional planning designs that support children's health and happiness. For example, a network of safe bicycle and walking trails connecting parks, playgrounds, schools, and public gardens to residential neighborhoods allows children to access local resources while exercising and enjoying the diversity found in their community.

While creating these special places at the regional or residential scale, designers, parents, teachers, and others should remember the principles of design and safety to assure that children will thrive, learn, and grow within a safe environment. Studying successful existing children's spaces can provide valuable insight into the creation of such spaces. The most successful children's gardens and schoolyards may vary dramatically in scale and budget, but they all share common elements: variety, discovery opportunities, appealing plants that are safe and sustainable in children's environments, and features that expand the power of imagination. Whether the garden's emphasis is play, education, emotional healing, or memorial tribute, it has great potential to foster childhood development and impact a young life in lasting ways.

After reading about the gardens in this book, consider visiting them and the myriad of others all over the world as you travel. Each garden is unique, a response to its soils, sun, wildlife, hydrology, and other site conditions. The children in your life will enjoy the great diversity and can be encouraged to look for the hand of the designer in each garden. To heighten their powers of observation and focus, encourage them to draw their favorite plants and other garden features in a journal or sketchbook.

The adventures, observations, and experiences found in public and private gardens can stimulate a child's senses and imagination, educate them in fun and engaging ways, and inspire them to create their own gardens. Three of the greatest gifts that designers, parents, and teachers can give a child are the space, time, and tools to design and build a garden of their own. Personal gardens can serve as landmarks in the life of children, providing an oasis where they can create, work, and play in sunlight or shade with seeds, plants, water, soil, and other natural materials.

Perhaps the most crucial reason to teach children a love of nature through garden experiences is in preparation for the future. Both present and future generations must actively seek solutions to the depletion of natural resources and degradation of our environment. Studies suggest that it is through an early bond with nature, as well as through the influence of nurturing adults, that children develop a sense of environmental stewardship. By instilling that responsibility and powerful bond in today's youth, those who provide gardens are protecting the future.

Childhood is a special time, one devoted to learning and experiencing joy and discovery. Children need spaces that they can make wholly their own in which to play, learn, laugh, think, and move. Providing well-designed outdoor spaces gives a child the freedom to explore life and develop into a healthy and unique individual.

"Study nature, love nature, stay close to nature. It will never fail you."
—Frank Lloyd Wright

Resources

Public Children's Gardens

ARIZONA

Children's Discovery Garden
2150 N. Alvernon Way
Tucson, AZ 85712
Phone: 520-326-9686
Website: http://www.tucsonbotanical.org/html/
    garden_children.html

ARKANSAS

Evans Children's Adventure Garden
Garvan Woodland Garden
550 Arkridge Road
University of Arkansas
Hot Springs National Park, AR 71913
Phone: 1-800-366-4664
Website: http://www.garvangardens.org/
    discover/gardens/gardens.asp

CALIFORNIA

Children's Garden
McConnell Arboretum & Gardens
Turtle Bay Exploration Park
840 Auditorium Drive
Redding, CA 96001
Phone: 1-800-887-8532
Website: http://www.turtlebay.org/

Helen and Peter Bing Children's Garden
Huntington Botanical Gardens
1151 Oxford Road
San Marino, CA 91108
Phone: 626-405-2100
Website: http://www.huntington.org/

Kids' Adventure Garden
The Conejo Valley Botanic Garden
P.O. Box 1382
Thousand Oaks, CA 91358
Phone: 805-376-6063
Website: http://www.conejogarden.com

Outdoor Learning Environments
Kidspace Children's Museum
480 N. Arroyo Blvd.
Pasadena, CA 91103
Phone: 626-449-9144
Website: http://www.kidspacemuseum.org/
    exhibits/gardens.asp

Seeds of Wonder
Quail Botanical Gardens
230 Quail Gardens Drive
Encinitas, CA 92023-0005
Phone: 760-436-3036
Website: http://www.qbgardens.com/
    qbgframed.html

WorldBeat Center's Children's Ethnobotany
  Garden
Balboa Park Gardens
1549 El Prado
San Diego, CA 92101
Phone: 619-239-0512
Website: http://www.balboapark.org/
  aboutgardens.html

COLORADO

Children's Secret Garden
Western Colorado Botanical Gardens
655 Struthers Avenue
Grand Junction, CO 81501
Phone: 970-245-9030
Website: http://www.wcbotanic.org/

Children's Secret Path
Denver Botanical Garden
1005 York Street
Denver, CO 80206
Phone: 720-865-3500
Website: http://www.botanicgardens.org/
  pageinpage/home.cfm

DELAWARE

The Delaware Center for Horticulture
1810 North Dupont Street
Wilmington, DE 19806
Phone: 302-658-6262
Website: http://www.dehort.org/

Enchanted Woods
Winterthur Museum and Country Estate
Winterthur, DE 19735
Phone: 1- 800-448-3883
Website: http://www.winterthur.org/

DISTRICT OF COLUMBIA

Seeds of Change Garden
Smithsonian Institute
P.O. Box 37012
SI Building, Room 153 MRC010
Washington, DC 26013-7012
Phone: 202-633-1000
Website: http://www.mnh.si.edu/archives/
  garden/

FLORIDA

Mounts Botanical Garden
531 N. Military Trail
West Palm Beach, FL 33415-1311
Phone: 561-233-1757
Website: http://www.mounts.org/

GEORGIA

Children's Garden
Dauset Trails Nature Center
360 Mt. Vernon Road
Jackson, GA 30233
Phone: 770-775-6798
Website: http://www.dausettrails.com/
  childgarden.htm

Children's Healthcare of Atlanta Garden
Atlanta Botanical Garden
1345 Piedmont Avenue, NE
Atlanta, GA 30309
Phone: 404-876-5859
Website: http://www.atlantabotanicalgarden.
  org/

IDAHO

Children's Garden
Idaho Botanical Garden
2355 N. Penitentiary Road
Boise, ID 83712
Phone: 208-343-8649
Website: http://www.idahobotanicalgarden.org/

ILLINOIS

Children's Garden
Chicago Botanic Garden
1000 Lake Cook Rd.
Glencoe, IL 60022
Phone: 847-835-5440
Website: http://www.chicagobotanic.org

Children's Garden & Maze Gardens
Morten Arboretum
4100 Illinois Route 53
Lisle, IL 60532-1293
Phone: 630-968-0074
Website: http://www.mortonarb.org/

Klehm Arboretum & Botanic Gardens
2701 Clifton Avenue
Rockford, IL 61102
Phone 815-965-8146
Website: http://www.klehm.org/

Lloyd C. Erickson Park
The Elwood Children's Garden
Elwood, Illinois 60421
Phone: 815-423-5520
Website: http://www.villageofelwood.com

Plants Alive! The Elizabeth Morse Genius
  Children's Garden
Garfield Conservatory
300 North Central Park Avenue
Chicago, Il 60624-1996
Phone: 773-638-1766
Website: http://www.klehm.org/

INDIANA

Foellinger-Freimann Botanical Conservatory
1100 South Calhoun Street
Fort Wayne, IN 46802-3007
Phone: 219-427-6440
Website: http://www.botanicalconservatory.org/

IOWA

Children's Garden
Cedar Valley Arboretum and Botanic Gardens
P.O. Box 1833
1927 East Orange Road
Waterloo, IA 50704
Phone: 319-226-4966
Website: http://www.cedarnet.org/gardens/

Iowa Arboretum Incorporated
1875 Peach Avenue
Madrid, IA 50156
Phone: 515-795-3216
Website: http://www.iowaarboretum.org/

Patty Jischke Children's Garden
Reiman Gardens
Iowa State University
1407 Elwood Drive
Ames, IA 50011
Phone: 515-294-2710
Website: http://www.reimangardens.
  iastate.edu/

LOUISIANA

Discovery Garden
Longue Vue House and Gardens
#7 Bamboo Road
New Orleans, LA 70124
Phone: 504-488-5488
Website: http://www.longuevue.com

MAINE

Children's Garden (Planned for 2006)
Coastal Maine Botanical Gardens
P.O. Box 234
Barters Island Road
Boothbay, ME 04537
Phone: 207-633-4333
Website: http://www.mainegardens.org

MARYLAND

Brookside Gardens Children's Garden
1800 Glenallan Avenue
Wheaton, MD 20902
Phone: 301-962-1400
Website: http://www.brooksidegardens.org

MASSACHUSETTS

Children's Garden
Berkshire Botanical Garden
P.O. Box 826
Routes 102 & 183
5 West Stockbridge Road
Stockbridge, MA 01262
Phone: 413-298-3926
Website: http://www.berkshirebotanical.org/

Weezie's Garden for Children
Massachusetts Horticultural Society
Elm Bank Horticulture Center
900 Washington Street (Rte. 16)
Wellesley, MA 02482-5725
Phone: 617-933-4925
Website: http://www.masshort.org

MICHIGAN

Children's Garden
Leila Arboretum Society
928 W. Michigan Avenue
Battle Creek, MI 49017
Phone: 269-969-0270
Website: http://www.leilaarboretumsociety.org/
    ChildrensGarden.htm

Discovery Garden
Fernwood Botanical Garden and Nature
    Preserve
13988 Range Line Road
Niles, MI 49120
Phone: 269-695-6491
Website: http://www.fernwoodbotanical.org/

Dow Gardens
1809 Eastman Avenue
Midland, MI 48640
Phone: 1-800-362-4874
Website: http://www.dowgardens.org/

Lena Meijer Children's Garden
Frederik Meijer Gardens & Sculpture Park
1000 E. Beltline, NE
Grand Rapids, MI 49525-5804
Phone: 888-957-1580
Website: http://www.meijergardens.org/

Michigan 4-H Children's Garden
Department of Horticulture
Michigan State University
A222 Plant and Soil Sciences Building
East Lansing, MI 48824-1325
Phone: 517-353-5191 X1327
Website: http://www.hrt.msu.edu/gardens/

Otsego County Alternative Landscaping
    Demonstration Gardens and Conservation
    Forest
225 West Main
Gaylord, MI 49735
Phone: 989-732-4021
Website: http://www.otsegocountymi.gov/
    conservation/programs.htm

Slayton Arboretum
Hillsdale College
Barber Drive
Hillsdale, MI 49242
Phone: 517-6-7-2241
Website: http://www.hillsdale.edu/arboretum/

MINNESOTA

Marion Andrus Learning Center
Sally Pegues Oswald Growing Place for Kids
Minnesota Landscape Arboretum
3675 Arboretum Drive
Chaska, MN 55318-9613
Phone: 952-443-1400
Website: http://www.arboretum.umn.edu/

MISSOURI

Doris I. Schnuck Childen's Garden
Missouri Botanical Garden
4344 Shaw Boulevard
St. Louis, MO 63110
Phone: 1-800-642-8842
314-577-5100
Website: http://www.mobot.org/

MONTANA

Children's Garden
Tizer Botanic Gardens & Arboretum
38 Tizer Road
Jefferson City, MT 59638
Phone: 1-866-933-8789
Website: http://www.tizergardens.com/

NEBRASKA

Arbor Day Farm Tree Adventure
National Arbor Day Foundation
100 Arbor Avenue
Nebraska City, NE 68410
Phone: 1-888-448-7337
Website: http://www.arborday.org/

NEW HAMPSHIRE

Summer Children's Garden
Derry Diggers Junior Garden Club
Robert Frost Homestead
Route 28
Derry, NH 63038
Phone: 603-432-3091
Website: http://www.derrygardenclub.org/
   activ.html

NEW JERSEY

Camden's Children Garden
Camden City Garden Club
3 Riverside Drive
Camden, NJ 08103
Phone: 856-365-8733
Website: http://www.camdenchildrensgarden.
   org/

Frelinghuysen Arboretum
53 East Hanover Avenue
Morristown, NJ 07926-1295
Phone: 973-326-7600
Website: http://www.morrisparks.org/parks/
   frelarbmain.htm

NEW MEXICO

Children's Fantasy Garden
Rio Grande Botanic Garden
2601 Central Avenue NW
Albuquerque, NM 87104
Phone: 505-764-6200
Website: http://www.cabq.gov/biopark/garden/
   fantacygarden.html

NEW YORK

Brooklyn Botanical Garden Children's Garden
1000 Washington Avenue
Brooklyn, NY 11225-1099
Phone: 718-623-7200
Website: http://www.bbg.org

Children's Garden
Genesee Country Village and Museum
P.O. Box 310
1410 Flint Hill Road
Mumford, NY 14511-0310
Phone: 585-538-6822
Website: http://www.gcv.org/attractions/
   heirloomGardens.shtml

Children's Play Garden
The Glass Garden
400 East 34th Street
New York, NY 10016
Phone: 212-263-6058
Website: http://www.med.nyu.edu/rusk/
   glassgardens/

Everett Children's Adventures Garden
Ruth Rea Howell Family Garden
The New York Botanical Garden
200th Street and Kazimiroff Boulevard
Bronx, NY 10458-5126
Phone: 718-817-8700
Website: http://www.nybg.org/

Ithaca Children's Gardens
Tompkins County Cooperative Extension
  Education Center
615 Willow Avenue
Ithaca, NY 14850
Phone: 607-272-2292
Website: http://www.cce.cornell.edu/tompkins/
  ithacachildrensgarden/

Queens Botanical Garden
43-50 Main Street
Flushing, New York 11355
Phone: 718-886-3800 Ext 229
Website: http://www.queensbotanical.org/
  education/childrengarden.html

NORTH CAROLINA

Children's Garden
Cape Fear Botanical Garden
536 N. Eastern Blvd.
Fayetteville, NC 28301
Phone: 910-486-0221
Website: http://www.capefearbg.org/
  childrengarden.html

OHIO

Children's Discovery Garden
Wegerzyn Gardens Metro Park
1375 E. Siebenthaler Avenue
Dayton, Ohio 45414
Phone: 937-277-6545
Website: http://www.metroparks.org/

Cox Arboretum & Gardens MetroPark
6733 Springboro Pike
Dayton, OH 45449
Phone: 937-434-9005
Website: http://www.coxarboretum.org/

Hershey Children's Garden
Cleveland Botanical Garden in University
  Circle
11030 East Boulevard
Cleveland, OH 44106
Phone: 216-721-1600
Website: http://www.cbgarden.org

The Sisters' Garden
Inniswood Metro Gardens
1069 W. Main Street
Westerville, OH 43081
Phone: 614-891-0700
Website: http://www.metroparks.net/
  featuregardens.aspx

OKLAHOMA

Oklahoma Botanical Garden and Arboretum
3425 West Virginia
Stillwater, OK 74078
Phone: 405-744-6460
Website: http://home.okstate.edu/Okstate/
  dasnr/hort/hortlahome.nsf/toc/obga

OREGON

Oregon Garden Children's Garden
879 W. Main Street
Silverton, OR 97381-0155
Phone: 877-674-2733
503-874-8100
Website: http://www.oregongarden.org/WYS_
  specialty.html

PENNSYLVANIA

Children's Creativity Garden
1875 Ritts Farm Road
Clarion County Park
Emlenton, PA 16373
Phone: 814-797-5028
Website: http://www.co.clarion.pa.us/

Children's Garden at Longwood Gardens
Route 1, P.O. Box 501
Kennett Square, PA 19348-0501
Phone: 610-388-1000
Website: http://www.longwoodgardens.com

Discovery Garden for Children
Phipps Conservatory and Botanical Gardens
One Schenley Park (Frank Curto Drive)
Pittsburgh, PA 15213-3830
Phone: 412-622-6914
Website: http://www.phipps.conservatory.org

Hershey Children's Garden
170 Hotel Road
Hershey, PA 17033
Phone: 717-534-3492
Website: http://www.hersheygardens.org/

National Resource Education Garden
Awbury Arboretum Association
The Francis Cope House
One Awbury Road
Philadelphia, PA 19138-1505
Phone: 215-849-2855
Website: http://awbury.org/

SOUTH CAROLINA

Carolina Children's Garden
Sandhill for Kids
Sandhills Research and Education Center
Clemson University
905 Clemson Road
Columbia, SC 29229
Phone: 803-788-5700 Ext 24
Website: http://www.clemson.edu/sandhill/
    html/kids/sand4kids.html

Greenville Children's Garden at Linky Stone
    Park
423 East Park Ave.
Greenville, SC 29601
Phone: 864-467-4350
Website: http://www.greatergreenville.com/
    city_services.asp

Philip Simmons Children's Garden
727-729 Eat Bay Street and Blake Street
Charleston, SC 29403
Phone: 843-853-0060
Website: http://www.simmonschildrensgarden.
    com/index2.htm

South Carolina Botanical Garden
102 Garden Trail
Clemson, SC 29634-0171
Phone: 864-656-3405
Website: http://www.clemson.edu/scbg/

SOUTH DAKOTA

Children's Maze
McCrory Gardens
South Dakota State University
Brookings, SD 57007
Phone: 1-800-952-3541
Website: http://www3.sdstate.edu/Academics/
    CollegeOfAgricultureAndBiological
    Sciences/HorticultureForestryLandscape
    andParks/McCroryGardens/Index.cfm

TEXAS

Aggie Horticulture Just for Kids
    KinderGARDEN
Children's Gardens at Texas A&M University
Texas A&M University Horticulture Program
College Station, TX 17843-2133
Phone: 979-845-5341
Website: http://aggie-horticulture.tamu.edu/
    kindergarden/index.html

Children's Discovery Garden
Aransas/San Patricio County Master Gardener
    Association
611 East Mimosa Street at Pearl Street
Rockport, TX 78382
Phone: 361-790-0103
Website: http://aggie-horticulture.tamu.edu/
    aransas/childga.htm

Clark Gardens Botanical Park
567 Maddux Road
Mineral Wells, TX
Phone: 940-682-4856
Website: http://www.clarkgardens.com/
    childrens.html

Kids Corner at CCBG
Corpus Christi Botanical Gardens and
    Nature Center
8545 S. Staples Street
Corpus Christi, TX 78413
Phone: 361-852-2100
Website: http://www.ccbotanicalgardens.org/
    kidscorner.html

Riverside Nature Center
150 Francisco Lemos St.
Kerrville, TX 78028
Phone: 830-257-4837
Website: http://www.riversidenaturecenter.org/

UTAH

Children's Discovery Garden
Thanksgiving Point
2095 N. West Frontage Road
Lehi, UT 84043
Phone: 801-768-2300
Website: http://www.thanksgivingpoint.com/
    gardens/children.html

Children's Garden Red Butte Botanic Garden
University of Utah
300 WaKara Way
Salt Lake City, UT 84108
Phone: 801-581-4747 - 801-581-IRIS
Website: http://www.redbuttegarden.org/
    Classes_and_Events/?c=Childrens_
    Garden.inc

VERMONT

Youth Garden Program
Friends of Burlington Gardens
33 Tracy Drive
Burlington, VT 05401
Phone: 802-658-5733
Website: http://www.burlingtongardens.org/
    youth.htm

VIRGINIA

The Children's Garden at Lewis Ginter
    Botanical Garden
1800 Lakeside Avenue
Richmond, VA 23228
Phone: 804-262-9887
Website: http://www.lewisginter.org/

The Growing Connection
Children's Gardens of the American
    Horticultural Society
7931 East Boulevard Drive
Alexandria, VA 22308-1300
Phone: 1-800-768-5700
Website: http://www.ahs.org/

World of Wonders
Norfolk Botanical Garden
6700 Azalea Garden Rd.
Norfolk VA 23518-5337
Phone: 757-441-5830 X335
Website: http://www.norfolkbotanicalgarden.
    org/

WASHINGTON

Raab Park Youth Garden
18349 Caldart Avenue NE
Poulsbo, WA 98370-8775
Phone: 360-337-7224
Website: http://kitsap.wsu.edu/hort/demo_
    gardens.htm

WISCONSIN

Field of Dreams Children's Garden
3003 30th Avenue
Kenosha, WI 53403
Phone: 262-857-1945
Website: http://www.uwex.edu/ces/cty/racine/
    hort/FieldofDreamsChildrensGardens
    INFO.html

WYOMING

Cheyenne Botanical Gardens
710 S. Lion Park Drive
Cheyenne, WY 82001
Phone: 307-637-6458
Website: http://www.botanic.com

Selected School Gardens and Youth Gardening Educational Programs

ALABAMA

Birmingham Botanical Gardens
2612 Lane Park Road
Birmingham, AL 35223
Phone: 205-414-3900
Website: http://www.bbgardens.org/media/
html/home/index.php

Children's Garden
Aldridge Botanical Garden
3530 Lorna Road
Hoover, AL 35216
Phone: 205-682-8019
Website: http://www.aldridgegardens.com/

Dothan Area Botanical Gardens
5130 Headland Avenue
Dothan, Alabama 36303
Phone: 334-793-3224
Website: http://www.dabg.com

Huntsville Botanical Garden
4747 Bob Wallace Avenue
Huntsville, AL 35805
Phone: 256-860-4447
Website: http://www.hsvbg.org/

Mobile Botanical Gardens
5151 Museum Drive
Mobile AL 36608
Phone: 251-342-0555
Website: http://www.mobilebotanicalgardens.
org/index.html

ALASKA

Alaska Botanical Garden
4516 Campbell Airstrip Road
Anchorage, AK 99507
Phone: 907-770-3692
Website: http://www.alaskabg.org

Babula Children's Garden
Georgeson Botanical Garden
University of Alaska
P.O. Box 757200
117 W. Tanana Drive
Fairbanks, AK 99775
Phone: 907-474-6921
Website: http://www.uaf.edu/salrm/gbg

ARIZONA

The Arboretum at Flagstaff
4001 South Woody Mountain Road
Flagstaff, AZ 86001-8776
Phone: 928-774-1442
Website: http://www.thearb.org/

Boyce Thompson Arboretum
37615 U.S. Highway 60
Superior, AZ 85273
Phone: 520-689-2723
Website: http://ag.arizona.edu/BTA/index.
html

Desert Botanical Garden
1201 N. Galvin Parkway
Phoenix, AZ 85008
Phone: 480-941-1225
Website: http://www.desertbotanical.org/

Youth Gardening
Home Horticulture in Maricopa County
4341 E. Broadway Road
Phoenix, AZ 85040
Phone: 602-470-8505
Website: http://cals.arizona.edu/youthgardens/
index.php

CALIFORNIA

The Anna Rainville Garden
Lakeside Elementary School
19621 Black Road
Los Gatos, CA 95033
Phone: 408-354-2372
Website: http://www.lakesidesd.K12.ca.us

Berkeley Community Gardening Collaborative
2530 San Pablo Avenue
Berkeley, CA 94702
Phone: 510-548-2220
Website: http://www.ecologycenter.org/bcgc/

Children's Garden
Strybing Arboretum and Botanical Gardens
9th Avenue at Lincoln Way
Golden Gate Park
San Francisco, CA 94122
Phone: 415-661-1316
Website: http://www.sfbotanicalgarden.org/

Courtyard Greening
Peralta Elementary School
460 63rd Street
Oakland, CA 94609
Phone: 510-879-1450
Website: http://www.geocities.com/
    peraltaschool/campus

Descanso Gardens
1418 Descanso Drive
La Canada Flintridge, CA 91011
Phone: 818-949-4200
Website: http://www.descansogardens.org

"Down to Earth" Garden
Buena Vista Elementary School
1330 Buena Vista Way
Carlsbad, CA 92008
Phone: 760-331-5400
Website: http://commserv.ucdavis.edu/
    cesandiego/schlgrdn/bv.html

The Edible Schoolyard
Martin Luther King Jr. Middle School
1781 Rose Street
Berkeley, CA 94703
Phone: 510-558-1335
Website: http://www.edibleschoolyard.org/
    homepage.html

Elizabeth Gamble Garden
1431 Waverly Street
Palo Alto, CA 94301
Phone: 650-329-1356
Website: http://www.gamblegarden.org/
    childrens/childrens.html

Green Schools Institute
Emery Unified School District
4727 San Pablo Avenue
Emeryville, CA 94608
Phone: 501-601-4000
Website: http://www.emeryusd.k12.ca.us

Tule Elk Park Child's Development Center
2110 Greenwood Street
San Francisco, CA 94123
Phone: 415-749-3551
Website: http://www.tuleelkpark.org/teptxp/
    index.php?s=introduction&id=6

Garden Classroom
Life Lab Science Program
University of California at Santa Cruz
1156 High Street
Santa Cruz, CA 95064
Phone: 831-459-2001
Website: http://www.lifelab.org/
Schools using the Life Lab Curricula:
http://www.lifelab.org/schools/index.html

The Gardens at Heather Farm
1540 Marchbanks Drive
Walnut Creek, CA 94598
Phone: 925-947-1678
Website: http://www.gardenshf.org/

Growing Green Kids
310 Lexington Street
San Francisco, CA 94110
Phone: 415-595-9484
Website: http://www.growinggreenkids.org/

The Learning Garden
Venice High School
13000 Venice Blvd.
Los Angeles, CA 90066
Phone: 310-722-3656
Website: http://www.thelearninggarden.org/

Los Angeles County Arboretum and
    Botanic Garden
301 N. Baldwin Avenue
Arcadia, CA 91007-2697
Phone: 626-821-3222
Website: http://www.arboretum.org/

Malcolm X Elementary School
90 Norwood Avenue
Kensington, CA 94707
Phone: 510-524-2916
Website: http://creec.edgateway.net/cs/creec7p/
    view/creec_res/695

Project OLE (Outdoor Learning
    Environment)
San Francisco Community School
San Francisco Unified School District
105 Aptos Avenue, Room 341
San Francisco, CA 94127
Phone: 415-452-4646
Website: http://www.learningindeed.org/
    slcommission/horace.html

Santa Barbara Botanic Garden
1212 Mission Canyon Road
Santa Barbara, CA 93105
Phone: 805-682-4726
Website: http://www.sbbg.org/

The Secret Garden
North Broadway Elementary School
2301 North Broadway
Escondido, CA 92026
Phone: 760-432-2479
Website: http://commserv.ucdavis.edu/
    CESanDiego/Schlgrdn/NB.html

UC Davis Arboretum
University of California
One Shields Avenue
Davis, CA 95616
Phone: 530-752-4880
Website: http://arboretum.ucdavis.edu

University of California Botanical Garden
200 Centennial Drive
Berkeley, CA 94720-5045
Phone: 510-643-2755
Website: http://botanicalgarden.berkeley.edu/
    education.shtml

Wonderland Gardens
3145 Rainbow Drive
Decatur, CA 30334
Phone: 404-286-6163
Website: http://www.wonderlandgardens.org/

COLORADO

Betty Ford Alpine Gardens
183 Gore Creek Drive
Vail, CO 81657
Phone: 970-476-0103
Website: http://www.bettyfordalpinegardens.
    org

Gardening with Children
Colorado State University / Denver County
    Cooperation Extension
201 W. Colfax Avenue Dept 107
Denver, CO 80262
Phone: 720-913-5278
Website: http://www.colostate.edu/Depts/
    CoopExt/4DMG/Children/ingarden.htm

The Hudson Gardens & Event Center
6115 South Santa Fe Drive
Littleton, CO 80120
Phone: 303-797-8565
Website: http://www.hudsongardens.org

CONNECTICUT

Youth Gardening
The Federated Garden Clubs of Connecticut,
  Inc.
P.O. Box 854
Branford, CT 06405
Phone: 203-488-5525
Website: http://www.ctgardenclubs.org/
  youth.html

DELAWARE

Imagination Garden
Forest Oak School
55 S. Meadowood Drive
Newark, DE 19711
Phone: 302-454-3420
Website: http://www.redclay.k12.de.us/
  Schools/ForestOak.htm

Plants for Kids/Outdoor Classroom
Claude E. Phillips Herbarium
Delaware State University
Department of Agriculture and Natural
  Resources
1200 N. DuPont Highway
Dover, DE 19901-2277
Phone: 302-857-6452
Website: http://herbarium.desu.edu

DISTRICT OF COLUMBIA

Agriculture in the Classroom
USDA Administration Bldg. Room 317-A
1400 Independence Avenue SW
Washington, DC 20250-2251
Phone: 202-720-5727
Website: http://www.agclassroom.org/aitc/
  contact.htm
For individual state websites:
http://www.agclassroom.org/state/websites.
  htm

United States Botanical Garden
245 First Street, SW
Washington, DC 20024
Phone: 202-225-8333
Website: http://www.usbg.gov/

Washington Youth Garden
U.S. National Arboretum
3501 New York Avenue NE
Washington, DC 20002-1958
Phone: 202-245-2726
Website: http://www.usna.usda.gov/Gardens/
  collections/youth.html

FLORIDA

Education Center for Teaching and Learning
Fairchild Tropical Botanic
10901 Old Cutler Road
Coral Gable, FL 33156
Phone: 305-667-1651
Website: http://www.fairchildgarden.org/
  education/n_education.html

Fairchild Tropical Botanic Garden
10901 Old Cutler Road
Coral Gables, Miami, FL 33156
305-667-1651
Website: http://www.ftg.org/education/
  n_education.html

Gator Gardening for Kids
University of Florida
IFAS Extension
P.O. Box 110210
Gainesville, FL 32611-0210
Phone: 352-392-1761
Website: http://hort.ifas.ufl.edu/ggk/

Heathcote Botanical Gardens
210 Savannah Road
Ft. Pierce, FL 34950
Phone: 772-464-4672
Website: http://www.heathcotebotanical
  gardens.org

Marie Selby Botanical Gardens
811 South Palm Avenue
Sarasota, FL 34236
Phone: 941-366-5731
Website: http://www.selby.org/

GEORGIA

Callaway Gardens
GA Hwy 18/354
Pine Mountain, GA 31822
Phone: 1-800-callaway (225-5292)
Website: http://www.callawaygardens.com/

Georgia Southern Botanical Garden
1505 Bland Avenue
Statesboro, GA 30458
Phone: 912-871-1149
Website: http://welcome.georgiasouthern.
   edu/garden/

Outdoor Classroom
Worth County Primary School
1304 N. Isabella Street
Sylvester, GA31791
Phone 229-776-8660
Website: http://www.worth.K12.ga.us/wcps/
   oc.html

The State Botanical Garden of Georgia
University of Georgia
2450 South Milledge Avenue
Athens, GA 30605-1624
Phone: 706-542-1244
Website: http://www.uga.edu/~botgarden/
   home2.html

HAWAII

Lyon Arboretum
University of Hawaii—Manoa
3860 Manoa Road
Honolulu, HI 96822-1198
Phone: 808-988-0456
Website: http://www.lyonarboretum.com/

ILLINOIS

Just for Kids
Urban Program Resource Network
University of Illinois Extension
547 Bevier Hall
905 S. Goodwin
Urbana, IL 61801
Phone: 217-265-6410
Website: http://www.urbanext.uiuc.edu/Kids/
   index.html

Luthy Botanical Garden
Peoria Park District
2218 N. Prospect
Peoria, IL 61603
Phone: 309-682-3362
Website: http://www.peoriaparks.org/luthy/
   luthymain.html

Quad City Botanical Center
2525 4th Avenue
Rock Island, IL 61201-3413
Phone: 309-794-0991
Website: http://www.qcgardens.com/

School Garden Wizard
School and Community Gardening
Chicago Botanic Garden
1100 Lake Cook Rd.
Glencoe, IL 60022
Phone: 847-835-5440
Website: http://www.schoolgardenwizard
   .org/

Theme Gardens
The Coyne Center Elementary School
Coyne Center Elementary
11310 16th Street
Milan, IL 61264
Phone: 309-787-1512
Website: http://cc.sherrard.us/tg/intro.html

Washington Park Botanical Garden
2500 South Eleventh Street
Springfield, IL 62703
Phone: 217-544-1751
Website: http://www.springfieldparks.org/
garden/

INDIANA

Educational EdVentures
Garfield Park Conservatory & Sunken
Gardens
2505 Conservatory Drive
Indianapolis, IN 46203
Phone: 317-327-7184
Website: http://www.garfieldgardens
conservatory.org/Educational_programs.htm

Hayes Arboretum
801 Elks Road
Richmond, IN 47374
Phone: 765-962-3745
Website: http://hayesarboretum.org

Youth Garden Program
Hilltop Garden and Nature Center
2301 E. 10th Street
Bloomington, IN 47405
Phone: 812-855-2799
Website: http://www.indiana.edu/~hilltop/

IOWA

Iowa Arboretum
1875 Peach Avenue
Madrid, IA 50156
Phone: 515-795-3216
Website: http://www.iowaarboretum.org/

Knee High Naturalist
The Brenton Arboretum
2629 Palo Circle
Dallas Center, IA 50063
Phone: 515-992-4211
Website: http://www.thebrentonarboretum.org/
kneehighnaturalist.htm.

KANSAS

Botanica, The Wichita Gardens
701 Amidon, in Sim Park at Amidon and
Murdock
Wichita, KA 67203-3162
Phone: 316-264-0448
Website: http://www.botanica.org/

KENTUCKY

Bernheim Arboretum and Research Forest
Highway 245
Clermont, KY 40110-0130
Phone: 502-955-8512
Website: http://www.bernheim.org/

Boone County Arboretum at Central Park
9190 Camp Ernst Road
Union, KY 41090
Phone: 859-384-4999
Website: http://www.bcarboretum.org/

University of Kentucky
4H & Youth Development
Dept. of Horticulture and Landscape
Architecture
N-318 Agri Science North—Room 212
Scorell Hall
Lexington, KY 40546-0064
Phone: 606-257-5961
Website: http://www.ca.uky.edu/agcollege/
4H/

MARYLAND

Adkins Arboretum
12610 Eveland Road
P.O. Box 100
Ridgely, MD 21660-0100
Phone: 410-634-2847
Website: http://www.adkinsarboretum.org/
child.html

MASSACHUSETTS

Arnold Arboretum of Harvard University
125 Arborway
Jamaica Plain, MA 02130
Phone: 617-524-1718
Website: http://www.arboretum.harvard.edu/

Kids Corner
Smith College Botanic Garden
Lyman Conservatory
Northhampton, MA 01063
Phone: 413-585-2740
Website: http://www.smith.edu/garden/
    kidscorner/index.htm

Tower Hill Farm School
Tower Hill Botanic Garden
11 French Drive, P.O. Box 598
Boylston, MA 01505-0598
Phone: 508-869-6111
Website: http://www.towerhillbg.org/
    thwebfarm_prog.html

MICHIGAN

Hidden Lake Gardens
6280 Munger Road (M50)
Tipton, MI 49287
Phone: 517-431-2060
Website: http://hiddenlakegardens.msu.edu/

Science Learning Lab
Anna Scripps Whitcomb Conservatory
Belle Isle Botanical Society
P.O. Box 14693
Detroit, MI 48214
Phone: 313-852-4065
Website: http://www.bibsociety.org/systmpl/
    sciencelearninglab/

Traverse Area District Library
Children's Learning Garden
505 Riverine Drive
Traverse City, MI 49684
Phone: 616-947-0422
Website: http://tadl.tcnet.org/garden.htm

W. J. Beal Botanic Garden
412 Olds Hall
Michigan State University
East Lansing, MI 48824
Phone: 517-355-9582
Website: http://www.cpa.msu.edu/beal/

MINNESOTA

Groveland's Outdoor Classroom
Groveland Elementary School
17310 Minnetonka Blvd.
Minnetonka, MN 55345
Phone: 952-401-5600
Website: http://www.minnetonka.k12.mn.us/
    grv/GOSHGOLLIE/HOME.HTM

MISSISSIPPI

Crosby Arboretum
370 Ridge Road
P.O. Box 1639
Picayune, MS 39466
Phone: 601-799-2311
Website: http://www.msstate.edu/dept/crec/
    catours.html

MISSOURI

National Garden Clubs
4401 Magnolia Avenue
St. Louis, MO 63110
Phone: 314-776-7574
Website: http://www.gardenclub.org/

MONTANA

The Bench Learning Garden
Bench Elementary
505 Milton Road
Billings, MT 59105
Phone: 406-255-3819
Website: http://www.billings.k12.mt.us/bench/
    garden.html

NEBRASKA

Lauritzen Gardens
Omaha's Botanical Center
100 Bancroft Street
Omaha, NE 68108
Phone: 402-346-4002
Website: http://www.omahabotanical
  gardens.org/

Teaching Youth about Trees
The National Arbor Day Foundation
100 Arbor Avenue
Nebraska City, NE 68410
Phone: 1-888-448-7337
Website: http://www.arborday.org/kids/
  TeachingYouth.cfm

NEW HAMPSHIRE

Family, Home and Garden Education
  Center
University of New Hampshire
Cooperative Extension
Durham, NH 03824
Phone: 877-EXT-GROW
Website: http://ceinfo.unh.edu/FHGEC/
  FHGEC.htm

Kirkwood Gardens
Squam Lakes Natural Science Center
23 Science Center Road
P.O. Box 173
Holderness, NH 03245
Phone: 603-968-7194
Website: http://www.nhnature.org/

Rockingham County Botanical Garden
113B North Road
Brentwood, NH 03833
Phone: 603-679-5616
Website: http://rockinghambotanical.org/
  youth.html

NEW YORK

Audubon International
46 Rarick Road
Selkirk, NY 12158
Phone: 518-767-9051
Website: http://www.auduboninternational.org/

6TH and B Community Garden
6th Street and Avenue B
New York, NY 10062
Website: http://www.6bgarden.org/

Buffalo and Erie County Botanical Gardens
2655 South Park Avenue
Buffalo, NY 14218-1526
Phone: 716-827-1584
Website: http://www.buffalogardens.com

The Children's Garden
Suffolk County Farm and Education Center
Yaphank Avenue, P.O. Box 129
Yaphank, NY 11980-0129
Phone: 631-852-4600
Sponsored by:
Cornell University Cooperative Extension of
  Suffolk County
423 Griffing Avenue, Suite 100
Riverhead, NY 11901-3071
Phone: 631-727-7850
Website: http://www.cce.cornell.edu/~suffolk/
  AGprograms/childrensgarden.htm

Explore
Cornell Plantations
One Plantations Road
Ithaca, NY 14850
Phone: 607-255-2400
Website: http://www.plantations.cornell.edu/

Garden Mosaics
101-A Rice Hall
Cornell University
Ithaca, NY 14853
Phone: 607-254-5479
Website: http://www.gardenmosaics.cornell.
  edu/index.htm

Gifford Garden
Institute of Ecosystem Studies
65 Sharon Turnpike
P.O. Box AB
Millbrook, NY 12545-0129
Phone: 845-677-5343
Website: http://www.ecostudies.org/ed.html

Greenschool Children Education
New York Botanical Garden
200th Street and Kazimiroff Blvd.
Bronx, NY 10458-5126
Phone: 717-817-8181
Website: http://www.nybg.org/chil_edu/

National Resource Directory
Agriculture in the Classroom
420 Kennedy Hall
Dept. of Education
Cornell University
Ithaca, NY 14853
Phone: 607-254-7442
Website: http://cerp.cornell.edu/directory/

Project Leap (Learning About Plants)
Cornell Plantations
One Plantations Road
Cornell University
Ithaca, NY 14850
Phone: 607-255-3020
Website: http://www.plantations.cornell.edu/
education/leap.cfm

Riley-Levin Children's Garden
Swindle Cove Park
Harlem River Drive and Dyckman Street
Manhattan, NY 11034
Sponsored by:
New York Restoration Project
31 West 56th Street
New York, NY 10019
Phone: 212-332-2552
Website: http://www.nyrp.org/rileylevin.htm

Youth Resources
Cornell Waste Management Institute
101 Rice Hall
Cornell University
Ithaca, NY 14583-5601
Phone: 607-255-1187
Website: http://cwmi.css.cornell.edu/youth.
html

Wave Hill
675 West 252nd Street
Bronx, NY 10471-2899
Phone: 718-549-3200
Website: http://www.wavehill.org/education/

NORTH CAROLINA

4-H Youth Horticulture
Department of Horticulture
North Carolina State University Cooperative
Extension
Raleigh, NC 27695-7609
Phone: 919-515-3131
Website: http://www.ces.ncsu.edu/index.php?
page=youth4h

Airlie Gardens
300 Airlie Road
Wilmington, NC 28403
Phone: 910-793-7700
Website: http://www.airliegardens.org/index.jsp

Daniel Stowe Botanical Garden
6500 New Hope Road
Belmont, NC 28012-8788
Phone: 704-825-4490
Website: http://www.dsbg.org/index.php

The Sarah P. Duke Gardens
426 Anderson Street
Box 90341
Duke University
Durham, NC 27708-0341
Phone: 919-684-3698
Website: http://www.hr.duke.edu/dukegardens/

OHIO

A Child's Garden of Herbs
The Herb Society of America
9019 Kirtland Chardon Road
Kirtland, OH 44094
Phone: 440-256-0514
Website: http://www.herbsociety.org/

Growing Students and Science
The Holden Arboretum
9500 Sperry Road
Kirtland, OH 44094
Phone: 440-946-4400
Website: http://www.holdenarb.org/index.html

Toledo Botanical Garden
5403 Elmer Drive
Toledo, OH 43615
Phone: 419-936-2986
Website: http://www.toledogarden.org/

OKLAHOMA

Li'l Green Thumbs Gardening Adventures
Tulsa Garden Center
2435 South Peoria Avenue
Tulsa, OK 74114-1350
Phone: 918-746-5125
Website: http://www.tulsagardencenter.com/

Myriad Botanical Gardens
100 Myriad Gardens
301 West Reno
Oklahoma City, OK 73102
Phone: 405-297-3995
Website: http://www.myriadgardens.com/
  education.html

PENNSYLVANIA

Bartram's Garden
54th Street and Lindbergh Blvd.
Philadelphia, PA 19143
Phone: 215-729-5281
Website: http://www.bartramsgarden.org/
  education/

Landscape Arboretum
Temple University Ambler
580 Meetinghouse Road
Ambler, PA 19002-3999
Phone: 215-283-1233
Website: http://www.ambler.temple.edu

Morris Arboretum of the University of
  Pennsylvania
100 Northwestern Avenue
Philadelphia, PA 19118
Phone: 215-247-5777
Website: http://www.business-services.upenn.
  edu/arboretum

Philadelphia Green's Youth Program
Pennsylvania Horticultural Society
100 North 20th Street—5th floor
Philadelphia, PA 19103-1495
Phone: 215-988-8800
Website: http://www.pennsylvaniahorticultural
  society.org/home/index.html

Strodes Mills Middle School
205 Chestnut Ridge Road
McVeytown, PA 17501
Phone: 717-248-5488
Website: http://www.mcsdk12.org/smms/
  garden_club.htm

Tyler Arboretum
515 Painter Road
Media, PA 19063-4424
Phone: 610-566-9134
Website: http://www.tylerarboretum.org/

RHODE ISLAND

Children's Garden Network
Rhode Island Center for Agricultural
  Promotion & Education
235 Promenade Street
Providence, RI 02908-5767
Phone: 401-222-2781 Ext 7104
Website: http://www.rifarmer.org/

SOUTH CAROLINA

Clemson Elementary School Outdoors
581 Berkeley Drive
Clemson, SC 29631
Phone: 864-654-2341
Website: http://www.pickens.k12.sc.us/
    clemson.es/CES/ClemsonElemOutdoors/
    CEOMain.htm

Landscapes for Learning
South Carolina Landscapes for Learning
    Collaborative
132 Brackett Hall
Box 341356-A
Clemson, SC 29634-1356
864-656-7988 or 864-656-3821
Website: http://business.clemson.edu/LFlearn/
    index.html

South Carolina Botanical Garden
102 Garden Trail
Clemson, SC 29634-0174
Phone: 864-656-3405
Children's Ethnobotany Gardens
Website: http://www.clemson.edu/scbg/sust/
    ethnobotany_garden.html

Sprouting Wings
Website: http://www.clemson.edu/scbg/
    pages/wings/program.htm

TEXAS

The Dallas Arboretum and Botanical Garden
8617 Garland Road
Dallas, TX 75218
Phone: 214-515-6500
Website: http://www.dallasarboretum.org/

Kids Corner of the Garden
Fort Worth Botanic Garden
3220 Botanic Garden Blvd.
Fort Worth, TX 76107-3496
Phone: 817-871-7686
Website: http://www.fwbg.org/kid_corner.htm

Lady Bird Johnson Wildflower Center
4801 La Cross Avenue
Austin, TX 78739
Phone: 512-292-4100
Website: http://www.wildflower.org/
    ?nd=children_family

Project WILD National Office
Council for Environmental Education
555 Morningside Drive, Suite 212
Houston, TX 77005
Phone: 713-520-8000
Website: http://www.projectwild.org/

San Antonio Botanical Garden
555 Funston Place
San Antonio, TX 78209
Phone: 210- 207-3250
Website: http://www.sabot.org/education/
    parkids.htm

Texas Discovery Gardens
3601 Martin Luther King Jr. Blvd.
Dallas, TX 75210
Phone: 214- 428-7476
Website: http://texasdiscoverygardens.org

VERMONT

National Gardening Association
GrowLab Program
1100 Dorset St.
So. Burlington, VT 05403
Phone: 802- 863-5251
Website: http://www.kidsgardening.com
Website: http://www.garden.org

VIRGINIA

Backyard Wildlife Habitat and Schoolyard
    Wildlife Habitats
National Wildlife Federation
11100 Wildlife Center Drive
Reston, VA 20190-5362
Phone: 1-800-822-9919
Website: http://www.nwf.org/backyard
    wildlifehabitat/
and http://www.nwf.org/backyard
    wildlifehabitat/creatinghabitatsites.cfm

Green Spring Gardens Park
4603 Green Spring Road
Alexandria, VA 22312
Phone: 703-642-5173
Website: http://www.fairfaxcounty.gov/parks/
  gsgp/index.htm

Hahn Horticulture Garden
Virginia Polytechnic Institute and State
  University Cooperative Extension
Department of Horticulture
301 Saunders Hall
Washington Street
Blacksburg, VA 24061-0327
Phone: 540-231-5970
Website: http://www.hort.vt.edu/VTHG/

Mattey's Garden
James City County/Williamsburg Master
  Gardner's
Matthew Whaley Elementary School
301 Scotland Street
Williamsburg, VA 23185
Phone: 757-221-0370
Website: http://jccwmg.org/matteys.htm

River Farm
American Horticultural Society
7931 East Boulevard Drive
Alexandria, VA 22308-1300
Phone: 1-800-777-7931, 703-768-5700
Website: http://www.ahs.org/river_farm/
  index.htm

Roots and Shoots Theme Gardens
Harrington Woddell Elementary School
100 Pendleton Place
Lexington, VA 24450
Phone: 540-463-6454
Website: http://rootsnshoots.info/

State Arboretum of Virginia
400 Blandy Farm Lane
Boyce, VA 22620
Phone: 540-837-1758
Website: http://www.virginia.edu/blandy/

Tuckahoe Discovery Schoolyard
6550 N. 26th Street
Arlington, VA 22213
Phone: 703-228-5288
Website: http://www.arlington.k12.va.us/
  schools/tuckahoe/schoolyard

WASHINGTON

Bellevue Botanical Garden Living Lab
12001 Main Street
Bellevue, WA 98005
Phone: 425-451-3755
Website: http://www.bellevuebotanical.org/

The Children's Center
Burke Gilman Gardens
5251 Sand Point Way NE
Building 5
Seattle, WA 98105
Phone: 206-729-0399
Website: http://bggardens.org

Plants Grow Children
Washington State University Cooperative
  Extension
5600-E West Canal Drive
Kennewick, WA 99336
Phone: 509-735-3551
Website: http://benton-franklin.wsu.edu/
  garden/plantsgrowchildren.htm

Seattle Tilth Association: Teaching Peace
  through Gardening
4649 Sunnyside Avenue, North, Rm. 120
Seattle, WA 98103
Phone: 206-633-0451
Website: http://www.seattletilth.org/

Washington Park Arboretum
2300 Arboretum Drive East
Seattle, WA 98112-2300
Phone: 266-325-4510
Website: http://www.arboretumfoundation.
  org/

WISCONSIN

Above and Beyond Children's Museum
902 North 8th Street
Sheboygan, WI 53082
Phone: 920-458-4263
Website: http://www.abkids.org/

Children's Horticulture Education
Boerner Botanical Gardens
9400 Boerner Drive
Hales Corner, WI 53130
Phone: 414-525-5650
Website: http://www.boernerbotanical
gardens.org/

Discovery Garden
Waisman Center
1500 Highland Avenue
Madison, WI 53705-2280
Phone: 608-263-5776
Website: http://www.waisman.wisc.edu/dg/

Gertrude B. Nielsen Children's Garden
Green Bay Botanical Garden
P.O. Box 12644
Green Bay, WI 54307-2644
Phone: 920-490-9457
Website: http://www.gbbg.org

Olbrich Botanical Gardens
3330 Atwood Avenue
Madison, WI 53704
Phone: 608-246-4550
Website: http://www.olbrich.org/

Organizations/Selected Internet Resources

Agriculture and Natural Resources
University of California, Davis
Website: http://commserv.ucdavis.edu

America the Beautiful Fund
Operation Green Plant
1730 K Street, NW, Suite 1002
Washington, DC 20006
Phone: 800-522-3557
Website: http://www.america-the-beautiful.org

American Association of Botanical Gardens
and Arboreta
Website: http://www.aabga.org/

American Community Gardening Association
Website: http://www.communitygarden.org/

American Horticultural Society
http://www.ahs.org/
7931 East Boulevard Drive
Alexandria, VA 22308-1300
Phone: 703-768-5700
National Registry of Childen's Gardens
Website: http://www.ahs.org/horticulture_
internet_community/national_
registry_of_childrens_gardens.htm

Youth Gardening Resource List
Website: http://www.ahs.org/youth_
gardening/youth_garden_resource_list.htm

National Youth Gardening Symposium
Website: http://www.ahs.org/youth_gardening/
national_youth_garden_symposium.htm

American Horticultural Therapy Association
909 York Street
Denver, CO 80206-3799
Phone: 301-948-3010
Website: http://www.ahta.org

American Society for Horticultural Science
113 South West Street, Suite 400
Alexandria, VA 22314-2824
Phone: 703-836-4606
Website: http://www.ashs.org/

At Your Fingertips WWW Links Directory—
Arboretums & Botanical Gardens
Website: http://www.millenium2.org/goodlife/
srlinks/arboresr.htm#us

Botanical Society of America
P.O. Box 299
St. Louis, MO 63166-0299
Phone: 314-577-9566
Website: http://www.botany.org/

Botanique: Portal to Gardens Arboretum &
    Nature Sites
Website: http://www.botanique.com/

The Captain Planet Foundation
133 Luckie Street, 2nd Floor
Atlanta, GA 30303
Phone: 404-522-4270
Website: http://www.captainplanetfdn.org/

Children's Gardens
A Guide to Selected Resources
Science Reference Section
Science, Technology and Business Division
Library of Congress
Website: http://www.loc.gov/rr/scitech/
    SciRefGuides/childrensgardens.html

Children's Gardens in the U.S. recommended
    by Sharon Lovejoy
Website: http://www.sharonlovejoy.com/
    cg.html

D.C. Greenworks
1701 6th Street, NW
Washington, DC 20001
Phone: 202-518-6195
Website: http://www.dcgreenworks.org/

Digital Librarian: Garden and Gardening
Website: http://www.digital-librarian.com/
    gardening.html#Gardens

Environment Directory for Education, K-12
Website: http://www.webdirectory.com/
    Education/K-12/

Garden Web
The Internet's Garden Community
Website: http://www.gardenweb.com/

The Gardening Launch Pad
Website: http://gardeninglaunchpad.com

Gardening for Kids
Website: http://www.geocities.com/
    enchantedforest/glade/3313/

Gardening with Kids
Website: http://www.emilycompost.com/
    kid_main_page.htm

Gardens in the USA
Website: http://www.internetfavorites.info/
    gardens.htm

I Love Gardens.com
Website: http://www.ilovegardens.com

Internet Directory for Botany
Website: http://botany.net/IDB/

Kids Gardening
Website: http://www.kidsgardening.com

Kids Valley Garden
Website: http://www.raw-connections.com/
    garden/

National 4-H Council
7100 Connecticut Avenue
Chevy Chase, MD 20815
Phone: 301-961-2934
Website: http://www.fourhcouncil.edu/

National Garden Bureau
Website: http://www.ngb.org/youth_
    resources/index.cfm

National Gardening Association
1100 Dorset Street
South Burlington, VT 05403
Phone: 802-263-5251
http://www.kidsgardening.com
http://www.garden.org

    School Garden Registry
    http://www.kidsgardening.com/School/
        searchform.asp

National Junior Horticulture Association
Executive Secretary
15 Railroad Avenue
Homer City, PA 15748
Phone: 724-479-9112
Website: http://www.njha.org/

State Program Leaders:
http://www.njha.org/stprldrs.htm

National Junior Master Gardener
225 Horticulture/Forestry Bldg.
Texas A&M University
College Station, TX 77843-2134
Phone: 979-845-8565
Website: http://www.jmgkids.us/

State Programs:
http://www.jmgkids.us/index.K2?did=
2025&sectionID=2019

National Park Service
U.S. Department of the Interior
1849 C Street, NW
Washington, DC 20240
Phone: 202-208-6843
Website: http://www.nps.gov/

National Sciences Resource Center
Smithsonian Institute
Room 1201, Arts and Industries
Washington, DC 20560
Phone: 202-357-2555
Website: http://www.nsrconline.org/

National Tree Trust
1120 G Street, NW, Suite 770
Washington, DC 20005
Phone: 800-846-TREE
Website: http://www.nationaltreetrust.org/

Ohio State University Web Garden
Website: http://webgarden.osu.edu

Open Directory Project: Botanical Gardens
and Arboreta
Website: http://dmoz.org/Science/Institutions/
Botanical_Gardens_and_Arboreta/

Open Directory Project: Kids Gardening
Website: http://dmoz.org/Home/Gardening/
Kids_Gardening/

Passport to America's Children's Gardens
Website: http://www.ces.purdue.edu/Hamilton/
ag/childgarden.html

Selected Educational Resources from the
AGRICOLA Database: Gardening for
Kids
Website: http://www.nal.usda.gov/outreach/
garden.htm

Sustainable Agricultural Resources for
Teachers, K-12
U.S. Department of Agriculture
Website: http://www.nal.usda.gov/afsic/
AFSIC_pubs/k-12.htm

The Virtual Library of Botany/Plant Biology
Website: http://www.ou.edu/cas/botany-
micro/www-vl/

Wikipedia's List of Botanical Gardens in the
U.S.
Website: http://en.wikipedia.org/wiki/
List_of_botanical_gardens_in_the_
United_States

WWW Virtual Library Gardening Links
Website: http://www.gardenweb.com/vl/

References

About the camden city garden club: Camden
Children's Garden [cited August 15 2005].
Available from http://www.camdenchildrens
garden.org.
Adventure playground at Huntington Beach.
Huntington Beach, CA [cited August 25
2005]. Available from http://www.ci.
huntington-beach.ca.us/CityDepartments/
comm_services/facilities/Huntington_
Central_Park/Adventure_Play ground.cfm.

Adventure playground at the Berkeley Marina. Berkeley, CA [cited August 25 2005]. Available from http://www.ci.berkeley.ca.us/marina/marinaexp/adventplgd.html.

Adventure playground in Irvine. In City of Irvine [database online]. Irvine, CA [cited August 25 2005]. Available from http://www.ci.irvine.ca.us/depts/cs/commparks/specialfac/adventure_playground.asp.

Akbari, Hashem, and United States Environmental Protection Agency Office of Policy Analysis. Climate Change Division. 1992. *Cooling Our Communities: A Guidebook on Tree Planting and Light-Colored Surfacing.* Lawrence Berkeley Laboratory Report. Vol. LBL-31587. Washington, DC: U.S. Environmental Protection Agency, Office of Public Analysis, Climate Change Division.

AkiB. Berlin, Germany [cited August 25 2005]. Available from http://www.akib.de/english/english.html.

Altman, I., and J. F. Wohlwill. 1983. *Behavior and the Natural Environment.* Human behavior and environment. Vol. 6. New York: Plenum Press.

———. 1978. *Children and the Environment.* Human behavior and environment. Vol. 3. New York: Plenum Press.

American Association of Botanical Gardens and Arboreta. 2001. *Reaching Out to the Garden Visitor: Informal Learning and Biodiversity.* Kennett Square, PA: American Association of Botanical Gardens and Arboreta.

American Association of Fund-Raising Counsel. 2004. *Giving USA 2004: The Annual Report on Philanthropy for the Year 2003.* 49th annual issue ed. Glenview, IL: AAFRC Trust for Philanthropy.

Anderson, E. 1995. Ethnobotany and liberal arts. In *Ethnobotany: Evolution of a Discipline.* Portland, OR: Dioscorides Press.

Atlanta Botanical Garden. Children's garden [cited August 1 2005]. Available from http://www.atlantabotanicalgarden.org/kidsgarden.htm.

Atlanta Botanical Garden: Garden map (brochure).

Atlanta Botanical Garden: School programs brochure, 2004–2005.

Atlanta Botanical Garden: Summer education brochure, July, August, September, 2005.

Atlanta Botanical Garden: Welcome to the garden brochure.

Awbury Arboretum. 2005. The arbor. *Newsletter of the Awbury Arboretum* (Spring).

———. [cited August 1 2005]. Available from http://www.awbury.org.

———. 2004a. *Awbury Arboretum: Field Trips (pamphlet).* Philadelphia, PA: Awbury Arboretum.

———. 2004b. *Welcome to Awbury Arboretum: Visitor Map (pamphlet).*

———. 2005. *Awbury arboretum: Summer nature program. (pamphlet).*

Balick, M. J., and P. A. Cox. 1999. *Plants, People, and Culture: The Science of Ethnobotany.* Scientific american library series; no. 60. 2nd printing, 1999 ed. New York: Scientific American Library.

Barrows, W. S. Sr. 1988. Trees, people, and the law. *Arbor Age* 8, (2) (April): 12–14, 16, 18.

Batmanghelidj, F. 2003. *Water for Health, for Healing, for Life.* New York: Warner Books.

Billig, S. H. 2000. The effects of service learning. 57(7): 14–18.

Bilski, N. 1994. The best children's gardens in the world. *American Horticulturist* 73(7), (July): 26.

Bixby, M. 2000. *Learning In College: I Can Relate.* Upper Saddle River, NJ: Prentice-Hall.

Bixler, R. D., C. L. Carlisle, W. E. Hammitt, and M. F. Floyd. 1994. Observed fears and discomforts among urban students on field trips to wildland areas. *Journal of Environmental Education* 26(1), (Fall): 24-33.

Bixler, R. D., and M. F. Floyd. 1997. Nature is scary, disgusting, and uncomfortable.

Environment and Behavior 29(4) (July): 443–467.

Brown, T., and W. J. Watkins. 1979. *The Tracker: The Story of Tom Brown, Jr., as Told to William Jon Watkins*. New York: Berkley Pub. Corp.

Buchanan, R. 1995. *Taylor's Guide to Herbs*. Taylor's guides to gardening. Boston: Houghton Mifflin.

Bund der Jungenfarmen, und Aktivspielplatze, eV. 2004. Adventure playgrounds and city farms in Europe and what they contribute to sustainable urban development [cited August 25 2005]. Available from http://www.bdja.org/oli/index.html.

———. 2004. *Youth Farms and Activity Playgrounds in Germany*. Stuttgart, Germany [cited August 25 2005]. Available from http://www.bdja.org/english.htm.

Burnett, F. H. 1987. *The Secret Garden*. Connecticut: Longmeadow Press.

Camden Children's Garden. 2005. *Camden Children's Garden Education Program: Distance Learning and Garden Lessons (flyer)*.

Camden Children's Garden Kid's Map (pamphlet).

The Camden City Garden Club and the Camden Children's Garden: History, Purpose, and Activities (handout).

Catterall, J. S. J. Iwanaga, and R. Chapleau. 1999. Involvement in the arts and human development. In *Champions of change: The impact of the arts on learning*, 1–18. Washington, D.C.: Arts Education Partnership: The President's Committee on the Arts and Humanities.

Center for Disease Control and Prevention National Center for Health Statistics. 2000 CDC growth charts: United States [cited September 3 2005]. Available from http://www.cdc.gov/growthcharts/.

Chawla, L. 2002. Spots of time: Manifold ways of being in nature in childhood. In *Children and Nature: Psychological, Sociocultural and Evolutionary Investigations*, P. H. Kahn, Jr. and S. R. Kellert, eds.

Cambridge, MA: Massachusetts Institute of Technology, 199–226.

Chawla, L. 1988. Children's concern for the natural environment. *Children's Environments Quarterly* 5(3): 13–20.

Chevallier, A. 1996. *Natural Health Encyclopedia of Herbal Medicine*. New York: DK Pub.

Children's environments research group. New York, NY [cited August 25 2005]. Available from http://web.gc.cuny.edu/che/cerg/.

The Children's Garden at Hershey Gardens: The Children's Garden $1.5 Million Campaign.

Cobb, E. 1993. *The Ecology of Imagination in Childhood*. 2nd ed. Dallas, TX: Spring Publications.

Coles, Robert. 1993. *The Call of Service: A Witness to Idealism*. New York: Houghton Mifflin.

Coley, R. L., F. E. Kuo, and W. C. Sullivan, 1997. Where does community grow? The social context created by nature in urban public housing. *Environment and Behavior* 29, (4) (July): 468–494.

Collins, A. 1993. *Design Issues for Learning Environments*. New York: Bank Street College of Education.

Collins, A., J. Hawkins, and J. R. Frederiksen. 1991. *Three Different Views of Students: The Role of Technology in Assessing Student Performance*. Technical report; no. 12. New York, NY; Washington, DC: Bank Street College of Education, Center for Technology in Education; U.S. Dept. of Education, Office of Educational Research and Improvement, Educational Resources Information Center.

Cooper's Ferry Development Association and Camden City Garden Club. 1999. Growing the Camden children's garden. VHS. VidComm for Cooper's Ferry Development Association.

Cowie, D. 2004. Children's garden a thriving 5-year-old. *The Philadelphia Inquirer*, August 13, 2004, sec Features Home and Design.

Crenson, M. 2001. New U.N. report profiles urbanizing world. *Associated Press*

Worldstream, June 4, 2001, sec International News.

Crosby, A. 1995. A critical look: The philosophical foundations of experiential education. In *The Theory of Experiential Education*, K. Warren, M. Sakofs, and J. S. Hunt, Jr., eds. 3rd ed. Dubuque, IA: Kendall/Hunt.

Dahlgren, A. 2003. Lecturer finds urban sprawl linked with obesity. *The Daily Free Press*, October 27.

Dannenmaier, M. 1998. *A Child's Garden: Enchanting Outdoor Spaces for Children and Parents*. New York: Simon and Schuster.

Dommert Phillips [cited August 15 2005]. Available from http://www.dommertphillips.com.

Eberbach, C. 2001. The children's adventure project. In *Reaching Out to the Garden Visitor: Informal Learning and Biodiversity*. Kennett Square, PA: American Association of Botanical Gardens and Arboreta, 71–74.

Eirhart, L. 2003. Change over time: Incorporating new gardens into historic landscapes.

Ellis, D. B. 1998. *Becoming a Master Student*, 8th ed. Boston, MA: Houghton Mifflin.

Environmental research foundation, and P. Montague ed. 2000. TV viewed as a public health threat. Rachel's Environment and Health Weekly 681, (Jan.6). http://www.sustainingwisconsin.org/issue.papers/pdf/bp-tune-2.pdf.

Ewing, R. H., R. Pendall, and D. T. Chen. 2002. *Measuring Sprawl and Its Impact*. Washington, DC: Smart Growth America, Access: http://www.smartgrowthamerica.org/sprawlindex/sprawlreport.html.

Eyler, J., Corporation for National Service, and Learn & Serve America. 2001. *At a glance*. 3rd ed. Nashville, Tenn.: Vanderbilt University, http://www.compact.org/resource/aag.pdf.

Fair play for children. West Sussex, UK [cited August 25 2005]. Available from http://www.arunet.co.uk/fairplay/home.htm.

Fishman, C. 1999. The smorgasbord generation. *American Demographics* 21, (5) (May): 54–60.

Folkard, R. 1884. *Plant Lore, Legends, and Lyrics: Embracing the Myths, Traditions, Superstitions, and Folk-Lore of the Plant Kingdom*. London: S. Low, Marston, Searle, and Rivington.

Fromme, T., M. Allison, and B. Ney. 1999. Longwood gardens: Opening the garden to children. Paper presented at the Youth Gardening Symposium, Denver, CO.

Garibaldi, A. 1999. *Medicinal Flora of the Alaska Natives: A Compilation of Knowledge from Literary Sources of Aleut, Alutiiq, Athabascan, Eyak, Haida, Inupiat, Tlingit, Tsimshian, and Yupik Traditional Healing Methods Using Plants*. Anchorage, AK: Alaska Natural Heritage Program, Environment and Natural Resources Institute, University of Alaska.

Ginsberg, O. Rediscovering the animation playground: Adventure playgrounds in Berlin. Available from http://www.cityfarmer.org/AnimationPlayground.html.

Glenn, J. L. 2000. *Environment-Based Education: Creating High Performance Schools and Students*. Washington, DC: National Environmental Education and Training Foundation (http://www.neetf.org/pubs/EnviroEdReport.pdf).

goCityKids attractions: Adventure playground. [cited August 21 2005]. Available from http://www.gocitykids.com/browse/attraction.jsp?id=224.

Grant, T., and G. Littlejohn. 2001. *Greening School Grounds: Creating Habitats for Learning*. Gabriola Island, BC: New Society Publishers.

Gray, M. J., E. H. Ondaatje, R. D. Fricker Jr., and S. A. Geschwind. 2000. Assessing learning-service. *Change*, 32, (2) (Mar/Apr2000): 30.

Graziano, A. B., M. Peterson, and G. L. Shaw. 1999. Enhanced learning of proportional math through music training and spatial-temporal training. *Neurological Research* 21, (2) (Mar): 139–152.

Grese, R. E. 1995. Reflections on community service learning in landscape architecture. In *Praxis III: Voices in Dialogue*, J. Galura, et al., eds. Ann Arbor, MI: OCSL Press, 69–81.

Growth charts for boys and girls [cited August 26 2005]. Available from http://pediatrics.about.com/od/growthcharts2/.

Hamel, P. B., and M. U. Chiltoskey. 1975. *Cherokee Plants and Their Uses: A 400 Year History*. Sylva, NC Herald Pub. Co.

Hamilton, A. C., S. Pei, J. Kessy, A. A. Kham, S. Logos-Witte, and Z. K. Shinwari. 2003. The purposes and teaching of applied ethnobotany [cited February 17 2005]. Available from http://peopleandplants.org/web-content%201/pdf/wp11.pdf.

Haque, M. T., L. Tai, D. Ham, D. Mizejdewski, and National Wildlife Federation. 2002. *National wildlife federation's tree conservation and home site development guide*. Reston, VA: National Wildlife Federation.

Healey, J. 1990. *Endangered Minds*. New York: Simon and Schuster, New York.

Heerwagen, J., and G. H. Orians. 2002. The ecological world of children. In *Children and Nature: Psychological, Sociocultural and Evolutionary Investigations*, P. H. Kahn, Jr., and S. R. Kellert, eds. Cambridge, MA.: Massachusetts Institute of Technology, 29–64.

Henniger, M. L. 1994. Enriching the outdoor play experience. *Childhood Education* 70(2): 87–90.

Herrington, S., and K. Studtmann. 1998. Landscape interventions: New directions for the design of children's outdoor play environments. *Landscape and Urban Planning* 42(2–4): 191–205.

Hershey Gardens. The children's garden at hershey gardens [cited August 1 2005]. Available from http://www.hersheypa.com/attractions/in_hershey/gardens.html.

Hershey's. Hershey industrial school: 1909 [cited August 1 2005]. Available from http://www.hersheys.com/discover/milton/hershey_ind_school.asp.

Holland, B. 1999. Factors and strategies that influence faculty involvement in public service. In *Service-learning toolkit: Readings and resources for faculty*, 147–150. Providence, RI: Campus Compact.

International Play Association. IPA world. Available from http://www.ipaworld.org/home.html.

International Play Association. Japan [cited August 25 2005]. Available from http://www.ipa-japan.org/.

James, J. 2005. A description and analysis of children's lived experiences from a social–historical–cultural context of their participation in a non-formal environmental learning program. PhD diss., Clemson University.

Jekyll, Gertrude. 1982. *Children and gardens*. Woodbridge, Suffolk: Antique Collectors' Club.

Kahn, P. H., Jr. 2002. Children's affiliations with nature: Structure, development, and the problem of environmental generational amnesia. In *Children and Nature: Psychological, Sociocultural and Evolutionary Investigations.*, P. H. Kahn, Jr. and S. R. Kellert, eds. Cambridge, MA: Massachusetts Institute of Technology.

Kaplan, R. and S. Kaplan. 1989. *The experience of nature: A psychological perspective*. Cambridge, New York: Cambridge University Press.

Kaplan, R. 1976. Wayfinding in the natural environment. In *Environmental Knowing: Theories, Research, and Methods*, G. T. Moore and R. G. Golledge, eds. Stroudsburg, PA: Dowden, Hutchinson and Ross.

Kellert, S. R. 1997. *Kinship to mastery: Biophilia in human evolution and development*. Washington, D.C.: Island Press, http://www.mannlib.cornell.edu/cgi-bin/toc.cgi?apm3905.

Kellert, S. R. 2002. Experiencing nature: Affective, cognitive, and evaluative development in children. In *Children and Nature: Psychological, Sociocultural and Evolutionary Investigations*, P. H. Kahn, Jr. and S. R. Kellert, eds. Cambridge, MA: Massachusetts Institute of Technology, 117–152.

Kellert, S. R., and Derr, V. 1998. *National Study of Outdoor Wilderness Experience*. New Haven: Yale University School of Forestry and Environmental Studies.

KIDS. Kidsactive: Play and opportunity for disabled children. London, UK [cited August 25 2005]. Available from http://www.kidsactive.org.uk/.

Kirkby, M. 1989. Nature as refuge in children's environments. *Children's Environments Quarterly*, 6(1), 7–12.

Knight, E. J. 2001. *Children and Landscapes: Environmental Education and Childhood Development*. Clemson, SC: Center for Electronic and Digital Publishing, College of Architecture, Arts, and Humanities, Clemson University.

Krist, J. 1993. Reclamation. *Sierra* 78(4) (Jul/Aug): 66.

Kuo, F. E., W. C. Sullivan, R. L. Coley, and L. Brunson. 1998. Fertile ground for community: Inner-city neighborhood common spaces. *American Journal of Community Psychology* 26, (6) (Dec): 823–851.

Laufer, G. 2001. Atlanta's newest family destination: The new children's healthcare of Atlanta children's garden keeps interest going, news release (January 18).

———. 1999. The children's garden is becoming a reality, news release, (March 18).

London play. London, UK [cited August 25 2005]. Available from http://www.londonplay.org.uk/.

Longwood Gardens. 2003. *Preserving the Past, Building the Future (brochure)*. Kennett Square, PA: Longwood Gardens.

———. What's new: The new indoor children's garden anticipated opening fall 2006. [cited August 1 2005]. Available from http://www.longwoodgardens.org/ WhatsNew/Renovations/ChildrensGarden Update.htm.

———. What's new: Bee-amazed children's garden opened May, 8, 2004 [cited August 1 2005]. Available from http://www.longwood gardens.org/WhatsNew/Renovations/Beea MazedChildrensGarden.htm.

Louv, R. 2005. *Last Child in the Woods: Saving Our Children from Nature-Deficit Disorder*. Chapel Hill, NC: Algonquin Books of Chapel Hill.

Lovejoy, S. 1999. *Roots, Shoots, Buckets and Boots: Gardening Together with Children*. New York: Workman Pub.

Magnani, D. 2001. *Discover Enchanted Woods: A Fairy-Tale Garden at Winterthur*. Discover Winterthur; variation: Discover Winterthur. Winterthur, DE: Henry Francis du Pont Winterthur Museum.

Malone, K., and P. J. Tranter. 2003. School grounds as sites for learning: Making the most of environmental opportunities. *Environmental Education Research* 9(3): 283–303.

Maps and Information: A Guide to Hershey Gardens and the Children's Garden.

Matheny, N. P., J. R. Clark, and International Society of Arboriculture. 1994. *A photographic guide to the evaluation of hazard trees in urban areas*. Urbana, IL: International Society of Arboriculture.

Maziak, P. Michigan 4H children's garden: Just imagine [cited August 25 2005]. Available from http://4hgarden.msu.edu.

McCafferty, K. 1995. Cross creek. *Field and Stream* 100(6) (October): 120(3).

McClendon, T. B. 2001. The children's healthcare of Atlanta children's garden. In *Reaching Out to the Garden Visitor: Informal Learning and Biodiversity*. Kennett Square, PA: American Association of Botanical Gardens and Arboreta, 1–5.

McGuiness, I. 1996. From skeptic to proponent: Faculty involvement in service learning. In *Service learning toolkit: Readings and resources for faculty*, 199–202. Providence, RI: Campus Compact.

Moffat, A. S., and M. Schiler. 1981. *Landscape Design That Saves Energy.* 1st ed. New York: Morrow.

Moore, R. C. 1997. The need for nature: A childhood right. *Social Justice* 24(3) (Fall): 203–220.

Moore, R. C. 2003. *How Cities Use Parks to Help Children Learn.* Chicago, IL: American Planning Association.

Moore, R. C., and H. H. Wong. 1997. *Natural Learning: The Life History of an Environmental Schoolyard: Creating Environments for Rediscovering Nature's Way of Teaching.* Berkeley, CA: MIG Communications.

Morton, J. F. 1974. *Folk Remedies of the Low Country.* Miami, FL: E. A. Seemann Pub.

Mott, A., K. Rolfe, and R. T. James. 1997. Safety of surfaces and equipment for children in playgrounds. *Lancet* 349, 1874–1876.

Music educators national conference (MENC). Music education facts and figures 2002. 2006 [cited august 15 2005]. Available from http://www.menc.org/information/advocate/facts.html.

Nabhan, G. P., and S. Trimble. 1994. *The Geography of Childhood: Why Children Need Wild Places.* The Concord Library. Boston: Beacon Press.

National Arbor Day Foundation. 1999. Arbor day (July/August): 4–5.

National Program for Playground Safety, School of HPELS, University of Northern Iowa. Playground-related statistics. Cedar Falls, Iowa 50614. Available from http://www.playgroundsafety.org/resources.statistics.htm.

National Wildlife Federation. 2001. *Schoolyard Habitats Planning Guide.*

Natural learning initiative. Raleigh, NC [cited August 25 2005]. Available from http://www.naturalearning.org/.

New York Botanical Garden. 2002. *School Programs for Grades Pre-K through 8 and Teachers 2002–03 (brochure).* Bronx, NY: New York Botanical Garden.

———. About the Everett children's adventure garden [cited August 15 2005]. Available from http://www.nybg.org/gardens/test_garden.php?id_gardens_collections=58.

———. The Everett children's adventure garden [cited August 15 2005]. Available from http://www.nybg.org/family/ecag.html.

———. *Guide to the Everett Children's Adventure Garden (pamphlet).* Bronx, NY: New York Botanical Garden.

Nilson, L. B. 1998. *Teaching at Its Best: A Research-Based Resource for College Instructors.* Bolton, MA: Anker Pub. Co.

Nixon, W. 1997. How nature shapes childhood: Personality, play and sense of place. *The Amicus Journal* 19(2) (Summer): 31(5).

Orr, D. W. 2002. Political economy and the ecology of childhood. In *Children and Nature: Psychological, Sociocultural and Evolutionary Investigations,* P. H. Kahn, Jr. and S. R. Kellert, eds. Cambridge, MA: Massachusetts Institute of Technology, 279–304.

Palmberg, I., and J. Kuru. 2000. Outdoor activities as a basis for environmental responsibility. *Journal of Environmental Education* 24: 26–30.

Palmer, J. A. 1993. Development of concern for the environment and formative experiences of educators. *Environmental Education* 24(3) (Spring): 26–30.

Penguin Group USA. 2005. Book Club Reading Guides: The Secret Garden. Available from http://www.penguinputnam.com/static/rguides/us/secret_garden.html

Pevec, I. 2003. Ethnobotanical gardens: Celebrating the link between human culture and the natural world. *Green Teacher* 70 (Spring): 25–28.

PLAYLINK [cited August 25 2005]. Available from http://www.playlink.org.uk/.

Project for Public Spaces. New York, NY [cited August 25 2005]. Available from http://www.pps.org/.

Pyle, R. M. 1998. *The Thunder Tree: Lessons from an Urban Wildland*. New York: Lyons Press.

Pyle, R. M. 2002. Eden in a vacant lot: Special places, species, and kids in the neighborhood of life. In *Children and Nature: Psychological, Sociocultural and Evolutionary Investigations*, P. H. Kahn, Jr. and S. R. Kellert, eds. Cambridge, MA: Massachusetts Institute of Technology, 305–328.

Ratey, J. J., and A. M. Galaburda. 2001. *A user's guide to the brain: Perception, attention, and the four theaters of the brain*. 1st ed. New York: Pantheon Books.

Rempel, G. The industrial revolution. Western New England College [cited August 15 2005] (http://mars.acnet.wnec.edu/~grempel/courses/wc2/lectures/industrialrev.html).

Rivkin, M. 1997. The schoolyard habitat movement: What it is and why children need it. *Early Childhood Education Journal* 25(1) (Fall): 61–66.

Robinette, G. O. 1972. *Plants, People, and Environmental Quality; A Study of Plants and Their Environmental Functions*. Washington, DC: U.S. Dept. of the Interior, National Park Service.

Robinson, R. Rodney Robinson, landscape architect. 2003 [cited September 5 2005]. Available from http://rrla.com/.

Robi-spiel aktionen. Basel, Switzerland [cited August 25 2005]. Available from http://www.robi-spiel-aktionen.ch/.

Rupp, J. 2005. Harvest benefits from kids' gardening. *MetroKids South Jersey* (March).

Santrock, J. W., and J. S. Halonen. 1999. *Your guide to college success: Strategies for achieving your goals*. Belmont, CA: Wadsworth Pub. Co.

Sawyers, J. K. 1994. The preschool playground: Developing skills through outdoor play. *The Journal of Physical Education, Recreation and Dance* 65(6) (August): 31–33.

Searles, H. F. 1960. *The nonhuman environment, in normal development and in schizophrenia*. New York: International Universities Press.

Shearer, A. 2004. New bee-amazed children's garden opens May 8 at Longwood Gardens, just in time for Mother's Day, press release (April 13).

Sobel, D. 1996. *Beyond ecophobia: Reclaiming the heart in nature education*. Nature literacy series; no. 1. Great Barrington, MA: Orion Society.

Sobel, D. 1993. *Children's Special Places: Exploring the Role of Forts, Dens and Bush Houses in Middle Childhood*. Tucson: Zephyr Press.

Sobel, David, and Orion Society. 2004. *Place-based education: Connecting classrooms & communities*. Nature literacy series; no. 4. Great Barrington, MA: Orion Society.

Sound Play: Outdoor musical instruments, [cited August 25 2005]. Available from http.www.soundplay.com.

Speux. Basel, Switzerland [cited August 25 2005]. Available from http://www.speux.ch/

Spyri, J., and C. Leslie. 1956. *Heidi*. Penguin popular classics. London: Penguin.

Stine, S. 1997. *Landscapes for Learning: Creating Outdoor Environments for Children and Youth*. New York: Wiley and Sons.

Sutton, L. Adventure play ground: A children's world in the city [cited August 21 2005]. Available from http://adventureplaygrounds.hampshire.edu/whyimportant.html.

Takahashi, N. 1999. *Educational Landscapes: Developing School Grounds as Learning Places*. Building blocks to better learning series. Charlottesville, VA: University of Virginia, Thomas Jefferson Center for Educational Design.

Tanner, T. 1980. Significant life experiences: A new research area in environmental education. *Journal of Environmental Education* 11(4) (Summer): 20–24.

Taylor, A. F., F. E. Kuo, and W. C. Sullivan. 2001. Coping with ADD: The surprising connection to green play settings.

Environment and Behavior 33(1) (January): 54–77.

Taylor, J. 2001. Creating magical spaces. Paper presented at the National Children and Youth Gardening Symposium, Lansing, MI.

Thompson, G. F., and F. R. Steiner. 1997. *Ecological Design and Planning.* The Wiley series in sustainable design. New York: John Wiley.

Tyler, C., and T. McClendon. 2005. Q and A with Tracy McClendon and Cindy Tyler. Presented at the American Horticultural Society Children's Symposium, Emory University, Atlanta, GA (July 28).

UN Secretary-General. 2005. *World Demographic Trends: Report of the Secretary-General.* New York: UN.

U.S. Consumer Product Safety Commission. 2003. *Handbook for public playground safety.* Washington, D.C.: U.S. Consumer Product Safety Commission.

Venturi, Scott, Brown and Associates, Inc. Projects: Camden Children's garden [cited August 15 2005]. Available from http://www.vsba.com/projects/index.html.

Verbeek, P., and F. B. M. deWaal. 2002. The primate relationship with nature: Biophilia as a general pattern. In *Children and Nature: Psychological, Sociocultural and Evolutionary Investigations,* P. H. Kahn, Jr. and S. R. Kellert, eds. Cambridge, MA.: Massachusetts of Technology, 1–28.

Wade, Beth. 1999. Playground design: it's more than child's play. *American City & County* 114, (3) (March): 24.

Wandsworth. 2005. Adventure playgrounds in Wandsworth. London, UK [cited August 2005]. Available from http://www.wandsworth.gov.uk/Home/Leisureand Tourism/Playandcommunityservices/Playservices/Adventure.htm.

Weinberger, N. 2000.The Impact of Arts on Learning, *MuSICa Research Notes* 7(2).

Wells, N. M. 2000. At home with nature: Effects of "greenness" on children's cognitive functioning. *Environment and Behavior* 32(6) (November): 775–795.

Wells, N. M., and G. W. Evans. 2003. Nearby nature: A buffer of life stress among rural children. *Environment and Behavior* 35(3) (May): 311–330.

White, R. 2004. *Young Children's Relationship with Nature: Its Importance to Children's Development and the Earth's Future.* Kansas City, MO: White Hutchinson Leisure and Learning Group (http://www.whitehutchinson.com/children/articles/childrennature.shtml).

White, R. 2005. *Benefits for children of play in nature.* Kansas City, MO: White Hutchinson Leisure and Learning Group, http: www.whitehutchinson.com/children/articles/benefits.shtml.

White, R., and L. S. Vicki. 1998. *Children's Outdoor Play and Learning Environments: Returning to Nature.* Kansas City, MO: White Hutchinson Leisure and Learning Group (http://www.whitehutchinson.com/children/articles/outdoor.shtml).

Whitman, W. 1999. Leaves of grass. In Bartleby.com [database online] [cited August 15 2005]. Available from http://www.bartleby.com/142/index.html.

Wieber, E. 2001. All about kids: Signage helps interpret and teach at the Camden children's garden. *Sign Business* (March): 20–26.

Williamson, C., and A. Hart. 2004. *Neighbourhood Journeys: Making the Ordinary Extraordinary: A Teacher's Guide to Using the Built Environment at Key Stage 2.* London: CABE Education Foundation.

Wilson, E.O. 1992. *The diversity of life.* Cambridge, Mass.: Belknap Press of Harvard University Press.

Winterthur. 2001. *Chat and Chew Report.*
———. 2001. *Preliminary Impressions of Enchanted Woods by Our Visitors (handout).*
———. Enchanted woods [cited August 8 2005]. Available from http://www.winterthur.org/for_families/enchanted_woods.asp.

Mushroom seating, 122
Music education, benefits of, 115–116
Music gardens, 115–120, 210
  benefits to children, 116
  funding, 117
  safety considerations in, 119–120
  Sound Play, 117

Nabham, Gary, 25
National Action Plan for the Prevention of Playground Injuries, 196
National Association for Education of Young Children, 196–197
National Center for Chronic Disease Prevention and Health Promotion, 26
National Center for Health Statistics, 26
National Environmental Education and Training Foundation, 272
National Gardening Association, 102
National Outdoor Leadership School, 15
National Parks, 24–25
National Program for Playground Safety, *National Action Plan for the Prevention of Playground Injuries,* 196–197
National Program for Playground Safety (NPPS), 182, 183, 190, 193
National Recreation and Park Association, 184, 196–197
National Safe Kids Campaign, 196–197

National Safety Council, 196–197
National Wildlife Federation, 31, 43, 224, 228, 295
Native American gardens
  Children's Healthcare of Atlanta Children's Garden, 86
  "three sisters" interplanting practice in, 106–107
Native Americans
  as educational field trip theme, 253, 254
  Lenape Indians, 253
  river cane use by, 314
Native plants, 8, 31, 96, 206, 214–215, 230, 246, 248
Native plant societies, 31, 246
Natural Water Garden, The (Burrell), 137
Nature, children's interaction with, 1–3
  effect on emotional development (affective maturation), 14–16
  effect on intelligence and cognitive development, 10, 11–12
  effect on physical development, 12–14
"Nature deficit disorder," 17
NatureScene (television program), 275
Nature trails, 218–219
The New Indoor Children's Garden. *See* Longwood Gardens, Kennett Square, PA, The New Indoor Children's Garden
New Jersey Department of Education Core Curriculum Content Standards, 144
Newsweek, 193

Plant disease control, 245

Plants. *See also* Edible gardens;
    Trees
  carnivorous, 91, 133, 134, 218
  for climate control, 239, 240
  as design element, 30–31
  in ethnobotany gardens,
      300–301, 305, 306
  hazardous or poisonous, 30
  maintenance of, 52–54
  in memorial gardens, 108, 111,
      114
  native, 8, 31, 96, 206, 214–215,
      230, 246, 248
    as lawn alternative, 230
  in storybook gardens, 124–125
  in water gardens, 126, 133–136
  as wildlife food and shelter, 31,
      32
  for wind control, 240
  in xeriscapes, 231–233

Plaques
  in memorial gardens, 109–110
  for recognition of fundraising
      donors, 280, 281

Play
  active, 28–29
  age-related, 192
  creative, 18, 29–30
  make-believe/fantasy, 28, 29,
      192
  outdoor, 9
  role of, 28–29
  role-play, 28

Playground equipment
  installation, 44, 45
  merry-go-rounds, 188, 194
  safety considerations for, 182,
      184–185, 186, 187–188, 192,
      193–194, 197
  seesaws, 188, 193, 194
  skywheels, 185

  slides, 184–188, 193, 194
  swings, 187–188, 193, 194

Playgrounds
  Clemson Elementary Outdoors,
      109, 198–221, 275
  design trends, 178–180
  hazardous, 8
  history of, 8–10, 177–178
  injuries in, 180, 182, 186,
      187–188, 189, 190, 194
    *National Action Plan for the
      Prevention of Playground
      Injuries,* 196
  maintenance, 52–54
  naturalistic approaches to, 178,
      179
  of park and recreation
      departments, 180–181
  safety considerations, 180,
      182–198
    for age-appropriate play areas,
        182, 186, 192–193
    alternative designs, 193–194
    design, 182, 183–185
    guidelines for, 183–189
    monitoring and promotion of
        safety, 196–197
    planning for, 182–183
    for playground equipment,
        182, 184–185, 186,
        187–188, 192, 193–194,
        197
    for safe play surfaces, 184,
        186–187, 189–191
    tree-related hazards, 194–196

"Playgrounds for the Future":
    they ain't got swing"
    (Hamilton and King), 193

Playhouses, 8

Play towers, 26–27. *See also*
    Treehouses

Plocek, Pat, 183

as habitats, 149
as "litter" problem, 246
in memorial gardens, 109, 111, 115
as noise buffers, 205
as playground safety hazards, 194–196
preservation of, 204–205
solar radiation control function, 239–240
in traditionally-designed neighborhoods, 14
Tree surveys, 33
"Tributes through Trees" programs, 109
Trimble, Stephen, 25
Turtles, 127
Tyler, Cindy, 82, 83, 84, 92

United Nations, *Report of the Secretary General on World Demographic Trends*, 2
United Nations Educational, Scientific, and Cultural Organization (UNESCO) Growing Up in Cities Program, 1–2
United States Consumer Products Safety Commission (CPSC), 182, 183, 184, 185–189, 190
United States Department of Agriculture, 224
University of California-Berkeley, 9, 99
University of California-Davis, 193
University of Georgia, Landscape Architecture Department, 113–114
Urban nature experiences, 11, 17
Urban population, 2, 9
Urban sprawl, 2, 13–14, 16
Urban Water Works, 136

Vanedemark & Lynch, 56, 61
Vegetable gardens, 96. *See also* Edible gardens
in storybook gardens, 124
Venturi, Scott, Brown and Associates, 145, 153
Versailles, Gardens of, 71
Vertical gardens, 96
Vestibular sense, 211
Victorian Days programs, 254, 257
Viehman, Elsie, 250
Villa D'Este, 71
Villa Lante, 71
Volunteers
for adventure gardens and playgrounds, 98
for fundraising, 282–283
for gardening projects, 217
for landscape installation, 44–49
for landscape maintenance, 49–54
for music garden development, 117, 118–119
for playground equipment installation, 185

Walking trails, 238–239
Walkways. *See also* Paths
in memorial gardens, 109
wheelchair-accessible, 36–37
Walls, in storybook gardens, 125
Washington, George, 43, 55
Washington Elementary School, Berkeley, CA, 9
Waste reduction, 227–228
Water
children's love for, 125–126
cooling effect of, 238
as design element, 26
to reduce watering, 244
as wildlife habitat component, 31, 32

Lolly Tai, PhD, RLA, FASLA, is professor and chair of the Department of Landscape Architecture and Horticulture at Temple University. She has been an educator and a practicing landscape architect for over two decades. Dr. Tai's teaching and professional work focuses on the role of the environment on landscape design. Throughout her teaching career, she has incorporated service learning into the curriculum where her students are exposed to hands-on learning while making significant contributions to communities. Designing schoolyard projects has been one of the focuses of her outreach. Dr. Tai and Mary Taylor Haque are coauthors and contributing writers of *Landscape Design for Energy Efficiency*, *Tree Conservation and Home Site Development Guide*, and *Service Learning Across the Curriculum: Case Studies*. Dr. Tai is a Fellow of the American Society of Landscape Architects, a recipient of the 2004 Bradford Williams Medal for Meritorious Writing in *Landscape Architecture Magazine* and a recipient of the 2005 Council of Educators in Landscape Architecture Award of Distinction in Teaching. She continues to foster service learning and sustainable design principles in her teaching and practice. She plans to contribute further to the research and advancement of children's learning environments in the future.

Mary Taylor Haque, RLA, ASLA is a registered landscape architect and Alumni Distinguished Professor of Horticulture at Clemson University. Utilizing a service learning model, she and her students and colleagues have partnered with USDA, the Sustainable Universities Initiative, and community partners to design children's gardens across the state of South Carolina. A primary focus area of her research and outreach has been Sustainable Schoolyard Habitats for K-12 schools. These outdoor classrooms incorporate design principles centered on sustainability and resource management as well as usefulness as a learning and play environment for children. She is a 2005 John Glenn Scholar in Service Learning and a recipient of the American Society for Horticulture Science Outstanding Undergraduate Educator Award.

Gina Kooiman McLellan, PhD, has been a professor of Parks, Recreation and Tourism Management at Clemson University for 25 years, with a teaching focus on recreation and leisure environments and natural resource management. She has also directed the U.S. Forest Service's national recreation management training program throughout her tenure at Clemson. She and her students, through service learning projects, have spent the last ten years working to design and develop creative, quality outdoor environments for children that help those children to develop respect for the outdoors, enhance their learning, and improve socialization through play. Her work with children's outdoor environments has led to numerous awards and to serving as an advisor to others developing children's environments. She plans to continue researching and advocating environment based education for schools around the country as a means of enhancing learning and environmental protection.

Erin Jordan Knight is Director of Natural Resource Protection at Upstate Forever, an organization that promotes sensible growth and protects special places in the Upstate region of South Carolina. Her public landscape designs include the Children's Garden at Linky Stone Park in Greenville, SC and the neighborhood park at Sliding Rock Creek, both community projects led by Leadership Greenville. Knight graduated Summa Cum Laude with Departmental Honors from Clemson University in 2001 with a degree in landscape architecture. Both her work in conservation and in landscape design is inspired by her own early nature experiences and her hope of providing the same opportunities for discovery for all children.